Creatspace Publishing

4900 La Ceross Road
North Charleston SC, 29406,

www.createspace.com

555 *ACT MATH*
1110 Questions with Solutions

- Second Edition -

Published by Creatspace: 12/01/2017

ISBN 13: 9781517619497
ISBN 10 : 1517619491

Tayyip Oral

555 ACT MATH

1110 Questions with Solutions

- Second Edition -

www.555mathbooks.com

www.555academy.com

555 Math Book series

* 555 GIFTED and TALENT for Elementary School Students

* 555 SAT Math (555 Questions with Solution)

* 555 GEOMETRY (555 Questions with Solution)

* 555 GEOMETRY Problems for High School Students

* 555 ACT Math (555 Questions with Solution)

* 555 ACT Math (555 Questions with Answer)

* 555 ADVANCED Math Problems - for Middle School Students

* 555 MATH IQ Questions for High School Students

* 555 MATH IQ Questions for Middle School Students

* 555 MATH IQ Questions for Elementary School Students

* 555 GEOMETRY Formula handbook for SAT, ACT, GRE

* GEOMETRY Formula Handbook.

* ALGEBRA Handbook for Middle School Students

Order the 555 Math Book series

www.555academy.com

www.amazon.com

and

www.barnesandnoble.com

www.555mathbooks.com

Table of Contents

INTRODUCTION

555 ACT Math skills for a high score 1110 math questions and solutions. 1110 questions cover all concepts. The book consists of 1110 number and word type math problems, the solutions to those problems are also included. The book covers basics of ACT preparation. Some of those questions are easy to solve even with the least knowledge of math, because all of them come with the easiest and shortest possible solution methods. Harder questions come with formulas and short tips explaining the answers. The index page for the book follows as

555 ACT Math

1110 Questions with Solutions

- Second Edition -

LEVEL 1: 555 Questions with Solutions

TEST – 1.1

- Questions -

1) $2(3x+4)+3(2x+4)=?$

   A) 12x+12   B) 12x+16   C) 14x+20   D)12x+20   E) 20x+12

2) $(8 - 4)^2+(4 - 8)^2=?$

   A) 30   B) 32   C) 0   D) 64   E) 80

3) If $x^2+8x+7=0$ which of the following show all of the possible value(s) of x?

   A) 7, 1   B) 1, 8   C) -7, -1   D) 8   E) 7

4) What is the least common denominator when adding three fractions with denominators of 4, 5, and 6?

   A) 60   B) 70   C) 72   D) 80   E) 84

5) If the width of a rectangle is 8 and its perimeter is 36, what is its length?

   A) 10   B) 9   C) 8   D) 7   E) 6

6) If the circumference of circle is 24π, what is the area?

   A) 48π B) 56π C) 120π D) 144π E) 164π

7) In the number sequence 2, 7, 22, 67, ___, 607, what number should be placed in the blank?

A) 170   B) 182   C) 192   D) 200   E) 202

8) In the number sequence 1, 4, 9, 16, 25, ___, 49, what number should be placed in the blank?

A) 36   B) 40   C) 64   D) 66   E) 68

9) $|-2\pi| + |2\pi-1|=?$

A) 1   B) 4π C) $4\pi-1$ D) $4\pi+1$ E) 2π

10) If $5x=7y$, find the min(x+y)=?

A) 12   B) 14   C) 16   D) 18   E) 20

11) Which number is divisibly by 3?

A) 9907   B) 9941   C) 99961   D) 99971   E) 99981

12) What is the greatest common factor of 14 and 21?

A) 1   B) 7   C) 3   D) 14   E) 21

13) Which percent of 400 is 100?

    A) 25%   B) 30%   C) 40%   D) 45%   E) 48%

14) Jack purchased a new ACT math book for $120; he bought book at a 20% discount. Find the original price of the book.

    A) 120   B) 130   C) 140   D) 150   E) 160

15) The school has a total of 120 students, 40 of whom are girls. What is the ratio of girls to boys?

    A) 1 to 5   B) 1 to 6   C) 1 to 2   D) 1 to 7   E) 2 to 5

16) Find the mean, median, and range for 5, 6, 8, 10, 13, 13, and 15.

    A) $\frac{71}{7}$, 10, 10   B) $\frac{71}{7}$, 10, 9   C) 10, 11, 13

    D) $\frac{71}{6}$, 10, 13   E) 8, 9, 10

17) Find the mean, median, mode, and range for 6, 6, 8, 12, 16, and 16.

    A) $\frac{32}{3}$, 10, 6, 10   B) $\frac{32}{3}$, 10, 6, 16, 10   C) 32, 10, 16, 6

    D) $\frac{32}{5}$, 10, 6, 16, 10   E) 10, 10, 6, 16, 10

18) If x=4, the value of $x^2 - 3x - 3$ is

    A) 4   B) 3   C) 2   D) 1   E) 0

19) Thirty students scored an 80, and 40 students scored a 90. Find the mean of all students' scores.

    A) 80   B) 81   C) 82   D) 83   E) 86

20) If 5, 7, a, b, and 17 are prime numbers, find 2a+b .

    A) 35   B) 37   C) 30   D) 28   E) 27

21) Which fraction is the largest?

    A) $\dfrac{3}{4}$ B) $\dfrac{7}{8}$ C) $\dfrac{7}{16}$ D) $\dfrac{8}{32}$ E) $\dfrac{17}{64}$

22) Find the mean of $\dfrac{2}{3}$ and $\dfrac{1}{5}$.

    A) $\dfrac{12}{29}$ B) $\dfrac{14}{27}$ C) $\dfrac{13}{28}$ D) $\dfrac{13}{30}$ E) $\dfrac{13}{29}$

23) If $2.24 = \dfrac{a}{b}$, then a-b=?

    A) 31   B) 32   C) 33   D) 34   E) 35

24) 99/66=a/b   if a+b=?

    A) 7   B) 5   C) 6   D) 4   E) 3

25) **Change 64% to a fraction.**

   A) $\frac{16}{44}$ B) $\frac{16}{50}$ C) $\frac{16}{25}$ D) $\frac{32}{75}$ E) $\frac{25}{16}$

26) **14% of what is 56?**

   A) 400   B) 380   C) 340   D) 350   E) 320

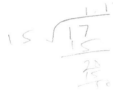

27) **17 is what percent of 15?**

   A) 105%   B) 110%   C) 111%   D) 118%   E) 113%

28) **The number of people who visited a museum increased from about 24,000 in 2011 to about 28,000 in 2012. Find the actual increase and the percent increase.**

   A) 22%   B) 20%   C) 18%`   D) 16%   E) 14%

29) **The book cost of a $300 is decreased by 20 if there is 3% sales tax, how much does cost?**

   A) 230   B) 240   C) 246,2   D) 245,3   E) 247,2

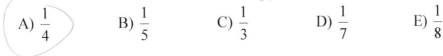

30) **A fraction between $\frac{7}{32}$ and $\frac{9}{32}$ is**

   A) $\frac{1}{4}$ B) $\frac{1}{5}$ C) $\frac{1}{3}$ D) $\frac{1}{7}$ E) $\frac{1}{8}$

31) A price increase of 30% followed by a decrease of 30% means the price is

   A) up 8%   B) up 3%   C) down 3%   D) down 9%   E) up 9%

32) Which is equivalent to 0.08333

   A) $\frac{1}{7}$ B) $\frac{1}{9}$ C) $\frac{1}{12}$ D) $\frac{1}{15}$ E) $\frac{1}{16}$

33) $(3a^2b^3)^3 = ?$

   A) $27a^6b^9$ B) $27a^7b^{27}$ C) $90a^6b^9$ D) $27a^6b^6$ E) $18a^2b^6$

34) $(6x^2)^3 : (3x^3)^2 = ?$

   A) $2x^6$ B) $12x^6$ C) $24x^6$ D) 24   E) 1

35) $3^m + 3^m + 3^m = ?$

   A) 3^{4m} B) 3^{3m+3} C) 3^{m+1} D) 3^m E) 3^{m+3}

36) $14^m : 7^m = ?$

   A) 7^m B) 7^{m+1} C) 2   D) 2^m E) 2^{m+1}

37) If -2≤x≤3, where is x^2 located?

 A) $4<x^2\leq9$ B) $4\leq x^2\leq9$ C) $4\leq x<9$ D) $2\leq x\leq9$ E) $9\leq x\leq4$

38) $\left(\sqrt{5}+\sqrt{2}\right)^2-2\sqrt{10}=?$

 A) 7   B) 6   C) $2\sqrt{10}$ D) $-4\sqrt{10}$ E) $3\sqrt{10}$

39) $99^2-90^2=9k$, k=?

 A) 199   B) 189   C) 174   D) 169   E) 159

40) If $(x+3)^2+(x-3)^2=2A$, then A=?

 A) $2x^2+9$ B) $2x+6$ C) $2x$ D) x^2-9 E) x^2+9

41) (24x+6):(4x+1)

 A) 8   B) 7   C) 6   D) 6x+1   E) 4x+1

42) Solve for x, given 6x-4=3x+8.

 A) 4   B) 5   C) 6   D) 7   E) 8

43) Solve for x, given |3x-6|=6.

 A) 4,1   B) 0;4   C) 3,0   D) 5,2   E) 6,0

44) The sum of two numbers is 16 and their difference is 2. The smaller number is

A) 10   B) 9   C) 8   D) 7   E) 6

45) A(6, 2), B(10, 4) find the distance AB.

A) 4   B) $3\sqrt{3}$ C) $2\sqrt{3}$ D) $\sqrt{5}$ E) $2\sqrt{5}$

46) Given $d_1 \| d_2$ in the image above, then y-x=?

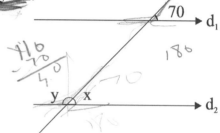

A) 40   B) 44   C) 50

D) 54   E) 60

47)

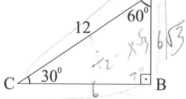

Given $\angle B=90^0$ and AC=12cm. The perimeter ABC=?

A) $18\sqrt{3}$ B) $18+6\sqrt{3}$ C) $17+6\sqrt{3}$

D) $8+8\sqrt{3}$ E) $24+7\sqrt{3}$

48)

 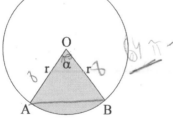

OA=OB=r=8cm, α=30⁰,

Find the area of the 30⁰ sector.

A) $\dfrac{15\pi}{3}$ B) 8π C) $\dfrac{16\pi}{3}$ D) 30π E) $\dfrac{16\pi}{5}$

49) For a cube with an edge of 4 meters, find (V):(SA)

A) $\dfrac{5}{2}$ B) $\dfrac{2}{5}$ C) $\dfrac{3}{2}$ D) $\dfrac{2}{3}$ E) 1

50) $\log_3 x = -3$, x=?

A) 27 B) 1 C) $\dfrac{1}{3}$ D) $\dfrac{1}{9}$ E) $\dfrac{1}{27}$

51) What is the distance of the point (8-4i)

A) $4\sqrt{5}$ B) $4\sqrt{9}$ C) $3\sqrt{5}$ D) $5\sqrt{3}$ E) 8

52) 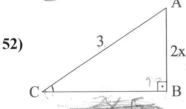 tanC=?

A) $\dfrac{2x}{\sqrt{9+4x}}$ B) $\dfrac{2x}{\sqrt{9-4x^2}}$ C) $\dfrac{3}{\sqrt{9+4x}}$ D) $\dfrac{3}{\sqrt{9-4x^2}}$ E) $\dfrac{3}{2}$

53) If the diagonal of square is 12, its area is

A) 164 B) 72 C) 84 D) 120 E) 144

54)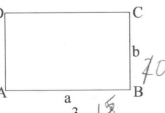

Given a:b=$\dfrac{3}{2}$ and perimeter ABCD=50cm, Area(ABCD)=?

A) 120 B) 130 C) 140 D) 150 E) 160

55) Given the line 7x+9y=63, find the slope.

    A) -7   B) $-\dfrac{9}{7}$ C) $\dfrac{9}{7}$ D) $-\dfrac{7}{9}$ E) $\dfrac{7}{9}$

56) The perimeter of a small rectangular garden is 44 feet and its area is 120 square feet. Find the length of the diagonal.

    A) $\sqrt{61}$ B) $2\sqrt{61}$ C) $3\sqrt{61}$ D) $\sqrt{5}$ E) $2\sqrt{51}$

57)

BD=8, DC=10, $\dfrac{A(ABD)}{A(ABC)}=?$

    A) $\dfrac{4}{9}$ B) $\dfrac{9}{4}$ C) $\dfrac{4}{5}$ D) $\dfrac{5}{4}$ E) 2

58) $\dfrac{x}{2}+\dfrac{x}{3}=8$, when x=?

    A) $\dfrac{24}{5}$ B) $\dfrac{48}{5}$ C) $\dfrac{48}{7}$ D) $\dfrac{36}{5}$ E) $\dfrac{18}{5}$

59) Find the center of circle $x^2+y^2+12x+10y+20=0$

    A) (6, 5)   B) (-6, 5)   C) (-6, -5)   D) (3, 5)   E) (-5, -6)

60) $A=\begin{bmatrix} 0 & 1 \\ 2 & 3 \end{bmatrix}$, $B=\begin{bmatrix} 4 & 5 \\ 6 & 7 \end{bmatrix}$, A+B=?

    A) $\begin{bmatrix} 4 & 6 \\ 8 & 9 \end{bmatrix}$ B) $\begin{bmatrix} 4 & 6 \\ 9 & 8 \end{bmatrix}$ C) $\begin{bmatrix} 4 & 6 \\ 7 & 7 \end{bmatrix}$ D) $\begin{bmatrix} 4 & 6 \\ 8 & 10 \end{bmatrix}$ E) $\begin{bmatrix} 5 & 7 \\ 9 & 10 \end{bmatrix}$

TEST – 1.2
- Questions -

1) If $3x-3y=12$, then $2x-2y=?$

   A) 8   B) 9   C) 10   D) 11   E) 7

2) If $2x-6=6-2x$, then $x^2=?$

   A) 11   B) 10   C) 9   D) 8   E) 7

3) The sum of two numbers is 32 and their difference is 2. What is the value of the smaller number?

   A) 20   B) 18   C) 17   D) 15   E) 13

Questions 4, 5, & 6 refer to line m: $2x+3y=12$

4) The slope of m is

   A) 6   B) $-\dfrac{3}{2}$ C) $\dfrac{3}{2}$ D) $\dfrac{2}{3}$ E) $-\dfrac{2}{3}$

5) The x–intercept of m is

   A) (6, 0)   B) (0, 6)   C) (0, 3)   D) (3, 0)   E) 3

6) The y–intercept of m is

   A) (4, 0)   B) (0, 3)   C) (0, 4)   D) (6, 0)   E) (0, 6)

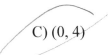

7) $(8) \cdot (0.004) : (0.32)$

A) $\dfrac{1}{8}$ B) 10   C) $\dfrac{2}{5}$ D) $\dfrac{1}{10}$ E) 16

8) $\left(\sqrt{9} + \sqrt{27}\right) : \left(\sqrt{9}\right)$

A) $3 - \sqrt{3}$ B) $3 + \sqrt{3}$ C) $\sqrt{3}$ D) $1 - \sqrt{3}$ E) $1 + \sqrt{3}$

9) **Find the arithmetic mean of the following four numbers:** $\sqrt{5}$, $\sqrt{20}$, $\sqrt{45}$, $\sqrt{80}$

A) $5\sqrt{5}$ B) $\dfrac{5\sqrt{5}}{2}$ C) $\dfrac{5\sqrt{5}}{3}$ D) $6\sqrt{5}$ E) $\dfrac{6\sqrt{5}}{7}$

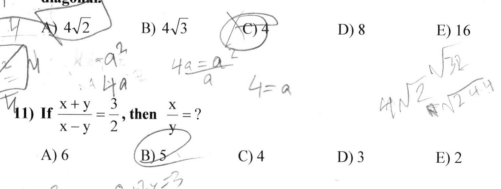

10) **The perimeter and area of a square are the same. Find the length of its diagonal.**

A) $4\sqrt{2}$ B) $4\sqrt{3}$ C) 4   D) 8   E) 16

11) **If** $\dfrac{x+y}{x-y} = \dfrac{3}{2}$, **then** $\dfrac{x}{y} = ?$

A) 6   B) 5   C) 4   D) 3   E) 2

12) $14^x = 7^x \cdot m$,   m=?

A) 1   B) 2   C) 2^x D) 7^x E) 4^x

13) $x^2 - y^2 = k,$ $(x+y)=m,$ $(x - y)=?$

A) $\dfrac{k}{m}$ B) $\dfrac{m}{k}$ C) mk   D) m   E) k

14) In an arithmetic progression, $a_1=3$, $a_2=6$,   then $a_8=?$

A) 12   B) 16   C) 18   D) 24   E) 30

15) $\sqrt{x + 3} = 3$, $x=?$

A) 8   B) 7   C) 6   D) 5   E) 4

16) Jack is 15 and his father 40. Find the sum of their ages after six years.

A) 60   B) 61   C) 62   D) 64   E) 67

17) Find the ratio of x to z if $3x=5y$ and $4y=7z$.

A) $\dfrac{36}{13}$ B) $\dfrac{12}{35}$ C) $\dfrac{35}{12}$ D) $\dfrac{13}{36}$ E) 4

18) $f(x)=x^2+3x$; $f(3x)=?$

A) $9+9x$ B) $9x^2+1$ C) $9x^2+9x$ D) $9x^2$ E) 9

19) $2(2x+4)=(x+5);$ $x=?$

A) 2   B) 1   C) 0   D) -1   E) -2

$4x+8=x+5$

$3x=-3$ $x=-1$

20) An arithmetic sequence is: 10, 4, -2,-8,-14,… $(a_5+a_{-6})=?$

A) -34   B) -42   C) -32   D) 32   E) 42

$a_n=a_1+(n-1)d$

$a_9=10+4=14$

21) $A = \begin{bmatrix} 4 & 2 \\ 3 & 1 \end{bmatrix}$, $B = \begin{bmatrix} 1 & 2 \\ 3 & 4 \end{bmatrix}$, $2A+3B=?$

A) $\begin{bmatrix} 11 & 10 \\ 15 & 14 \end{bmatrix}$ B) $\begin{bmatrix} 10 & 10 \\ 15 & 14 \end{bmatrix}$ C) $\begin{bmatrix} 9 & 10 \\ 15 & 14 \end{bmatrix}$ D) $\begin{bmatrix} 13 & 14 \\ 14 & 13 \end{bmatrix}$ E) $\begin{bmatrix} 10 & 12 \\ 13 & 15 \end{bmatrix}$

22) $A = \begin{bmatrix} 9 & 8 \\ 7 & 6 \end{bmatrix}$, $B = \begin{bmatrix} 1 & 2 \\ 3 & 4 \end{bmatrix}$, $A-B=?$

A) $\begin{bmatrix} 8 & 6 \\ 3 & 3 \end{bmatrix}$ B) $\begin{bmatrix} 8 & 6 \\ 4 & 2 \end{bmatrix}$ C) $\begin{bmatrix} 8 & 6 \\ 3 & 4 \end{bmatrix}$ D) $\begin{bmatrix} 7 & 3 \\ 2 & 1 \end{bmatrix}$ E) $\begin{bmatrix} 1 & 3 \\ 6 & 2 \end{bmatrix}$

23) $\dfrac{2+\sqrt{5}}{2-\sqrt{5}}+9=?$

A) $\left(2+\sqrt{5}\right)^2$ B) $2\sqrt{5}$ C) $3\sqrt{5}$ D) $4\sqrt{5}$ E) $-4\sqrt{5}$

24) f(x)=3x+3,   g(x)=2x+2,   f(g(2))=?

A) 18   B) 19   C) 20   D) 21   E) 22

25) $(i)^{-8} - (i)^{-6} = ?$

    A) 1   B) 2   C) 0   D) -2   E) -1

26) Find the sum of the number of diagonals in a square and in a trapezoid.

    A) 8   B) 7   C) 6   D) 5   E) 4

27) Two squares are similar, with a ratio of ¾. If the perimeter of the smaller square is 24, find the perimeter of larger square.

    A) 30   B) 31   C) 32   D) 34   E) 36

28)   tanC+cotC=?

    A) $\dfrac{4m^2 + 9n^2}{6mn}$ B) $\dfrac{4m^2 + 6n^2}{4mn}$ C) $\dfrac{3m^2 + 4n^2}{6mn}$

    D) $\dfrac{4m^2 - 9n^2}{6mn}$ E) $\dfrac{4m^2 - 6n^2}{4mn}$

29) $\left(x\sqrt{5} + x\sqrt{20}\right) : \sqrt{5} = ?$

    A) $\sqrt{5}$ B) x   C) 2x   D) 3x   E) $3x\sqrt{5}$

30) $f(x) = \dfrac{x^2 + 2x + 3}{9x^2 - 9}$,   f(x) is undefined if x=?

    A) 0, 9   B) -1, 1   C) 9, 1   D) 3, 2   E) -2, 3

31) 4% of 4% of 4 =

   A) 0.16   B) 0.00000064   C) 0.0016

   D) 0.0000064   E) 0.000032

32) In a large university stadium the ratio of men to women is 4:5. If there are 3,600 people in the stadium, find the difference between the number of women and men.

   A) 400   B) 500   C) 600   D) 700   E) 800

33) If a circle has an area of $\sqrt{5}$, find its radius.

   A) $\dfrac{\pi}{\sqrt{5}}$ B) $\sqrt{\dfrac{5}{\pi}}$ C) $\sqrt{\dfrac{\pi}{5}}$ D) π E) 5π

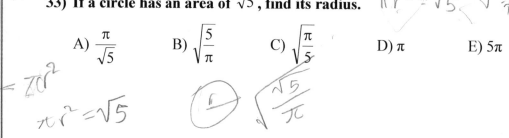

34) $(14)^x : 7^x = ?$

   A) 7^x B) 2^x C) 2   D) 7   E) 1

35) $(5^2 - 5^1) \cdot (4^2 - 4^1) \cdot (3^2 - 3^1) = ?$

   A) 1240   B) 1340   C) 1440   D) 1560   E) 1640

36) $\left(\sqrt{5} + \sqrt{10}\right) : \left(1 + \sqrt{2}\right) = ?$

   A) 2   B) 3   C) $1 + \sqrt{2}$ D) $1 - \sqrt{2}$ E) $\sqrt{5}$

37) Enlarge the fraction $\dfrac{4}{5}$ by 9.

    A) $\dfrac{4}{45}$ B) $\dfrac{36}{5}$ C) $\dfrac{45}{36}$ D) $\dfrac{36}{45}$ E) 1

38) The difference of the squares of two consecutive odd numbers is 24. Find the value of these numbers.

    A) 5, 7   B) 5, 6   C) 7, 4   D) 7, 3   E) 6, 3

39) $0.(22) = \dfrac{a}{b}$ if a+b=?

    A) 7   B) 8   C) 9   D) 10   E) 11

40) Round 0.87 into its tenths place.

    A) 0.9   B) 0.8   C) 0.88   D) 1.0   E) 0.92

41) If x-6=y, then evaluate the value of $|4x-4y| + |6y-6x|$.

    A) 60   B) 50   C) 40   D) 30   E) 20

42) Calculate the geometric mean of 100 and 169

    A) 110   B) 120   C) 130   D) 140   E) 150

43) A TV plaza cost $800 after a 20% discount. Originally the cost was

    A) $1000   B) $900   C) $800   D) $700   E) $750

44) $(x-2)^2=(x-4)^2$, x=?

    A) 1   B) 2   C) 3   D) 4   E) 5

45) $\left(\dfrac{3}{2}-\dfrac{2}{3}\right)\cdot\left(\dfrac{3}{2}+\dfrac{2}{3}\right)=?$

    A) $\dfrac{25}{7}$ B) $\dfrac{36}{25}$ C) $\dfrac{12}{25}$ D) $\dfrac{25}{36}$ E) 65/36

46) $\log_9 x^2=2$, $\sqrt{x}$ =?

    A) 5   B)   C) 6   D) 8   E) 9

47) **A circle whose center is at the point (9, 12) and is tangent to the y-axis has a radius of**

    A) 12   B) 9   C) 6   D) 4.5   E) 6

48) $\sin 2x=2\sin x\cdot\cos x$;   if $\sin x=5/6$,   find $\sin 2x$.

    A) $\dfrac{6\sqrt{11}}{5}$ B) $\dfrac{10\sqrt{11}}{18}$ C) $\dfrac{5\sqrt{11}}{18}$ D) $\dfrac{\sqrt{11}}{18}$ E) $\dfrac{3\sqrt{11}}{17}$

49) $\left.\begin{array}{l} 2a+3b=12 \\ 3a+2b=13 \end{array}\right\}$ a+b=?

    A) 5   B) 6   C) 7   D) 4   E) 3

50) 4/7 and $-\dfrac{2}{7}$ are two solutions to a quadratic equation. Find the equation.

A) $49x^2-14x-8$ B) $49x^2+14x+8$ C) $7x^2+14x+8$

D) $29x^2-14x+8$ E) $7x^2-14x-8$

51) $f(x) = \dfrac{(x-3)^2}{x^2+12x}$, **f(x) is undefined if**

A) x=3 only B) x=3 and x=-12 only
C) x=1 and x=12 D) x=0 and x= -12 only
E) x=3, x=0, and x=-12

* $\sqrt{(a+b)+2\sqrt{ab}} = \sqrt{a} + \sqrt{b}$

52) $\sqrt{7+2\sqrt{12}} = ?$

A) $2+\sqrt{3}$ B) $4+\sqrt{3}$ C) $1+\sqrt{3}$ D) $\sqrt{3}+\sqrt{2}$ E) $\sqrt{2}+\sqrt{5}$

53) $x^2+5x+3m=(x+3)\cdot(x+n)$, n=?

A) 1   B) 2   C) 3   D) 4   E) 5

54) **Three brothers' ages form the ratio of 2:4:6. Their ages sum to 60. Find the eldest brother's age.**

A) 20   B) 25   C) 30   D) 32   E) 33

55)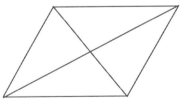

How many triangles are there?

A) 8   B) 7   C) 6   D) 5   E) 4

56)

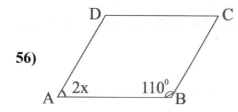

ABCD is a parallelogram. $\angle A=2x$, $\angle B=110^o$, x=?

A) 30   B) 32   C) 35   D) 36   E) 40

57)

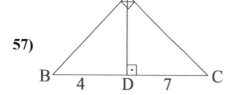

$\angle A=\angle ADC=90^o$, BD=4, DC=7, AD=?

A) 14   B) 28   C) $4\sqrt{7}$ D) $2\sqrt{7}$ E) $3\sqrt{7}$

58) A rectangle has sides 12 inches and 4 inches. Determine the length of the diagonal, in inches.

A) $5\sqrt{5}$ B) $6\sqrt{10}$ C) $2\sqrt{10}$ D) $3\sqrt{10}$ E) $4\sqrt{10}$

59) $\left(\dfrac{a}{b}+\dfrac{b}{a}\right)^2-2=?$

A) $\dfrac{a^2}{b^2}+\dfrac{b^2}{a^2}$ B) $\dfrac{a^2}{b^2}+\dfrac{a^2}{b^2}+2$ C) $\dfrac{a^2}{b^2}-\dfrac{b^2}{a^2}+2$

D) $\dfrac{a^2}{b^2}+2$ E) $\dfrac{a^2}{b^2}-2$

60) d_1: $2x+3y=12$ and d_2: $y=3x+4$. Sum the slopes of lines d_1 and d_2.

A) $\dfrac{7}{3}$ B) $\dfrac{6}{5}$ C) $\dfrac{11}{3}$ D) $\dfrac{7}{6}$ E) 0

TEST – 1.3
- Questions -

1) **Find the different.**

   A) $\dfrac{3}{4}$ 　　 B) $\dfrac{9}{12}$ 　　 C) $\dfrac{2}{3}$ 　　 D) $\dfrac{15}{20}$ 　　 E) $\dfrac{12}{16}$

2) $\sqrt{(a+b)+2\sqrt{a\cdot b}}=\sqrt{a}+\sqrt{b}$, $\sqrt{9+2\sqrt{18}}=?$

   A) $\sqrt{6}-\sqrt{2}$ 　 B) $\sqrt{6}+\sqrt{3}$ 　 C) $\sqrt{6}-\sqrt{3}$ 　 D) $3+\sqrt{6}$ 　 E) $3-\sqrt{6}$

3) **Given $f(x)=2x^2+4$ and $g(x)=x^2+2$, which of the following relationships between $f(x)$ and $g(x)$ is true?**

   A) $f(x)=g(x)$ 　　　　 B) $f(x)=g(x)-2$ 　　　　 C) $f(x)=2g(x)$
   D) $g(x)=3f(x)$ 　　　　 E) $f(x)=3g(x)$

4) **Given $f(x)=x^2+16$ and $g(x)=(x+4)^2$, which of the following relationships between $f(x)$ and $g(x)$ is true?**

   A) $g(x)=f(x)+8x$ 　　　 B) $g(x)=f(x)-8x$ 　　　 C) $g(x)=2f(x)+4$
   D) $g(x)=3f(x)$ 　　　　 E) $g(x)=2f(x)-4$

In Questions 5-6, A={1, 2, 4, 8, 16, 27, 30, 36, 64}.

5) **How many perfect squares are in sequence A?**

   A) 5 　　　 B) 4 　　　 C) 3 　　　 D) 2 　　　 E) 1

6) **How many perfect cubes are in sequence A?**

   A) 6 　　　 B) 5 　　　 C) 4 　　　 D) 3 　　　 E) 2

7) **Find the different.**

   A) $\dfrac{4^x}{2^{2x}}$ B) $\dfrac{14^x}{7^x}$ C) $\dfrac{3^{2x}}{9^x}$ D) $\dfrac{5^{2x}}{25^x}$ E) $\dfrac{6^{2x}}{36^x}$

8) **What percent of 800 is 600?**

   A) 45%   B) 55%   C) 60%   D) 75%   E) 80%

9) **What is the value of x   if   4x+4=2x+16?**

   A) 6   B) 7   C) 8   D) 9   E) 10

10) **What is the value of $4a^2$-2ab+b^2 if   a=2, and b=-3?**

   A) 30   B) 29   C) 24   D) 20   E) 18

11) **Which of the following expressions is equivalent to 4x+3y+6xy-x-6y-3xy?**

   A) x-y+3xy   B) 3(x-y+xy)   C) 2(x-y+xy)
   D) 4(x-y+xy)   E) 3(x-y-xy)

12) **a^2-b^2=2x,   (a-b)=y   , a+b=?**

   A) 2xy   B) $\dfrac{y}{2x}$ C) $\dfrac{2x}{y}$ D) $\dfrac{2y}{x}$ E) xy

13) If $\dfrac{6n+3}{4} = \dfrac{2n-5}{5}$, then $22n = ?$

   A) -33   B) -44   C) -35   D) -66   E) -55

14) Which of the following values satisfies the equation $\sqrt{3x+12} - 4 = x$?

   A) (-4, -1)   B) (-4, 0)   C) (-1, 0)   D) (-1, 2)   E) (-2, -1)

15) $4(x^2+3)=2(2x^2+2x)$, $x=?$

   A) 3   B) 4   C) 5   D) 6   E) 7

16) 14, 13, 26, 25, 50, x, y;   x+y=?

   A) 140   B) 147   C) 148   D) 149   E) 152

17) $ax+by+cx=my$, then $y=?$

   A) $\dfrac{m+b}{a+c}$ B) $\dfrac{x(a-c)}{m+b}$ C) $\dfrac{x(a+c)}{m+b}$ D) $\dfrac{x(a+c)}{m-b}$ E) $\dfrac{m-b}{a+c}$

18) Which is the smallest?

   A) $\dfrac{\pi}{\sqrt{13}}$ B) $\dfrac{\pi}{4}$ C) $\dfrac{\pi}{\sqrt{17}}$ D) $\dfrac{\pi}{\sqrt{18}}$ E) $\dfrac{\pi}{\sqrt{22}}$

19) Enlarge the fraction $\dfrac{5}{9}$ by 12.

    A) $\dfrac{108}{60}$ B) $\dfrac{60}{54}$ C) $\dfrac{60}{108}$ D) $\dfrac{70}{108}$ E) $\dfrac{80}{108}$

20) Find positive proper divisors of go 40.

    A) 10   B) 9   C) 8   D) 7   E) 6

21) A tin contains 84 lb. of olive oil and another tin contains 106 lb. of flare oil. Both oils will be mixed and filled into bottles of equal volume such that there will be no remaining oil. At least how many bottles will be needed?

    A) 12   B) 10   C) 9   D) 8   E) 7

22) 5!-4!-2!-1!=?

    A) 90   B) 92   C) 93   D) 97   E) 98

23) What is the product of the solutions to the equation $|x-3|=4$?

    A) -8   B) -7   C) -6   D) 6   E) 8

24) If $x-4=y$, then evaluate the value of $|6x-6y|=?$

    A) 12   B) 26   C) 24   D) 28   E) 32

25) Calculate the geometric mean of 49 and 100.

    A) 70   B) 74   C) 78   D) 84   E) 94

26) Calculate the ratio of milk in the mixture when 30 lb of water is mixed with 70 lb of milk.

A) $\frac{5}{2}$ B) $\frac{2}{5}$ C) $\frac{10}{3}$ D) $\frac{3}{10}$ E) 1

27) The perimeter of a rectangle is 80cm, and the proportion of sides is 3:7. Calculate the length of the shorter side.

 A) 10   B) 12   C) 14   D) 16   E) 18

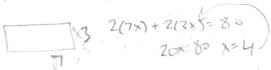

28) Numbers x and y are directly proportional. If y=8 when x=4, then what is the value of x when 24?

A) 44   B) 42   C) 48   D) 50   E) 52

29) What is the value of 30% of 40?

A) 16   B) 14   C) 12   D) 10   E) 8

30) What is the difference $\frac{1}{3}$ and $\frac{1}{4}$ of a number is 5 what is this number?

A) 90   B) 80   C) 70   D) 60   E) 50

31)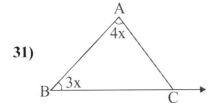

AB=AC, ∠A=4x, ∠B=3x, x=?

A) 30° B) 25° C) 20° D) 18° E) 16°

32)

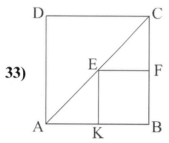

AB=6, AC=6, BD=3, DC=4, AD=4,
Find the sum of all three triangles' perimeters.

A) 36   B) 49   C) 50   D) 52   E) 54

33)

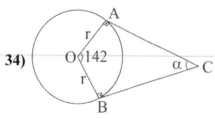

ABCD is square. Find the perimeter KBFE if AB=16cm.

A) 32   B) 34   C) 36   D) 38   E) 40

34)

O is the center of the circle. $\angle AOB=142^0$, $\angle A=\angle B=90^0$, $\angle C=\alpha=$?

A) 34   B) 36   C) 38   D) 40   E) 42

35) Find the surface area of a rectangular prism, with shorter side 7 cm., longer side 8 cm., and height 5 cm..

A) 248cm^2 B) 262cm^2 C) 280cm^2 D) 290cm^2 E) 300cm^2

36) A line passes through points A(9, 3) and B(12, 6). Find the slope of this line.

A) 4   B) 3   C) 2   D) 1   E) 5

37) The sum of the ages of 6 siblings now is 80. Calculate the sum of their ages 4 years ago.

A) 50   B) 56   C) 58   D) 60   E) 64

38) Jack can complete a task in 12 days. George can complete the same task in 16 days. If they work together, what percentage of the task can they complete at the end of 1 day?

A) $\dfrac{7}{48}$ B) $\dfrac{7}{43}$ C) $\dfrac{48}{7}$ D) $\dfrac{6}{43}$ E) $\dfrac{8}{43}$

39) The first pipe fills an empty pool in 12 hours, and a second pipe fills the same pool in 20 hours. If both pipes are turned on, in how many hours will the pool be filled?

A) 6   B) 7.5   C) 8   D) 9   E) 10

40) In how many different ways can 5 people sit around a round table?

A) 24   B) 28   C) 30   D) 36   E) 40

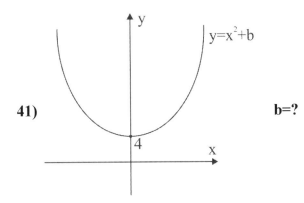

41)   b=?

A) 1   B) 2   C) 4   D) 0   E) 3

42) If $2a+b+c=14$, $a+2b+c=16$, $a+b+2c=18$, then $a+b+c=?$

A) 10   B) 11   C) 16   D) 13   E) 16

43) One sack of feed will last a canary, pigeon, and chicken 100, 60, and 40 days respectively. With one sack of feed, for how many days can all 3 birds eat?

A) 25   B) 22   C) 21   D) 19   E) 1 5

44) Create different 3 digit numbers by using the numbers 2, 4 and 3. Find the sum of all the numbers created.

A) 2644   B) 2654   C) 2544   D) 2444   E) 2254

45) What is the sum of the divisors of 24?

A) 60   B) 54   C) 50   D) 48   E) 44

46) Which of the following is a rational number?

A) $\dfrac{\sqrt{3}}{\sqrt{2}}$ B) $\sqrt{5}$ C) $\sqrt{7}$ D) $\dfrac{\sqrt{100}}{\sqrt{289}}$ E) $\sqrt{13}$

47)

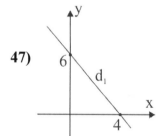

Find the equation of the line d_1.

A) $\dfrac{x}{4}+\dfrac{y}{6}=2$ B) $\dfrac{x}{4}+\dfrac{y}{6}=1$ C) $\dfrac{x}{2}+\dfrac{y}{3}=1$ D) $\dfrac{x}{4}-\dfrac{y}{6}=1$ E) $\dfrac{x}{2}-\dfrac{y}{3}=1$

48) If $\log_3 x = 4$, the $x^2 = ?$

A) 81   B) 3^5 C) 3^6 D) 3^8 E) 3^{16}

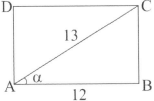

49)

Find the sin2α=?

A) $\dfrac{60}{169}$ B) $\dfrac{120}{169}$ C) $\dfrac{60}{159}$ D) $\dfrac{120}{26}$ E) $\dfrac{26}{169}$

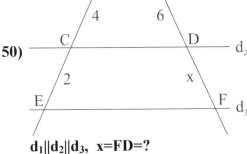

50)

$d_1 \| d_2 \| d_3$, x=FD=?

A) 3 B) 4 C) 5 D) 6 E) 7

51) Which of the following gives the solutions to the equation $x^2+4x=12$?

A) 6 and -2 B) 4 and -2 C) -6 and 2 D) -6 and 3 E) -4 and 2

52) In the (x, y) coordinate plane, what is the y- intercept of the line 12x-9y=17?

A) $\dfrac{17}{9}$ B) $\dfrac{9}{17}$ C) $\dfrac{6}{17}$ D) $-\dfrac{17}{9}$ E) $-\dfrac{6}{17}$

53) For the complex number i such that $i^2=-1$, what is the value of $i^8+i^4+4i^2=?$

A) 2 B) -2 C) 3 D) -3 E) 4

54) If 6x-2x-4=12, then x=?

    A) 4   B) 3   C) 2   D) 1   E) 0

55) If P=4x+4, and Q=4y+8 then what is the value of 2P-Q=?

    A) 8x-4y   B) 8x+8y   C) 4x+8y   D) 8x-4y-4   E) 8x+4y

56) The expression 6a+6b-6c+12d is equivalent to which of the following?

    A) 6(a+b+c+d)   B) 6(a+2b-c+d)   C) 6(2a+b+c-d)

    D) 6(a+b-c-2d)   E) 6(a+b-c+2d)

57) If m=-11, what is the value of |2m+20|=?

    A) 8   B) 6   C) 4   D) 2   E) 0

58) Simplify 6-3(2x-2)+6x.

    A) 10   B) 12   C) 6x   D) 6x+6   E) 6x+12

59) If $0^0 \le x \le 90^0$ and tanx=2, then sinx=?

    A) $\dfrac{\sqrt{5}}{2}$ B) $\dfrac{1}{\sqrt{2}}$ C) $\dfrac{2\sqrt{5}}{5}$ D) $\dfrac{\sqrt{5}}{5}$ C) $\dfrac{\sqrt{5}}{2}$

60) What is the slope of the line of the equation 7x-6y=15?

    A) $\dfrac{6}{7}$ B) $\dfrac{-6}{7}$ C) $\dfrac{7}{6}$ D) $\dfrac{-7}{6}$ C) $-\dfrac{15}{7}$

TEST – 1.4

- *Questions* -

1) If a bookstore sells every book for \$5 each, the store will make a \$120 profit, and if the bookstore sells every book for \$4 each, the store will make a \$100 loss. With the information given, how many books does the bookstore have?

   A) 100   B) 110   C) 180   D) 200   E) 220

2) There are 64 men and 16 women in a room. How many married couples should join the room to make the number of men 3 times greater than the number of women?

   A) 6   B) 8   C) 10   D) 12   E) 14

3) If y=-4, what is the value of $\dfrac{y^2 - 9}{y - 3} = ?$

   A) -1   B) -2   C) -3   D) -4   E) -5

4) A and B are positive whole numbers, if a number's 30 times more than the big number and 70 times more than the other number the two number will be equal to each other then what will be minimum value of (A+B)=?

   A) 14   B) 12   C) 10   D) 9   E) 8

5) There are 4 yellow, 7 red, 5 green, and 4 blue marbles in one box. What is the probability of a randomly chosen marble to be green?

   A) $\dfrac{1}{2}$ B) $\dfrac{1}{3}$ C) $\dfrac{1}{4}$ D) $\dfrac{1}{5}$ C) $\dfrac{1}{6}$

6) What is the perimeter of a rectangle with width 2^x and length 2^y?

   A) $2^x + 2^y$ B) 2^{x+y} C) 2^{2x+2y} D) 2^{x-y} E) $2^{x+1} + 2^{y+1}$

7) If there is a 25% clearance on an item that was priced for \$160, how much money would the clearance price be?

    A) 75   B) 80   C) 100   D) 110   E) 120

8) What is the value of (4m+1) given the equation $\dfrac{7}{m} = \dfrac{28}{5}$?

    A) 5   B) 6   C) 7   D) 8   E) 9

9) If -6(m+n-3)=-6n-18, then m=?

    A) -5   B) -6   C) -7   D) 5   E) 6

10)

120^0

$\alpha=?$

α

140^0

    A) 100   B) 110   C) 120   D) 130   E) 140

11) If $f(x)=3^x+x^3$, then f(3) - f(2)=?

    A) 17   B) 27   C) 37   D) 47   E) 57

12) What is the least common multiple of 12, 18, and 20?

    A) 80   B) 100   C) 120   D) 160   E) 180

13)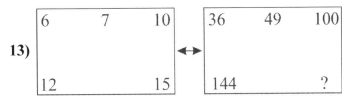

A) 60   B) 120   C) 125   D) 225   E) 230

14) If 3A+3B-3C=21, then 5A+5B-5C=?

A) 30   B) 35   C) 40   D) 45   E) 50

15)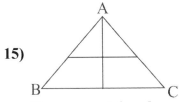

How many triangles are in the figure?

A) 6   B) 7   C) 8   D) 9   E) 10

16)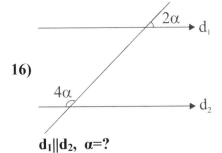

$d_1 \| d_2$, α=?

A) 20   B) 30   C) 40   D) 45   E) 60

17) $43\Delta \rightarrow 71$,
$62\Delta \rightarrow 84$
$94\Delta \rightarrow 135$
$75\Delta \rightarrow ?$

A) 22   B) 102   C) 122   D) 132   E) 135

18)

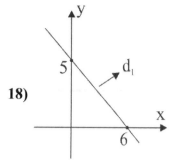

Find the liner equation for d_1.

A) 5x+6y=30   B) 5x+6y+30=0   C) 5x+6y=12

D) 3x+6y=30   E) 6x+5y=20

19) The difference of $\dfrac{x}{2}$ and $\dfrac{x}{3}$ is 20. Which of the following equations represents this relationship?

A) $\dfrac{x}{2}-\dfrac{x}{3}=20$ B) $\dfrac{x}{2}+\dfrac{x}{3}=20$ C) $\dfrac{x}{4}-\dfrac{x}{6}=10$

D) $\dfrac{x}{2}-\dfrac{x}{3}=10$ E) $\dfrac{x}{2}+\dfrac{x}{3}=10$

20) a, b∈N, $a^2-b^2=29$, then calculate a^2+b^2.

A) 320   B) 380   C) 421   D) 432   E) 532

21)

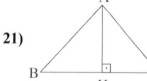

A(ABC)=A(DEF),
If BC=12, AH=8, EF=16, AG=?

A) 9   B) 8   C) 7   D) 6   E) 5

22) The expression 6(y+4) – 4(2y-2) is equivalent to which of the following?

A) 2y-32   B) 2y+16   C) 32   D) 32-2y   E) 16-2y

23) If x+2y=3m and x-2y=m, then x=?

    A) 4m   B) 3m   C) 2m   D) m   E) $\dfrac{m}{2}$

24) If $x = \sqrt{7} - 3$, then what is the value of x^2+6x+9?

    A) 9   B) $\sqrt{3}$ C) 3   D) $\sqrt{7}$ E) 7

25)

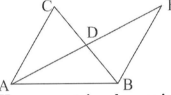

How many triangles are in the figure above?

    A) 5   B) 6   C) 9   D) 10   E) 11

26) d_1 equation: 8y-6x=12   slope: m_1
d_2 equation: 7y+4x=14   slope: m_2
m_1+m_2=?

    A) $-\dfrac{5}{28}$ B) $\dfrac{5}{28}$ C) $\dfrac{4}{17}$ D) $\dfrac{17}{4}$ E) 4

27) If $3x^2+19x+20=(ax-4)(bx+5)$, then $2a+3b$=?

    A) 11   B) 10   C) 9   D) 8   E) 6

28)

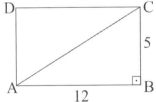

BC=5, AB=12, $\dfrac{P(ABCD)}{P(ABC)}=?$

    A) $\dfrac{30}{17}$ B) $\dfrac{17}{30}$ C) $\dfrac{17}{15}$ D) $\dfrac{30}{19}$ E) 3

29) Which number times $\dfrac{6}{7}$ is equal to 36?

    A) 34   B) 38   C) 40   D) 42   E) 44

30) The sum of the ages of 6 siblings now is 77. Calculate the sum of their ages after 7 years.

    A) 105   B) 106   C) 107   D) 18   E) 119

31) Given the geometric sequence: a, 6, 4a, 24, 16a, and x. Find the value of x.

    A) 96   B) 90   C) 84   D) 80   E) 78

32) If $\dfrac{1}{a}+\dfrac{1}{b}+\dfrac{1}{c}=3x$, then $\dfrac{3}{a}+\dfrac{3}{b}+\dfrac{3}{c}=?$

    A) 4x   B) 5x   C) 6x   D) 9x   E) $\dfrac{1}{x}$

33) Circle 1 contains: 2, 3, 4, 5, 6. Circle 2 contains: 125, x, 64, 27, 8. $x = ?$

    A) 216   B) 217   C) 108   D) 36   E) 172

34) $\dfrac{13^n+13^{n+1}}{13^n+13^n}=?$

    A) 8   B) 7   C) 6   D) 5   E) 4

35) If $\tan\alpha=3a$, then $\sin\alpha=?$

    A) $\dfrac{1}{30}$ B) $3a^2-11$ C) $9a^2+1$ D) $\dfrac{3a}{\sqrt{9a^2+1}}$ E) $\dfrac{a}{9a+1}$

36) $\sqrt{4} + \sqrt{9} + \sqrt{16} + \sqrt{25} = \sqrt{14}\,x$ **if x=?**

    A) 10   B) 12   C) 13   D) 14   E) $\sqrt{14}$

37)

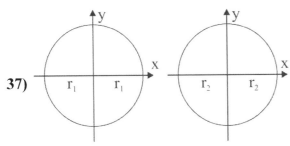

    $x^2+y^2=16$ $x^2+y^2=36$ $2r_2-r_1=?$

    A) 2   B) 3   C) 4   D) 5   E) 6

38) **Turn the number 3.175 to a mixed number, of the form:** $a\dfrac{b}{c}$. **Then find a+b+c.**

    A) 36   B) 40   C) 42   D) 44   E) 50

39) **If a+b=16, a+c=14, and b+c=12, then a+b+c=?**

    A) 20   B) 21   C) 22   D) 23   E) 24

40) **Create different 3 digit numbers by using the numbers 1, 2, and 3. Find the sum of all the numbers created.**

    A) 1224   B) 1320   C) 1332   D) 1440   E) 1312

41)

Books	Price
Math	100
Physics	95
Chemistry	150
Biology	170

The chart above shows the prices of some of the books sold at a local bookstore. A student buys 4 books, 3 which are the same. The student pay $470. Which books did the student buy?

A) Chemistry and Biology   B) Chemistry and Math
C) Math and Biology   D) Math and Physics
E) All Math

42) Given f(x)=(x+3)^2 and q(x)=2x^2+12x+18, which of the following relationships between f(x) and q(x) is correct?

A) f(x)=q(x)   B) f(x)=2q(x)   C) q(x)=2f(x)

D) f(x)+q(x)=0   E) f(x)=3q(x)

43)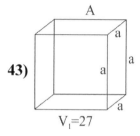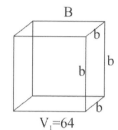

A and B are cubes. The volume of cube A is 27, and the volume of cube B is 64. Find a:b.

A) $\dfrac{3}{2}$ B) $\dfrac{2}{3}$ C) $\dfrac{4}{3}$ D) $\dfrac{3}{4}$ E) $\dfrac{27}{64}$

44)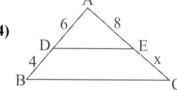

DE∥BC, AD=6, BD=4, AE=8, EC=x, x=?

A) 6   B) 5   C) $\dfrac{16}{5}$ D) $\dfrac{16}{3}$ E) 7

45)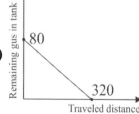

With the information given, at what mile will be vehicle have 25 litres in tank?

A) 100   B) 110   C) 120   D) 125   E) 130

46) If $\dfrac{17}{3} - 3x = \dfrac{11}{3} + 3y$, then x+y=?

   A) 3   B) $\dfrac{3}{2}$ C) 2   D) $\dfrac{2}{3}$ E) 1

47) Write the equation of the circle with a radius of 6cm and center at (5, 4).

   A) $(x-5)^2+(y-4)^2=36$ B) $(x-5)^2+(y+4)^2=36$
   C) $(x+5)^2+(y-4)^2=36$ D) $(x-5)^2+(y+4)^2=25$
   E) $(x+5)^2+(y+6)^2=16$

48) $\ln(5e^3)-3=?$

   A) ln3+5   B) ln5+3   C) ln3+3   D) ln5+5   E) ln15

49) If $3^4 4^4 5^4 = (ab)^c$, then ab+c=?

   A) 54   B) 60   C) 64   D) 66   E) 70

50) A= {2, 3, 4, 5, 6, 7, 8, 9, 10, 11, 12, 13, 14, 15}
   How many prime numbers are in set A?

   A) 6   B) 7   C) 8   D) 9   E) 10

51) Two vehicles drive around a circular track with a perimeter of 280 meters. One vehicle travels 16m/s and the other 12 m/s in opposite directions around the track. In how many seconds will they meet?

   A) 10   B) 11   C) 12   D) 13   E) 14

52) How many even numbers could the value of x be if $14 \leq x \leq 84$?

   A) 30   B) 32   C) 34   D) 35   E) 36

53) How many more is the expression 18a-14b than 14b-18a=?

  A) 32a   B) 16a   C) 32a-4b   D) 28b-16a   E) 36a-28b

54) (6!+8!):6!

  A) 50   B) 52   C) 54   D) 57   E) 60

55) Eight times a number and 8 more is 88. What is the total of its digits?

  A) 1   B) 2   C) 3   D) 4   E) 5

56) Difference of a number 14% and 4% is 30. What is the number?

  A) 400   B) 470   C) 300   D) 320   E) 340

57) Three teachers and 5 students sit around a table. How many different ways can be chosen for their seating arrangement?

  A) 6!   B) 7!   C) 8!   D) 9!   E) 10!

58) $11^{0.32} \cdot 11^{0.26} \cdot 11^{0.42}$, what is result of the operation?

  A) 1   B) 0   C) 11   D) 11^2 E) 22

59) Given |4x-8|=8, find the values of x.

  A) 4; 2   B) 3; 2   C) 0; 4   D) 0; 3   E) 0; 7

60) Find the geometric average of 7 and 4.

  A) 28   B) $\sqrt{14}$ C) 14   D) $2\sqrt{7}$ E) $7\sqrt{2}$

TEST – 1.5

- Questions -

1) **If 6x-6=6-6x,   then x=?**

   A) 1   B) 2   C) 3   D) 4   E) 5

2) **If 3x+3y=9,   then 2x+2y=?**

   A) 10   B) 9   C) 8   D) 6   E) 4

3) **Arrange** $\dfrac{\pi}{\sqrt{13}}, \dfrac{\pi}{\sqrt{17}}, \dfrac{\pi}{\sqrt{25}}, \dfrac{\pi}{\sqrt{10}}$ **in descending order.**

   A) $\dfrac{\pi}{\sqrt{25}} > \dfrac{\pi}{\sqrt{17}} > \dfrac{\pi}{\sqrt{13}} > \dfrac{\pi}{\sqrt{10}}$ B) $\dfrac{\pi}{\sqrt{25}} > \dfrac{\pi}{\sqrt{13}} > \dfrac{\pi}{\sqrt{17}} > \dfrac{\pi}{\sqrt{10}}$

   C) $\dfrac{\pi}{\sqrt{17}} > \dfrac{\pi}{\sqrt{25}} > \dfrac{\pi}{\sqrt{13}} > \dfrac{\pi}{\sqrt{10}}$ D) $\dfrac{\pi}{\sqrt{10}} > \dfrac{\pi}{\sqrt{13}} > \dfrac{\pi}{\sqrt{17}} > \dfrac{\pi}{\sqrt{25}}$

   E) $\dfrac{\pi}{\sqrt{17}} = \dfrac{\pi}{\sqrt{13}} > \dfrac{\pi}{\sqrt{25}} > \dfrac{\pi}{\sqrt{10}}$

4) **What is the value of   70%   of $70\sqrt{7}$?**

   A) $28\sqrt{7}$ B) $14\sqrt{7}$ C) $70\sqrt{7}$ D) $49\sqrt{7}$ E) $69\sqrt{7}$

5) **A father is 34 and his daughter is 10 years old. After how many years will the ratio of their ages be 5:2?**

   A) 5   B) 6   C) 7   D) 8   E) 9

6) **The sum of two consecutive ~~even~~ numbers is 34, and their difference is 2. Find the ratio of the two numbers.**

   A) $\dfrac{9}{3}$ B) $\dfrac{9}{8}$ C) $\dfrac{8}{7}$ D) $\dfrac{7}{5}$ E) $\dfrac{5}{7}$

7) If $P=3^x-1$ and $Q=3^x+1$, then what is the value of P•Q?

    A) 3^x+2 B) $3^{2x}+1$ C) $3^{2x}-1$ D) 3^x+4 E) 3^{2x}

8)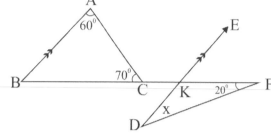

AB||KE, $\angle A=60$, $\angle C=70$, $\angle F=20$, $\angle D=x=?$

    A) 10   B) 20   C) 25   D) 30   E) 40

9) If x=4, then $x^2 - \sqrt{2} + \dfrac{\sqrt{x}}{2} - 4 = ?$

    A) 8   B) 9   C) 10   D) 11   E) 12

10) Calculate arithmetic mean of numbers $\sqrt{7}$, $\sqrt{28}$, and $3\sqrt{7}$.

    A) $2\sqrt{7}$ B) $3\sqrt{7}$ C) $4\sqrt{7}$ D) $7\sqrt{2}$ E) $7\sqrt{3}$

11) The expression $3^x+x^3•3^x$ is equivalent to which of the following?

    A) $x^3•3^x$ B) $3^x(1+x^3)$ C) $x^3(3x+1)$ D) $3^{x+2}•x^3$ E) 3^{2x+3}

12) When 10kg of fresh apricots are dried, 8kg of dried apricots are obtained. How many kilograms of fresh apricots do we need in order to obtain 24kg of dried apricots?

    A) 25   B) 28   C) 30   D) 32   E) 34

13) $-3 < x \leq 7$ **given. Evaluate the largest solution set for x^2.**

    A) $9 < x < 49$ B) $9 < x^2 < 49$ C) $9 < x^2 \leq 49$ D) $49 < x^2 < 9$ E) $49 < x \leq 9$

14) $4\square3 \to 71$, $7\square2 \to 95$, $6\square3 \to 93$, $6\square2 \to ?$

    A) 82   B) 84   C) 83   D) 28   E) 81

15)

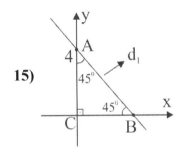

Find the equation of the line d_1.

    A) $x+y=2$ B) $x+y=-2$ C) $x+y=-4$ D) $x+y=4$ E) $x+y=1$

16) Which of the following is a factored form of $ab+a^2b^2+a^3b^3$?

    A) $ab(2+a^2b^2+a^3b^3)$ B) $ab(1+ab+a^2b^2)$

    C) $ab(2+ab+a^2b^2)$ D) $ab(ab+a^2b^2)$

    E) $ab(3+ab+a^2b^2)$

17) If $\dfrac{4}{11}$ of a number is 60, then what is the value of this number?

    A) 125   B) 135   C) 145   D) 155   E) 165

18) If 10% of x equals 10^9, then x=?

    A) 10^{10} B) 10^9 C) 10^8 D) 10^7 E) 10^6

19) **Ahmet alone can complete a job in 10 days, and Mehmet alone can complete the same job in 15 days. If they work together, in how many days can they finish the job?**

A) $\dfrac{60}{17}$　　　B) 6　　　C) $\dfrac{11}{60}$　　　D) $\dfrac{30}{11}$　　　E) $\dfrac{11}{30}$

20) $\dfrac{3^n + 3^n + 3^n}{2^n + 2^n + 2^n} = ?$

A) $\dfrac{3}{2}$　　　B) $\dfrac{2}{3}$　　　C) $\dfrac{3^{n+1}}{2^n}$　　　D) $\left(\dfrac{3}{2}\right)^n$　　　E) $\left(\dfrac{2}{3}\right)^n$

21) $\dfrac{60}{40}$　$\dfrac{30}{70}$　$\dfrac{75}{25}$　$\dfrac{64}{x}$　　x=?

A) 32　　　B) 36　　　C) 40　　　D) 42　　　E) 48

22) $\left(\sqrt{88} + \sqrt{66}\right) = A\sqrt{11}$　　**If A=?**

A) $\sqrt{8} + \sqrt{7}$　　　　　B) $\sqrt{6} + \sqrt{7}$　　　　　C) $\sqrt{8} + \sqrt{6}$
D) $\sqrt{9} + \sqrt{8}$　　　　　E) $\sqrt{10} + \sqrt{11}$

23) **If Ahmet works alone, he complete a task in 18 days, and Mehmet alone completes the same task in 24 days. If they work together 6 days, what percent of the task will be completed?**

A) $\dfrac{11}{24}$　　　B) $\dfrac{13}{24}$　　　C) $\dfrac{6}{13}$　　　D) $\dfrac{7}{12}$　　　E) $\dfrac{7}{11}$

24) **300 grams of fruit juice containing 30% sugar is mixed with 500 grams of fruit juice containing 50% of sugar. What is the percentage of sugar in the obtained mixture?**

A) 38%　　　B) 39%　　　C) 40%　　　D) 41%　　　E) 42.5%

25) **Which of the following gives all the solutions of $x^2+4x=12$?**

   A) -6 and 3   B) -6 and 2   C) -2 and 6   D) -4 and 3   E) -3 and 4

26) **If a=77 and b=33, then $\dfrac{(a-b)^2 + 4ab}{(a+b)^2 - 4ab} = ?$**

   A) 77   B) 33   C) $\dfrac{25}{4}$ D) $\dfrac{4}{25}$ E) $\dfrac{36}{25}$

27) **If $\dfrac{a}{7} + \dfrac{b}{14} + \dfrac{c}{28} = 12$, then 4a+2b+c=?**

   A) 336   B) 326   C) 316   D) 306   E) 236

28) **For the complex number i such that $i^2 = -1$, what is the value of $i^2+i^4+i^6+i^8=?$**

   A) 1   B) 2   C) 3   D) 4   E) 0

29) **In the (x; y) coordinate plane, what is the x-intercept of the line $3x+2y=5$?**

   A) $\dfrac{3}{5}$ B) $\dfrac{5}{3}$ C) $\dfrac{5}{2}$ D) $\dfrac{2}{5}$ E) $\dfrac{3}{2}$

30) **$\dfrac{3!+4!}{4!-3!} = ?$**

   A) $\dfrac{2}{3}$ B) $\dfrac{3}{2}$ C) $\dfrac{5}{3}$ D) $\dfrac{3}{5}$ E) 3

31) **What is the radius of a circle with the equation: $(x+4)^2+(y+5)^2=13$?**

   A) 4   B) 5   C) 13   D) $\sqrt{13}$ E) $2\sqrt{13}$

32)

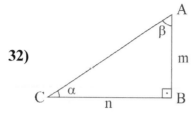

$\sin\alpha + \cos\beta = ?$

A) $\dfrac{m}{m^2 + n^2}$

B) $\dfrac{2m}{m^2 + n^2}$

C) $\dfrac{2m}{\sqrt{m^2 + n^2}}$

D) $\dfrac{2n}{m^2 + n^2}$

E) $\dfrac{2n}{\sqrt{m^2 + n^2}}$

33) For all nonzero x and y, $\dfrac{(6x^2 y) \cdot (-3x^3 y^3)^2}{54x^2 y^2} = ?$

A) $3x^6 y^5$ B) $x^6 y^5$ C) $6x^5 y^6$ D) $6x^4 y^7$ E) $8x^5 y^6$

34) If the fraction $\dfrac{a+b}{a-b} = \dfrac{11}{7}$, then evaluate a•b=?

A) 12   B) 14   C) 15   D) 16   E) 18

35)

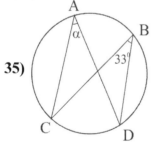

$\angle B = 33^0$, $\angle A = \alpha = ?$

A) 33   B) 66   C) 23   D) 44   E) 46

36)

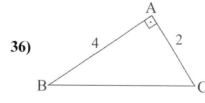

$\angle A = 90^0$, AB=4, AC=2, $\dfrac{A(ABC)}{P(ABC)} = ?$

A) $\dfrac{6}{6 + 2\sqrt{5}}$ B) $\dfrac{4}{6 + 2\sqrt{5}}$ C) $\dfrac{8}{4 + 2\sqrt{5}}$ D) $\dfrac{4\sqrt{2}}{6 + 2\sqrt{5}}$ E) $\dfrac{3\sqrt{2}}{6 + 2\sqrt{5}}$

37)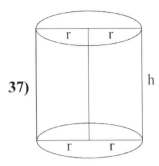

r=4cm, h=6cm, V=?

A) 76π B) 86π C) 96π D) 98π E) 100

38) $\dfrac{11x}{2}+\dfrac{7x}{3}$, then what is the maximum value of the expression can take?

A) 27   B) 37   C) 47   D) 18   E) 36

39) d_1 line: 6x+4y=24
d_2 line: 3x+ay=18
$d_1\|d_2$, if a=?

A) 1   B) 2   C) 3   D) 4   E) 5

40)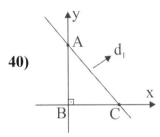

Given line d_1: 3x+2y=12, find the A(ABC)=?

A) 6   B) 8   C) 10   D) 12   E) 14

41) △, □, ⌂, ?

A) □   B) ⬡   C) △   D) ▱   E) ○

42) $\dfrac{△}{3}, \dfrac{⧄}{5}, \dfrac{⧅}{4}, \dfrac{⊠}{?}$

A) 4   B) 5   C) 6   D) 7   E) 8

43)

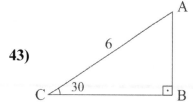

Find the perimeter ABC?

A) $3+3\sqrt{3}$ 　　B) $6+6\sqrt{3}$ 　　C) $9+3\sqrt{3}$ 　　D) $12+\sqrt{3}$ 　　E) $9+4\sqrt{3}$

44)

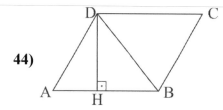

Given: ABCD is a parallelogram, DC=10, and DH=6; $\dfrac{A(ABCD)}{A(ADB)}=?$

A) 2 　　　　B) 3 　　　　C) 4 　　　　D) 5 　　　　E) 6

45)

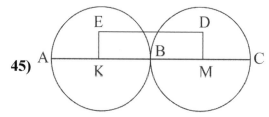

Given: AB=BC=$4\sqrt{2}$ cm; K and M are the centers of each circle; and BE=BD=$2\sqrt{3}$ cm; find the A(KMDE).

A) $3\sqrt{3}$ 　　B) $8\sqrt{2}$ 　　C) $4\sqrt{3}$ 　　D) $4\sqrt{5}$ 　　E) $4\sqrt{6}$

46)

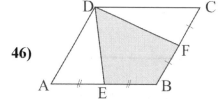

Given: ABCD is a parallelogram, AE=EB, BF=FC, and A(ABCD)=$12\sqrt{2}$ cm²; find A(DEBF).

A) 6 　　　　B) $6\sqrt{3}$ 　　C) $6\sqrt{2}$ 　　D) $6\sqrt{5}$ 　　E) 8

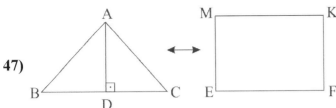

47) If A(ABCD)=A(EFKM), BC=20, AD=4, and EF=10, then FK=?

    A) 10   B) 9   C) 8   D) 7   E) 6

48) If $a=2+x$, then $x^2-4=$?

    A) a^2+4a B) a^2-4a C) a^2+6a D) a^2+2a+2 E) a^2+4a+4

49) If $\log_2 x=6$, then $x/2+X/4=$?

    A) 12   B) 16   C) 32   D) 48   E) 2^8

50) Given the sequence: 7, 11, 13, 17, x, y;   y-x=?

    A) 6   B) 7   C) 8   D) 9   E) 10

51) If $0^o \leq x \leq 90^o$ and $\tan x = \dfrac{3}{2}$, then $\sin 2x=$?

    A) $\dfrac{13}{12}$ B) $\dfrac{12}{13}$ C) $\dfrac{11}{13}$ D) $\dfrac{2\sqrt{3}}{3}$ E) $\dfrac{2\sqrt{3}}{7}$

52)

A(3, 4) has a symmetry x=6, find the $A^{/}$ point.

    A) (8, 4)   B) (7, 4)   C) (9, 4)   D) (6, 3)   E) (6, 2)

53) Evaluate the sum of values for x, which are solutions to the equation $|x-7|+|7-x|=10$

    A) 10   B) 11   C) 13   D) 14   E) 16

54) If $a_2+a_6=20$ and a_2 and a_6 are from an arithmetic sequence, then what is a_3+a_5?

    A) 20   B) 24   C) 26   D) 30   E) 40

55) The number of the subsets of a set is 64. What is the number of the elements?

    A) 3   B) 4   C) 5   D) 6   E) 7

56) A={natural numbers smaller than 12}
B={prime numbers smaller than 10}
A∩B=?

    A) 2, 3, 5   B) 2, 3, 4, 5, 7   C) 2, 3, 5, 7

    D) 3, 5, 7, 11   E) 3, 5, 9, 11

57) $3^n \cdot 7^n = k$, $3^{2n} \cdot 7^{2n} = ?$

    A) k   B) k^2 C) $\dfrac{k}{2}$ D) 2k   E) 21k

58)

6	2	8	x
4	12	3	24

$x=?$

    A) 1   B) 2   C) 3   D) 4   E) 6

59) 27   64   125   ?

    A) 126   B) 156   C) 180   D) 211   E) 216

60) Solve $\sqrt{m} + \sqrt{n} = a$ for m.

    A) $a^2 + 2a\sqrt{n} + n$ B) $a^2 - 2a\sqrt{n} + n$ C) $a^2 + 2an + n$

    D) $a^2 + 4a\sqrt{n} + n$ E) $a^2 - 2n + 4$

TEST – 1.6
- Questions -

1) If $3x+3=6x-6$, then $x=$?

   A) 3   B) 4   C) 5   D) 6   E) 7

2) $\square\Delta \rightarrow 12$, $\square\square \rightarrow 16$, $\Delta\Delta \rightarrow$?

   A) 10   B) 9   C) 8   D) 7   E) 6

3) If $x=2a+b$ and $y=2b+a$, then $x-y=$?

   A) $2a+2b$ B) $2b$ C) $2a$ D) $a+b$ E) $a-b$

4) **Ahmet is 14 and Mehmet is 12 years old. Find the sum of their ages after 6 years.**

   A) 38   B) 36   C) 34   D) 32   E) 30

5)

   ABCD is a rectangle and EFKL is a square. Find the ratio of their perimeters: P(ABCD):P(EFKL).

   A) 110%   B) 125%   C) 130%   D) 140%   E) 145%

6) If $a^2=289$ and $b^2=169$, then $(a+b):(a-b)=$?

   A) $\dfrac{4}{15}$ B) $\dfrac{15}{4}$ C) $\dfrac{15}{2}$ D) $\dfrac{7}{2}$ E) 6

7)

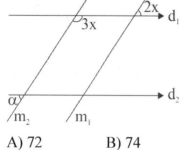

$d_1 \| d_2$ and $m_1 \| m_2$

$\alpha = ?$

A) 72   B) 74   C) 77   D) 80   E) 82

8) If x=-2, then $x^3+x^2+x+12=?$

A) 10   B) 8   C) 7   D) 6   E) 5

9) If |2x-2a|=14 , then |3x-3a|=?

A) 18   B)21   C)23   D) 24   E) 26

10) If ax+bx=m+n, then x=?

A) $\dfrac{m+n}{a+b}$ B) $\dfrac{m-n}{a+b}$ C) $\dfrac{m-n}{a-b}$ D) $\dfrac{m}{a}$ E) $\dfrac{n}{b}$

11) If $(x^4)^{12}=(x^{16.m})$, then m=?

A) 8   B) 6   C) 5   D) 4   E) 3

12) If x is a prime number such that 2≤x≤12. Find the sum of all possible values of x.

A) 30   B) 28   C) 26   D) 24   E) 22

13)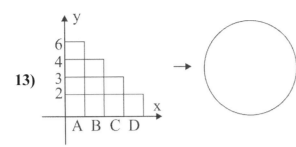

A) 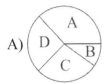   B) 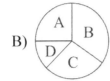   C)

D) 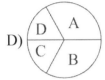   E)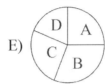

14) Which of the following equations has both $x = -\sqrt{3}$ and $x = +\sqrt{2}$ as solutions?

A) $(x-3)\cdot(x+2)=0$ B) $(x+3)\cdot(x-2)$ C) $(x+\sqrt{3})(x+\sqrt{2})$

D) $(x+\sqrt{3})(x-\sqrt{2})$ E) $(x+\sqrt{3})(x-2)$

15) The number of books printed each day for one week is represented in the table below. Determine the average number of books printed per day for the given week.

Day	Number of Books
Mon	244
Tues	240
Wed	260
Thurs	280
Fri	300

A) 260   B) 264.8   C) 274,4   D) 268.8   E) 270

16) Simplify $3(3x+3)-2(2x+2)$.

A) $5x+5$ B) $5x-5$ C) $4x+4$ D) $4x-4$ E) $x+2$

17) If 40% of x equals 2^{10}, then x=?

    A) 2^9 B) 2^8 C) $3 \cdot 2^9$ D) $5 \cdot 2^8$ E) $5 \cdot 2^9$

18) The price of two math books and one chemistry book is \$12. The price of two math books and two chemistry books is \$15. What is the cost of one math and one chemistry book?

    A) 10   B) 9   C) 8   D) 6   E) 5

19) Ahmet paints a wall alone in 8 hours. Mehmet paints the same wall alone in 12 hours. If they work together, in how many hours they will they finish?

    A) 3.2   B) 3.8   C) 4   D) 4.2   E) 4.8

20)

x	y	z
2	a	c
4	9	d
8	b	216

a+b+c+d=?

    A) 70   B) 72   C) 74   D) 76   E) 78

21) $\dfrac{\pi}{3} + \dfrac{3}{\pi} = ?$

    A) $\dfrac{\pi^2 + 3}{3\pi}$ B) $\dfrac{9 + \pi}{3\pi}$ C) $\dfrac{\pi^2 + 9}{3\pi}$ D) $\dfrac{\pi - 9}{3\pi}$ E) $\dfrac{\pi^2 - 9}{\pi}$

22) If $A=9+a^2$, $B=18+2a^2$, then which is correct?

    A) $A=2B$ B) $A=B^2 \text{-} 2$ C) $A=4B$ D) $A=2B$ E) $B=2A$

23) In the standard (x, y) coordinate plane, what is the slope of the line joinery the points (7; 3) and (3; 9)?

    A) $-\dfrac{3}{2}$ B) $\dfrac{3}{2}$ C) $-\dfrac{2}{3}$ D) $\dfrac{2}{3}$ E) $\dfrac{7}{3}$

24) If A·B=77, A·C=55, then B+C=?

    A) 10   B) 12   C) 13   D) 14   E) 15

25) If $2^a+3^a=m$, then $4^a+9^a=?$

    A) $m+6^a$ B) $m-6^a$ C) $m^2-2\cdot6^a$ D) $m^2+2\cdot6^a$ E) m^2+6^a

26) $\left(x^{\sqrt{2}}\right)^{\sqrt{3}}=x^m$, $y^{\left(\sqrt{3}-1\right)^{\left(\sqrt{3}+1\right)}}=y^n$,   **m+n=?**

    A) $\sqrt{6}+1$ B) $\sqrt{6}+4$ C) $\sqrt{6}+2$ D) $\sqrt{3}+\sqrt{2}$ E) $\sqrt{6}+5$

27) $\log_3 5=a$, If $\log_3 25+\log_3 125=?$

    A) a^2 B) a   C) 5a   D) 2a+1   E) 8a

28)

    A(8, 7)   C(6, 4)   B(x, y)

    If AC=BC, find (x, y).

    A) (1, 4)   B) (2, 3)   C) (3, 2)   D) (4, 1)   E) (1, 4)

29) In the coordinate plane, what is the radius of the circle formed by the equation: $(x-5)^2+(y-2)=15$?

    A) 15   B) 225   C) $\sqrt{15}$ D) 30   E) 22

30)

In the right triangle shown, $\dfrac{1}{\cos\alpha}+\dfrac{1}{\sin\alpha}=?$

    A) $5\sqrt{13}$ B) $6\sqrt{13}$ C $5\sqrt{13}/\dfrac{}{6}$ D) $\dfrac{6\sqrt{3}}{7}$ E) $\dfrac{3\sqrt{5}}{6}$

31) For all nonzero a and b, $\dfrac{(3a^3b^3)^2 \, 4a^4b^4}{(2a^2b^2)^2} =$

    A) a^6b^6 B) $9a^6b^6$ C) $-9a^6b^6$ D) $-a^6b^6$ E) 1

32)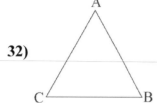

ABC is a triangle. AC=6cm. AB=AC=BC.
A(ABC):P(ABC)=?

    A) $3\sqrt{3}$ B) $5\sqrt{3}$ C) $\dfrac{2\sqrt{3}}{3}$ D) $\dfrac{2}{\sqrt{3}}$ E) $\dfrac{\sqrt{3}}{2}$

33)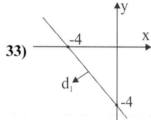

Find the liner equation for d_1.

    A) x+1=0   B) x+y=4   C) x+y=-4   D) x+y=-3   E) x+y=-1

34)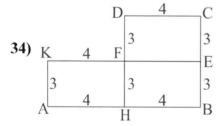

Find the all rectangle perimeter.

    A) 80   B) 81   C) 82   D) 83   E) 84

35) $A = \begin{bmatrix} 1 & 2 \\ 3 & 4 \end{bmatrix}$, $B = \begin{bmatrix} 5 & 6 \\ 7 & 8 \end{bmatrix}$, $C = \begin{bmatrix} 6 & 8 \\ 10 & 2x \end{bmatrix}$, **A+B=C if x=?**

    A) 4   B) 5   C) 6   D) 7   E) 8

36) Solve $x^2+y^2=a^2+b$ for x=?

A) $\sqrt{a^2-y^2+b}$ B) $\sqrt{a^2+y^2+b}$ C) $\sqrt{a^2-y^2+2b}$

D) a^2-y^2+b E) a^2+y^2+b

37) m_1: $3x+2y=6$
m_2: $4x+ay=10$
Line m_1 is perpendicular to line m_2. Find the value of a.

A) $\dfrac{7}{3}$ B) $\dfrac{3}{7}$ C) $\dfrac{8}{3}$ D) $-\dfrac{8}{3}$ E) 4

38) y=x and y=-2x. Find the slope lines.

A) (3; -2)   B) (2; 1)   C) (1; -2)   D) (-1; -1)   E) (1; 1)

39)

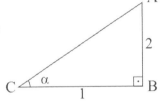

Find the $\dfrac{\tan\alpha+\cot\alpha}{\sin\alpha}=?$

A) $5\sqrt{5}$ B) $3\sqrt{5}$ C) $\dfrac{5\sqrt{5}}{2}$ D) $\dfrac{5\sqrt{5}}{4}$ E) 4

40) Ahmet can write a 3 page letter in 33 minutes. How many pages can he write in 77 minutes?

A) 6   B) 7   C) 8   D) 9   E) 10

41) The swimming pool contains 2400 gallons of water. A gallon of water is about 3.8 liters. How many liters of water are in the swimming pool?

A) 8120   B) 9120   C) 9200   D) 9320   E) 9360

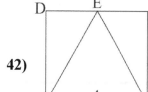

42)

ABCD is square. AB=BE=AE=4cm. A(ABE):P(ABCD)=?

A) $\dfrac{\sqrt{3}}{4}$ B) $\dfrac{\sqrt{3}}{2}$ C) $\dfrac{\sqrt{3}}{3}$ D) $2\sqrt{3}$ E) $3\sqrt{3}$

43) In the standard (x, y) coordinate plane, which of the following lines goes through (2, 4) and is parallel to 3x+4y=12?

A) $y = -3x + 11$ B) $-y = \dfrac{-3x}{4} + 3$ C) $y = \dfrac{2x}{7} + \dfrac{11}{2}$

D) $y = \dfrac{-3x}{4} + \dfrac{11}{2}$ E) $y = \dfrac{3x}{4} + \dfrac{11}{2}$

44) If $4.25 = \dfrac{a}{b}$, then (a+b)²=?

A) 440   B) 441   C) 443   D) 436   E) 448

45) If $\dfrac{a}{5} + \dfrac{b}{7} = 15$, then 7a+5b=?

A) 625   B) 620   C) 615   D) 525   E) 500

46) What is the result of   875·889 − 874·888?

A) 1567   B) 1763   C) 1165   D) 1666   E) 1760

47) Following the pattern given in the table, determine the value of x.

72	84	93	61
5	4	6	x

A) 1   B) 2   C) 3   D) 4   E) 5

48) There are 5 yellow, 4 red, 6 green, and 5 blue marbles in one box. What is the probability of a randomly chosen marble to be green?

   A) $\dfrac{6}{17}$ B) $\dfrac{3}{10}$ C) $\dfrac{7}{14}$ D) $\dfrac{5}{14}$ E) $\dfrac{6}{23}$

49) What is the sum of the divisors of 35?

   A) 48   B) 44   C) 40   D) 36   E) 32

50) In a class of 50 students, everyone plays at least one sport. Eighteen students play only basketball and 8 students play both basketball and football. How many students only play football?

   A) 20   B) 22   C) 24   D) 26   E) 28

51)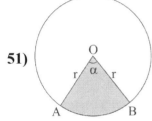

   O is the center of the circle. Given: AO=r=4cm. α=45°, what is the area of sector AOB?

   A) 6π   B) 5π   C) 4π   D) 3π   E) 2π

52) A taxi stops every 30 and a bus stops every 45 minutes at a station. If they both leave the station at 10 a.m., then at what time will they both be at the station again?

   A) 11:00   B) 11:30   C) 11:45   D) 12:00   E) 12:30

53) If $0°\leq x\leq 90°$ and tanx=3, then sinx+cosx=?

   A) $\dfrac{4}{\sqrt{10}}$ B) $\dfrac{3}{\sqrt{10}}$ C) $\dfrac{1}{\sqrt{10}}$ D) $\dfrac{4}{\sqrt{7}}$ E) $\dfrac{5}{\sqrt{7}}$

54) $2x-4y+3z=3$
$6x-4y+3z=7$ What is the value of x?

   A) 4   B) 3   C) 2   D) 1   E) $\dfrac{1}{2}$

55) When a chest with apples are splice up in 6's and 7's every time3 apples are left. In this case what is the minimum amount of apples in the chest?

    A) 41   B) 42   C) 43   D) 44   E) 45

56) If 400 grams of apricots cost $1.60, then how much is 900 grams?

    A) $3.20   B) $3.40   C) $3.60   D) $3.80   E) $4.00

57) Ahmet has $600 more than Mehmet. If Ahmet spends $200, he has 4 times as much money as Mehmet. How much money does Mehmet have?

    A) $300   B) $200   C) $100   D) $90   E) $80

58) There is a league with 9 teams. If each team plays another team only once, then how many matches will they have played in all?

    A) 30   B) 32   C) 34   D) 36   E) 40

59)

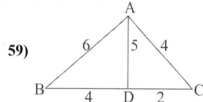

AB=6, AC=BD=4, AD=5, DC=2. Find the sum of all three triangles' perimeters.

    A) 42   B) 43   C) 44   D) 45   E) 46

60)

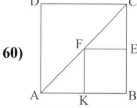

ABCD and KBEF are squares. KB=4cm. Find the perimeter ABCD.

    A) 24   B) 28   C) 30   D) 32   E) 64

TEST – 1.7

- Questions -

1)

123	324	442	552
6	9	10	?

    A) 12   B) 11   C) 10   D) 9   E) 8

2) **What is the value of $(888-886)^2 + (777-775)^2 = ?$**

    A) 6   B) 8   C) 10   D) 12   E) 14

3) **What is the solution set of $4(4x+4)=3(3x+3)$?**

    A) 3   B) 2   C) 1   D) -1   E) -2

4) **What percent of 3^{x+2} is 3^{x+1}?**

    A) 40%   B) 38%   C) 36%   D) 33%   E) 30%

5) **Round 0.68 into its tenths place.**

    A) 0.4   B) 0.5   C) 0.6   D) 0.8   E) 0.7

6) **Given: $4-4(4x+4)=5-5(x+5)$, find the value of x.**

    A) -10   B) -9   C) -8   D) -7   E) -6

7) **Find the difference.**

A) $\dfrac{1}{2}$ B) $\dfrac{14}{28}$ C) $\dfrac{\sqrt{50}}{\sqrt{200}}$ D) $\dfrac{\pi}{2\pi}$ E) $\dfrac{\sqrt{3}}{\sqrt{6}}$

8)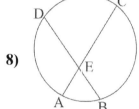

DE=8, BE=3, CE=6, AE=?

A) 1   B) 2   C) 3   D) 4   E) 5

9) **If x=2 and y=-2, then $x^3y^3+x^2y^2-xy=$?**

A) -32   B) -36   C) -40   D) -44   E) 40

10)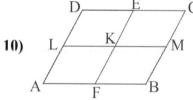

ABCD is parallelogram. Find the number of parallelograms?

A) 9   B) 10   C) 11   D) 12   E) 13

11) $\sqrt[3]{ab}\sqrt[3]{a^2b^2}\sqrt[3]{a^3b^3} = ?$

A) ab   B) a^2b C) ab^2 D) $(ab)^2$ E) $(ab)^3$

12) **Find the different number.**

A) $\sqrt{289}$ B) $\sqrt{900}$ C) $\sqrt{400}$ D) $\sqrt{200}$ E) $\sqrt{100}$

13) What is the expanded form of the expression $(3^x+3)^2$?

    A) 9^x+6^x+9 B) $9^x+3^{x+1}+9$ C) $9^x+2\cdot3^{x+1}+9$

    D) $9^x+3\cdot6^x+9$ E) $3^x+3^{x+1}+9$

14) If $3!+4!=6A$, then $A=?$

    A) 3   B) 5   C) 6   D) 7   E) 8

15)

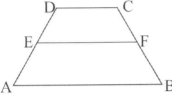

ABCD is trapezoid. AB=12, DC=8, AE=ED, BF=FC, EF=?

    A) 10   B) 9   C) 8   D) 7   E) 6

16) $|\pi-4|+|4-\pi|=?$

    A) 0   B) 2π C) 8   D) $8+2\pi$ E) $8-2\pi$

17)

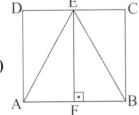

How many triangles are in the figure above?

    A) 4   B) 5   C) 6   D) 7   E) 8

18)

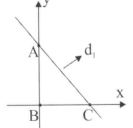

The equation for line d_1 is $2x+3y=24$ Find the area of triangle ABC.

    A) 36   B) 38   C) 40   D) 42   E) 48

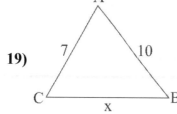

19)

ABC is a triangle. If AB=7 and AC=10, what is the range of the possible values of x?

A) 2<x<16   B) 3<x<17   C) 3≤x≤17   D) 4≤x≤16   E) 2≤x≤16

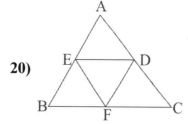

20)

ABC is a triangle. Given: ED‖BC, AE=BE, AD=DC, BF=FC, and A(AED)=6cm², find the A(ABC).

A) 22   B) 24   C) 28   D) 30   E) 36

21) △□→3/4, □◊→4/5, △◊→?

A) 5/3   B) 3/4   C) 3/5   D) 2/5   E) 2/7

22) If $\frac{8}{3}+\frac{7}{5}+\frac{9}{7}-\left(\frac{9}{7}+\frac{7}{5}-\frac{8}{3}\right)=a\frac{b}{c}$, then a+b+c=?

A) 10   B) 9   C) 8   D) 7   E) 6

23) What is the value of $\log_2 256$?

A) 6   B) 7   C) 8   D) 9   E) 10

24) For 0°<α<90°, if $\sin\alpha=\frac{2}{3}$, then tanα-cosα=?

A) $-2\sqrt{5}$ B) $\frac{1}{2\sqrt{5}}$ C) $-\frac{1}{2\sqrt{5}}$ D) $-2\sqrt{3}$ E) $-\frac{1}{2\sqrt{3}}$

25)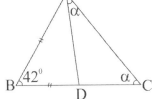

AB=BD, AD=DC, ∠B=42°, 2α=?

A) 49   B) 59   C) 60   D) 69   E) 70

26) The ratio of two supplementary angles is 1:4. Determine the value of the smaller angle.

A) 16   B) 18   C) 20   D) 22   E) 24

27) Which is the largest of the following numbers?

A) $\sin 30^{\circ}$ B) $\dfrac{\pi\sqrt{12}}{2\pi 2\sqrt{3}}$ C) $\dfrac{0!}{2!}$ D) $\cos 60^{\circ}$

E) All these numbers are equal

28) Using the letters from the word *Texas*, how many meaningful or meaningless words can be made?

A) 120   B) 110   C) 100   D) 80   E) 90

29) Which of the following equations is not a function?

A) 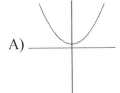   B) 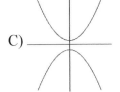   C)

D) 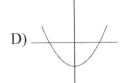   E)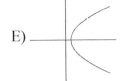

30) Following the pattern given in the table, determine the value of x.

2	3	5	4
8	27	x	64

A) 25   B) 45   C) 120   D) 125   E) 130

31) What is the solution to this system of equations?

$$2x+3y=12$$
$$x+y=5$$

A) {2, 3}   B) {3, 2}   C) {-3, 2}   D) {3, -2}   E) {1, 2}

32) If $x^2y+y^2x=6$ and $x+y=3$, then $xy=$?

A) 1   B) 2   C) 3   D) 4   E) 5

33) If $a<3$, then $\dfrac{|a-3|+|a+3|}{a+3}=$?

A) 2   B) $a+3$ C) $\dfrac{3}{a+3}$ D) $\dfrac{6}{a+3}$ E) $-\dfrac{6}{a+3}$

34) What is the set of prime factors of 145?

A) {3, 29}   B) {5, 29}   C) {6, 24}   D) {6, 29}   E) {7, 45}

35)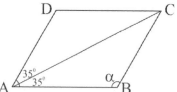

ABCD is parallelogram. Find the value of α.

A) 100°   B) 105°   C) 110°   D) 115°   E) 120°

36) If $\dfrac{1}{a}+\dfrac{1}{b}+\dfrac{1}{c}=4$, then $\dfrac{3}{a}+\dfrac{3}{b}+\dfrac{3}{c}=$?

A) 9   B) 10   C) 11   D) 12   E) 14

37) What is the degree of the polynomial: $(3xy)^2+4x^4y^3+3xy$?

    A) 7   B) 8   C) 9   D) 10   E) 11

38) What is the value of $\left(\sqrt{3}\right)^{(\sqrt{3}-1)^{(\sqrt{3}+1)}}$

    A) $\sqrt{3}$ B) $\dfrac{1}{\sqrt{3}}$ C) 3   D) $\dfrac{1}{3}$ E) $-\dfrac{1}{3}$

39) What is the sum of the roots of $x^2+9x+20$?

    A) 9   B) 20   C) -9   D) -20   E) 11

40) $81^{1/4}+9^{1/2}+3^{1/2}=$?

    A) 6   B) $3+\sqrt{3}$ C) $4+\sqrt{3}$ D) $6+\sqrt{3}$ E) $6+2\sqrt{3}$

41) Which of the following is not correct?

    A) sin10=cos80   B) sin15=cos75   C) sin5=cos85

    D) sin20=cos70   E) sin40=cos40

42) $-4^{-4}+3^{-3}-3^{-3}=$?

    A) $\dfrac{1}{64}$ B) $-\dfrac{1}{64}$ C) $\dfrac{1}{32}$ D) $-\dfrac{1}{32}$ E) 64

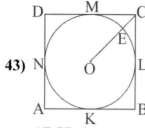

43) ABCD is a square. AB=6cm. O is the center of the circle. Find the length of EC.

A) $3\sqrt{2}$ B) $3\sqrt{2} - 2$ C) $3\sqrt{2} - 3$ D) $3\sqrt{2} + 1$ E) $3\sqrt{2} + 3$

44) What is the center of the circle whose equation is $x^2+y^2+6x-12y+64=0$?

A) (-3; 6)   B) (3; 6)   C) (6; 3)   D) (-6; 3)   E) (3; 7)

45) What is the distance between (6, 2) and (8, 4)?

A) $4\sqrt{2}$ B) $3\sqrt{2}$ C) $2\sqrt{2}$ D) $\sqrt{2}$ E) 2

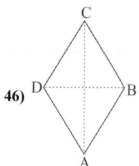

46) ABCD is rhombus. AC=10. BD=6. Find the area of ABCD.

A) 60   B) 45   C) 30   D) 24   E) 20

47)

ABC is a right triangle. Given: $\angle B=90^{o}$, AC=13, BA=5, and BC=3x. Determine the value of x.

A) 8   B) 7   C) 6   D) 5   E) 4

48)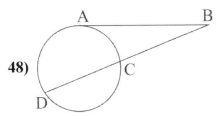

BC=4, DC=3, AB=?

A) $\sqrt{7}$ B) $2\sqrt{7}$ C) $3\sqrt{7}$ D) $2\sqrt{5}$ E) 5

49)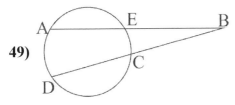

AD=80°, EC=20°, ∠B=?

A) 10   B) 15   C) 20   D) 25   E) 30

50) If $\dfrac{8x+m}{16x-4}$ simplifies to a fraction that is a constant, then what is the value of m?

A) 2   B) -2   C) 4   D) -4   E) 3

51) If $0.\overline{6} - 0.\overline{4} = \dfrac{a}{b}$, then a+b=?

A) 10   B) 11   C) 12   D) 13   E) 14

52) What is the product of the solutions to the equation |x-3|=5?

A) -16   B) 16   C) 12   D) -12   E) 14

53) If |a-3|+|b-4|+|c-6|=0, then evaluate (a+b):c.

A) $\dfrac{7}{2}$ B) $\dfrac{7}{3}$ C) $\dfrac{10}{7}$ D) $\dfrac{7}{6}$ E) $\dfrac{6}{7}$

54) The red pipe fills an empty pool in 12 hours, and the blue pipe fills the same pool in 18 hours. If the both pipes are turned on, in how many hours will the pool be filled?

A) $\dfrac{12}{17}$ B) $\dfrac{17}{12}$ C) $\dfrac{36}{13}$ D) $\dfrac{36}{7}$ E) $\dfrac{36}{5}$

55) In how many different ways can 12 people sit in an armchair for two people?

A) 132   B) 122   C) 112   D) 98   E) 88

56) Create different 3 digit numbers by using the numbers 1, 2, and 5. Find the sum of all of the numbers created.

A) 1475   B) 1555   C) 1666   D) 1776   E) 1700

57) 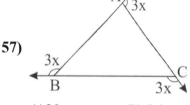 x=?

A) 30   B) 36   C) 40   D) 100   E) 120

58) $0<x<1$, $a=x$, $b=x^2$, $c=2x$. List a, b, and c in order.

A) a>b>c   B) a>c>b   C) b>a>c   D) c>a>b   E) a=b>c

59) Find the number between $\dfrac{1}{3}$ and $\dfrac{3}{7}$ in numerical axis.

A) $\dfrac{8}{23}$ B) $\dfrac{8}{21}$ C) $\dfrac{7}{20}$ D) $\dfrac{7}{19}$ E) $\dfrac{1}{2}$

60) What is the ratio of two natural numbers with a difference of 6 and sum of 22?

A) $\dfrac{4}{7}$ B) $\dfrac{4}{5}$ C) $\dfrac{5}{7}$ D) $\dfrac{7}{9}$ E) $\dfrac{3}{5}$

TEST – 1.8

- Questions -

1) $0.2\overline{1} = ?$

   A) $\dfrac{17}{90}$
   B) $\dfrac{19}{90}$
   C) $\dfrac{23}{90}$
   D) $\dfrac{29}{90}$
   E) $\dfrac{19}{99}$

2) **Find the number which 8% of it is 16.**

   A) 100
   B) 150
   C) 180
   D) 200
   E) 220

3) **Find the geometric mean of $9x^2$ and $4y^2$.**

   A) 3xy
   B) 13xy
   C) $6\sqrt{xy}$
   D) 6xy
   E) 8xy

4) **If $x^2+8x-33=A\cdot(x-3)$, then A=?**

   A) x+11
   B) x-11
   C) x+10
   D) x-10
   E) x+7

5) **Given: $6x^2y^4+5x^4y^6+3x^2y^2+10$, find polynomial's degree.**

   A) 12
   B) 10
   C) 9
   D) 8
   E) 7

6) **If $(4x-4)^9=(3x+8)^9$, then x=?**

   A) 10
   B) 11
   C) 12
   D) 13
   E) 14

7) If an equation has roots 1 and 3, find the equation with leading coefficient of one.

A) $x^2-4x-3=0$ B) $x^2-4x-2=0$ C) $x^2-4x+3=0$

D) $x^2-3x-4=0$ E) $x^2+3x+4=0$

8)

If two object are moving face to face, then t=?

A) $t = \dfrac{x}{v_1 - v_2}$ B) $t = \dfrac{x}{v_1 + v_2}$ C) $t = \dfrac{x}{2v_1 + v_2}$

D) $t = \dfrac{x}{2v_2 + v_1}$ E) $t = \dfrac{x}{v_1}$

9) In an arithmetic sequence $a_1=4$ and $a_8=25$. Find the common difference.

A) 1   B) 2   C) 3   D) 4   E) 5

10) Find the period of the function $f(x)=\tan 5x$.

A) π B) 2π C) $\pi/2$ D) $\pi/4$ E) $\pi/5$

11) $\log_3 30=?$

A) $2\log_3 10$ B) 3   C) $3\log_3 10$

D) $1+\log_3 10$ E) $2+\log_3 10$

12) The expression: $3^0+3^1+3^2+27-3^3=?$

A) 8   B) 9   C) 10   D) 12   E) 13

13) What is the complex factorization of the polynomial $2x^2-9y^2$?

A) $\left(\sqrt{2}x - 3y\right)\left(\sqrt{2}x + 3y\right)$ B) (x-3y)(x+3y)   C) (2x-3y)(2x+3y)

D) (2x-y)(2x+3y)   E) (x-3y)(2x+3y)

14) $\dfrac{(a-b)^2 + 2ab}{(a+b)^2 - 2ab} = ?$

A) 1   B) 2   C) 3   D) a^2+b^2 E) $\dfrac{a^2 - b^2}{a^2 + b^2}$

15) Which of the following is an arithmetic sequence?

A) 3, 6, 8, 12, 24, 48,…   B) 2, 4, 8, 10, 16, 32, ...

C) 7, 14, 28, 52, 104,…   D) 6, 12, 18, 24, 30, ...

E) 5, 10, 15, 21, 25, 30,…

16) Which is the solution set of the equation:
6x-(5x+5)=-7x-(6x-6)

A) $\dfrac{11}{14}$ B) $\dfrac{11}{13}$ C) $\dfrac{14}{11}$ D) $-\dfrac{14}{11}$ E) $-\dfrac{6}{7}$

17)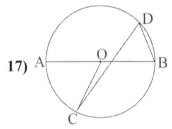

O is the center of this circle.
AOC=82º, ∠CDB=?

A) 44º   B) 45º   C) 46º   D) 48º   E) 49º

18) Which of the following numbers is the smallest?

A) 2π B) $\sqrt{72}$ C) $(\pi)^2$ D) $3\pi-3$ E) $2\pi-4$

19) **Out of 6 books in how many different ways can 3 books be chosen?**

A) 10   B) 20   C) 21   D) 22   E) 23

20) **In how many different ways can 7 people sit around a round table?**

A) 240   B) 210   C) 200   D) 180   E) 160

21) **Determine the sum of the two given permutations.** $_7P_3 + _6P_3 =$?

A) 300   B) 310   C) 330   D) 340   E) 350

22) **What is the solution set of the following equation?**

$$\frac{3x+1}{3} + \frac{4x+1}{4} = \frac{1}{8}$$

A) $\frac{11}{45}$ B) $-\frac{11}{45}$ C) $-\frac{11}{48}$ D) $\frac{11}{48}$ E) $\frac{11}{49}$

23)

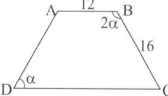

In the figure above, ABCD is an isosceles trapezoid. Find the length of DC.

A) 18   B) 20   C) 24   D) 26   E) 28

24) **What is the degree of the expression: $(2xy^2+xy+4x)^3$?**

A) 10   B) 9   C) 8   D) 7   E) 6

25) What is the product of the roots of $x^2-13+42=0$?

    A) 13   B) -13   C) -42   D) 42   E) $\dfrac{13}{42}$

26) $2 \cdot 10^4 + 3 \cdot 10^3 + 5 \cdot 10^2 + 6 \cdot 10 = ?$

    A) 23560   B) 23460   C) 22560   D) 21560   E) 2360

27) Find the LCM of 12 and 18.

    A) 20   B) 32   C) 36   D) 40   E) 48

28) What is the average of the numbers $\sqrt{2}, 4\sqrt{2}, \sqrt{8}, \sqrt{50}$?

    A) $4\sqrt{2}$ B) $3\sqrt{2}$ C) $2\sqrt{2}$ D) $5\sqrt{2}$ E) $\dfrac{7\sqrt{2}}{2}$

29) Calculate the ratio of milk in the mixture to the mixture when 25 gallons of water is mixed with 45 gallons of milk.

    A) $\dfrac{9}{13}$ B) $\dfrac{9}{11}$ C) $\dfrac{9}{14}$ D) $\dfrac{8}{7}$ E) $\dfrac{7}{8}$

30) $\dfrac{\dfrac{1}{3^x}+\dfrac{1}{2^x}}{\dfrac{1}{3^x}-\dfrac{1}{2^x}}=?$

    A) $\dfrac{2^x}{3^x}$ B) $\dfrac{3^x}{2^x}$ C) $\dfrac{2^x-3^x}{2^x+3^x}$ D) $\dfrac{2^x+3^x}{2^x-3^x}$ E) $\dfrac{2^x-3}{2^x-2}$

31) When $36^{2x+3}=1$, find the value of x that satisfies the equation.

    A) $\dfrac{2}{3}$ B) $\dfrac{3}{2}$ C) $\dfrac{1}{2}$ D) 2   E) $-\dfrac{3}{2}$

32) $\dfrac{144 \cdot 10^{-8}}{24 \cdot 10^{-4}} = ?$

    A) 10^4 B) $3 \cdot 10^4$ C) $6 \cdot 10^{-4}$ D) $8 \cdot 10^{-4}$ E) $3 \cdot 10^{-4}$

33) Given: A(8, 2) and B(-3, -4), find the slope of the line AB.

    A) $\dfrac{11}{6}$ B) $-\dfrac{11}{6}$ C) 2 D) $-\dfrac{6}{11}$ E) $-\dfrac{7}{3}$

34) In a rectangular prism with dimensions 18cm, 24cm, and 16cm, cubes are placed in such way that no empty space is left. According to this, what is the minimum number of cubes that can be placed?

    A) 800   B) 864   C) 868   D) 870   E) 880

35)

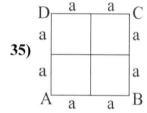

ABCD is a square. Find the number of squares .

    A) 5   B) 6   C) 7   D) 8   E) 9

36)

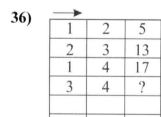

    A) 20   B) 21

    C) 23   D) 25

    E) 30

37) AB∥DC, AE=7, BE=9, CE=x, DE=3, x=?

    A) $\dfrac{17}{7}$ B) $\dfrac{27}{7}$ C) $\dfrac{18}{7}$

    D) $\dfrac{19}{7}$ E) $\dfrac{7}{17}$

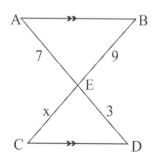

38)

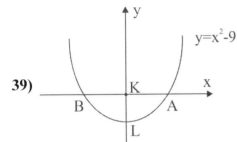

In the figure above ∠y-∠x=22. Find the value of ∠y.

A) 100   B) 101   C) 102   D) 112   E) 122

39) $\dfrac{|AK|}{|KL|} = ?$

A) 9   B) 6   C) 3   D) 1   E) $\dfrac{1}{3}$

40) In △ABC, ∠A=105°, ∠B=45°, and AC=12cm, find the area of △ABC.

A) $18\sqrt{3}$ B) $18+18\sqrt{3}$ C) $12+12\sqrt{3}$ D) $6+6\sqrt{3}$ E) $4+4\sqrt{3}$

41) What is the standard form of $\dfrac{4-3i}{4+3i}$?

A) $\dfrac{16i+9}{25}$

B) $\dfrac{16+24i+9}{25}$

C) $(7+24i)/25$

D) $\dfrac{12-24i}{25}$

E) $\dfrac{16i-9}{25}$

42) There are 3 yellow, 6 blue, and 7 red marbles out of 16 marbles in a bag. What is the probability of a randomly chosen marble from the bag to be blue or red?

A) $\dfrac{16}{13}$ B) $\dfrac{11}{13}$ C) $\dfrac{14}{15}$ D) $\dfrac{13}{16}$ E) $\dfrac{13}{17}$

43) What is the value of $\log_4 64+\log_5 25=$?

A) $\dfrac{1}{3}$ B) $\dfrac{1}{2}$ C) $\dfrac{1}{4}$ D) 4   E) 5

44) The ratio of the perimeters of similar squares is 4 to 9. What is the ratio of the areas of these squares?

A) $\dfrac{16}{18}$ B) $\dfrac{16}{36}$ C) $\dfrac{16}{81}$ D) $\dfrac{81}{16}$ E) $\dfrac{81}{4}$

45) If $\sin 10^{\circ}=\cos x$, then x=?
   A) 10° B) 20° C) 60° D) 70° E) 80°

46) What is the period of function $y=-6\sin(5x+\pi)$?

   A) -6   B) 6   C) 5   D) $\dfrac{\pi}{5}$ E) $\dfrac{\pi}{-6}$

47)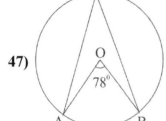

   O is the center of the circle. If $\angle AOB=78^{0}$ and $\angle C=2\alpha$, then α=?

   A) 30   B) 39   C) $\dfrac{39}{2}$ D) 37   E) $\dfrac{37}{2}$

48)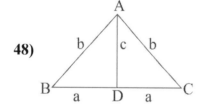

   Find the sum of all three triangles' perimeters.

   A) 3a+3b+3c   B) 4a+4b+4c   C) 4a+4b+2c
   D) 4a+3b+3c   E) 2a+2b+2c

49)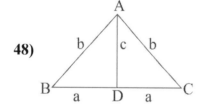

   ABCD is a square. Find the sum of all possible squares' area

   A) 12a   B) 16a   C) 10a   D) $8a^2$ E) $16a^2$

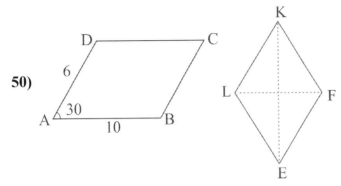

50)

ABCD is a parallelogram. EFKL is a rhombus. AB=10, AD=6, ∠A=30°, KF=8, LF=8, A(ABCD)=A(EFKL). sin30=1/2.

A) $\dfrac{17}{2}$ B) $\dfrac{15}{2}$ C) $\dfrac{14}{9}$ D) $\dfrac{14}{5}$ E) $\dfrac{17}{4}$

51) $(4^2+4^1+4^0)-(3^2+3^1+3^0)=?$

A) 10 B) 9 C) 8 D) 7 E) 6

52)

A) B) C) D) E)

53) $\dfrac{7^x+7^x+7^x+7^x}{14^x}=?$

A) 2^x B) $\dfrac{1}{2^x}$ C) $\dfrac{3}{2^x}$ D) $\dfrac{4}{2^x}$ E) $\dfrac{7^x}{2^x}$

54) If 3x+2y-z=9, then 6x+4y-2z=?

A) 10 B) 12 C) 16 D) 17 E) 18

55) What is expanded form of $\left(x+\sqrt{x}\right)^2$?

    A) $x(x+2\sqrt{x}+1)$ B) $x(x+\sqrt{x}+1)$ C) $x(2x+\sqrt{x}+1)$

    D) $x(x^2+2\sqrt{x}+1)$ E) $x^2+2\sqrt{x}+x$

56) A={2, 3, 4, 5, 7, 11, 13, 23, 29, 30, 37, 47, 61, 64}
How many prime numbers are in set A?

    A) 9   B) 10   C) 11   D) 12   E) 13

57)

$$\begin{array}{|cc|}\hline 12 & 15 \\ 24 & 43 \\ 64 & 79 \\ \hline \end{array} \leftrightarrow \begin{array}{|cc|}\hline 21 & 51 \\ 42 & 34 \\ 46 & x \\ \hline \end{array} \quad x=?$$

    A) 46   B) 96   C) 95   D) 97   E) 98

58) P_1: $4x^4+3x^3+2x$ P_1 polynomial degree: d_1
P_2: $3x^2+3x+3$ P_2 polynomial degree: d_2
P_3: $3x+4x^2+8x^5$ P_3 polynomial degree: d_3
$d_1+d_2+d_3=?$

    A) 14   B) 13   C) 12   D) 11   E) 10

59) If $\sqrt{2}+\sqrt{6}+\sqrt{18}+\sqrt{32}=A\cdot\sqrt{2}$, then A=?

    A) $4+\sqrt{3}$ B) $6+\sqrt{3}$ C) $7+\sqrt{3}$ D) $8+\sqrt{3}$ E) $9+\sqrt{3}$

60) If x+y=a, then x^2+y^2=?

    A) a^2+2x-y B) a^2-2xy C) $a^2+2\sqrt{xy}$ D) 2xy   E) a-2xy

TEST – 1.9

- *Questions* -

1) If $A^2-5=B$, then $A=$?

    A) B-5   B) B+5   C) $\sqrt{B-5}$ D) $\sqrt{B+5}$ E) B^2-5

2) If $3^x+3^x+3^x=9$, then $x=$?

    A) 0   B) 1   C) 2   D) 3   E) 4

3) $(99^2-88^2):11^2=$?

    A) 15   B) 16   C) 17   D) 18   E) 20

4) **Paul read 92 pages of his book on the first day. He read 114 pages on the second day. What is the percent increase of the number of pages read from the first to second day?**

    A) 23.9%   B) 24.6%   C) 25%   D) 26%   E) 28%

5) $\dfrac{1}{\pi}+\dfrac{1}{2\pi}+\dfrac{1}{3\pi}+\dfrac{1}{4\pi}=$?

    A) $\dfrac{23}{8\pi}$ B) $\dfrac{25}{12\pi}$ C) $\dfrac{23}{12\pi}$ D) $\dfrac{22}{12\pi}$ E) $\dfrac{6}{13\pi}$

6) $34\triangle43,\ 63\triangle36,\ 45\triangle54,\ 75\triangle$?

    A) 54   B) 56   C) 57   D) 58   E) 67

7)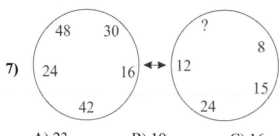

    A) 23   B) 19   C) 16   D) 20   E) 21

8) **If 3<x<5 and 6<y<8, then which of the following is true?**

    A) 4<x+y<3   B) 9<x+y<12   C) 9<x+y<11
    D) 9<x+y<13   E) 13<x+y<9

9) **What is the complete factorization of the polynomial : $3x^2+12xy+24x$?**

    A) $3x(x-4y+8)$ B) $3x(x+4y+4)$ C) $3x(x-3y+4)$

    D) $3x(x+4y+8)$ E) $2x(x+4y+8)$

10) **If a=4 and b=3, then $ab^2+(a+2b)-(2b+a)=$?**

    A) 36   B) 32   C) 30   D) 28   E) 24

11) $\sqrt{12\pi x^2}\ \sqrt{24\pi 4x^3y^3}$ =?

    A) $12\pi x^2 y\sqrt{xy}$ B) $24\pi x^2 y\sqrt{2xy}$ C) $12\pi x^2 y^2\sqrt{2xy}$

    D) $48\pi x^2 y^2\sqrt{xy}$ E) $24\pi x^2 y$

12) $\sin 2^\circ = \cos x$, x=?

    A) 80° B) 82° C) 84° D) 86° E) 88°

13) $\sqrt{1-\sin x} \cdot \sqrt{1+\sin x} + \cos x = ?$

    A) $\cos^2 x$ B) $\sin^2 x$ C) $2\cos x$ D) $2\sin x$ E) 0

14) Simplify the following expression: $\dfrac{1}{a} + \dfrac{2}{b} + \dfrac{3}{c}$.

    A) $\dfrac{2b+3c+a}{abc}$ B) $\dfrac{bc+2ac+3ab}{abc}$ C) $\dfrac{bc+2ac+2ab}{ab}$

    D) $bc+2ac+2ab$ E) $\dfrac{6}{abc}$

15) $\dfrac{3 \cdot 3^x + 9 \cdot 3^{2x}}{3 \cdot 3^x} = ?$

    A) $1+3^{x+2}$ B) $1+3^{x+3}$ C) 3^x D) 3^x+2 E) 3

16) $A = 0.\overline{3} + 0.\overline{2}$ **if 9A+9=?**

    A) 10 B) 12 C) 13 D) 14 E) 16

17) Evaluate the sum of prime factors of 90.

    A) 10 B) 11 C) 12 D) 13 E) 14

18) Find the prime factor(s) of 17.

    A) 17 B) 1 C) $17; 1$ D) $17; 2$ E) $3; 17$

19) Find the number of positive proper divisors of 40.

    A) 10   B) 9   C) 8   D) 7   E) 6

20) A carpenter wishes to cut equally sized wooden cubes from a wooden rectangular solid whose edges' lengths are 6, 8, and 10cm. How many equally sized cubes, with greatest volume, can this carpenter obtain?

    A) 20   B) 25   C) 30   D) 35   E) 60

21) Evaluate geometric mean $\sqrt{7}+2$ and $\sqrt{7}-2$.

    A) 3   B) 2   C) 1   D) $\sqrt{3}$ E) $\sqrt{2}$

22) If $\dfrac{a+b}{a} = 9$, then $\dfrac{a+b}{b} = ?$

    A) $\dfrac{3}{2}$ B) $\dfrac{9}{8}$ C) $\dfrac{2}{3}$ D) $\dfrac{8}{9}$ E) 1

23) The difference of $\dfrac{1}{3}$ of and $\dfrac{1}{7}$ of a number is 8. What is the number?

    A) 42   B) 40   C) 38   D) 36   E) 32

24) A vehicle travels with an average speed of 130km/h. In how many hours will this vehicle travel the distance of 780km?

    A) 3   B) 4   C) 5   D) 6   E) 7

25) Find the sum of the x and y values of the solution to the system of equations:

$$\left.\begin{array}{l} 2x + 3y = 28 \\ 3x + 2y = 27 \end{array}\right\}$$

A) 12   B) 11   C) 13   D) 14   E) 15

26) If $f(x)=x^2+2x+a$ and $f(2)=10$, then $a=?$

A) 6   B) 5   C) 4   D) 3   E) 2

27) $\dfrac{a}{\sqrt{900}} + \dfrac{b}{\sqrt{400}} + \dfrac{c}{\sqrt{100}} = ?$

A) $\dfrac{2a + 2b + 6c}{30}$ B) $\dfrac{2a + 3b + 6c}{60}$ C) $\dfrac{2a + 3b + 3c}{60}$

D) $\dfrac{a + 3b + 6c}{60}$ E) $\dfrac{4a + 3b + 2c}{60}$

28) $(5^2+5^1+5^0)-(4^2+4^1+4^0)=?$

A) 10   B) 11   C) 12   D) 13   E) 14

29) 25, 35, and 45 by of three different sugar types will be put in bags in equal weights without mixing each other. Here under how many bags will be needed at least?

A) 24   B) 23   C) 22   D) 21   E) 20

30) The average of three consecutive positive integers is 16. According to that, what is the minimum integer?

A) 20   B) 18   C) 16   D) 15   E) 12

31) Ahmet's working speed is 4 times that of Mehmet's. They can finish a job together in 20 days. Accordingly, how many days will it take for Mehmet to finish the job if he works alone?

    A) 60   B) 70   C) 80   D) 100   E) 110

32) In a school, the ratio of girls to boys is 7:4. If there are a total of 55 students in the school, how many girls are there?

    A) 30   B) 32   C) 35   D) 25   E) 20

33) If $x \neq 0$ and $4x^2 - 4x = 4x$, then x=?

    A) 0   B) 1   C) 2   D) 3   E) 4

34)

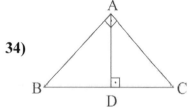

    $\angle A = 90$, BD=3, DC=8 units, AD=?

    A) $2\sqrt{2}$ B) $3\sqrt{2}$ C) $2\sqrt{6}$ D) $2\sqrt{5}$ E) 24

35) At which y-coordinate does the line described by the equation 4x-3y=24 intersect the y-axis?

    A) 6   B) -6   C) 8   D) -8   E) 12

36) If $3^a - 3^b = x$ and $3^a + 3^b = y$, then $3^{2a} - 3^{2b} = ?$

    A) $x^2 + y^2$ B) x+y   C) x-y   D) xy   E) y-x

37) If $0^{o}<x<90^{o}$ and $\sin x = \dfrac{5}{7}$, then $\cos^2 x=$?

    A) $\dfrac{24}{49}$ B) $\dfrac{24}{47}$ C) $\dfrac{25}{49}$ D) $\dfrac{25}{39}$ E) $\dfrac{23}{24}$

38) $\dfrac{\dfrac{3}{4}+\dfrac{4}{3}}{\dfrac{3}{4}-\dfrac{4}{3}}=$?

    A) $\dfrac{25}{6}$ B) $-\dfrac{25}{6}$ C) $\dfrac{27}{-7}$ D) $\dfrac{27}{7}$ E) $\dfrac{25}{-7}$

39)

Given AB=4x, DC=2x, and DH=x, find the area of ABCD.
A) 4x   B) 3x   C) $3x^2$ D) $4x^2$ E) 6x

40) If ax+by=cx+dy, then which of the following equations expresses x in terms of a, b, c, d, and y?

    A) $\dfrac{y(d-b)}{a-c}$ B) $\dfrac{y(d+b)}{a+c}$ C) $\dfrac{y(d+b)}{a-c}$

    D) $\dfrac{a-c}{y(d-b)}$ E) $\dfrac{a+c}{y(d-b)}$

41) For all x≠1, $\dfrac{x^2-x-30}{x-6}=$?

    A) x+3   B) x+4   C) x+5   D) x+6   E) x-5

42) If $0^{o}<x<90^{o}$ and $\cos x = \dfrac{2}{7}$, then $\sin^2 x=$?

    A) $\dfrac{25}{29}$ B) $\dfrac{35}{39}$ C) $\dfrac{42}{47}$ D) $\dfrac{44}{49}$ E) $\dfrac{45}{49}$

43) Which of the following inequalities is equivalent to $-3-5x \leq -7x$?

   A) $x \geq 2$ 　　 B) $x \leq 2$ 　　 C) $x \leq \dfrac{3}{2}$ 　　 D) $x \leq -\dfrac{3}{2}$ 　　 E) $x \leq 1$

44) The regular price for new math book is \$60. If that price is reduced by 30% what is the new price?

   A) \$32 　　 B) \$42 　　 C) \$44 　　 D) \$46 　　 E) \$47

45) If $x=3$, then $3x^2+3x-9=$?

   A) 20 　　 B) 22 　　 C) 23 　　 D) 24 　　 E) 27

46) For all x, $2x \cdot 3x^2 \cdot 8x^3 =$?

   A) $24x^4$ 　　 B) $24x^5$ 　　 C) $48x^4$ 　　 D) $48x^5$ 　　 E) $48x^6$

47) Which of the following is the solution for the inequality $-6 < 6x-12$?

   A) $x>1$ 　　 B) $x<1$ 　　 C) $x>-1$ 　　 D) $x<-1$ 　　 E) $x>2$

48) In a school of 60 students, 26 students play only soccer and 20 students play only basketball. All other students play both sports. How many students play both sports?

   A) 14 　　 B) 15 　　 C) 16 　　 D) 17 　　 E) 18

49) One car travels 300 miles in 5 hours. A second car travels 500 miles in 5 hours. Find the ratio of the speed of the first car to the speed of the second car.

    A) 5/3   B) 3/5   C) 3/4   D) 4/3   E) 1

50) If $f(x)=x^2-2x-2$, what is the value of $f(-2)$?

    A) 6   B) 5   C) 4   D) 3   E) -2

51)

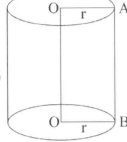

If AO=r=6cm and AB=8cm, then what is the volume of the cylinder?

    A) 188π B) 200π C) 220π D) 260π E) 288π

52)

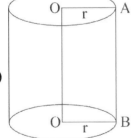

Given AO=r=2π and AB=3π, find the volume of the cylinder.

    A) $12\pi^2$ B) $12\pi^3$ C) $12\pi^4$ D) $14\pi^2$ E) $15\pi^3$

53) If $f(x)=4x+4$, then $f(x+4)=?$

    A) $4x+20$ B) $3x+17$ C) $2x+16$ D) $x+16$ E) x^2+20

54) **What is the equation of circle in the coordinate plane with center (-3, 4) and radius of 10 units?**

    A) $(x+3)^2+(y+4)^2=10$ B) $(x+3)^2+(y+4)^2=100$

    C) $(x+3)^2+(y-4)^2=10$ D) $(x+3)^2+(y-4)^2=100$

    E) $(x+2)^2+(y-4)^2=100$

55) **In the complex number system, $i^2=-1$; $(2+i)^2+(2-i)^2=?$**

    A) 6   B) 7   C) 8   D) 9   E) 10

56) **The ratio of the radius of two circles is 4:11. What is the ratio of perimeters of these circles?**

    A) 4:12   B) 11:4   C) 4:11   D) 15:11   E) 11:15

57) **Find the solution set to the equation $x^2-10x+24=0$.**

    A) {3, 6}   B) {4, 6}   C) {-4, 6}   D) {4, -6}   E) {3, 7}

58) **Point A(3, 4) and point B(8, 11) are points on the coordinate plane. What is the length of the AB=?**

    A) $\sqrt{70}$ B) $\sqrt{71}$ C) $\sqrt{72}$ D) $\sqrt{73}$ E) $\sqrt{74}$

59) **If ax+by=mx, then b=?**

    A) $\dfrac{m-a}{y}$ B) $\dfrac{m-a}{b}$ C) $\dfrac{x(m-a)}{y}$ D) $\dfrac{x(m+a)}{y}$ E) x(m-a)

60) $A = \begin{bmatrix} 3 & 4 \\ 5 & 6 \end{bmatrix}$, $B = \begin{bmatrix} 1 & 3 \\ 4 & 2 \end{bmatrix}$, **2A+3B=?**

    A) $\begin{bmatrix} 9 & 17 \\ 22 & 16 \end{bmatrix}$ B) $\begin{bmatrix} 9 & 17 \\ 20 & 18 \end{bmatrix}$ C) $\begin{bmatrix} 9 & 17 \\ 22 & 20 \end{bmatrix}$ D) $\begin{bmatrix} 17 & 12 \\ 13 & 8 \end{bmatrix}$ E) $\begin{bmatrix} 14 & 13 \\ 2 & 8 \end{bmatrix}$

TEST – 1.10
- Questions -

1) **f(x)=x+1 and q(x)=x²+2x+1. Find the relationship between f(x) and q(x).**

   A) f(x)=q(x)　　　　　B) f(x)=2q(x)　　　　　C) q(x)=2f(x)

   D) q(x)=f(x)²　　　　　E) q(x)=2f(x)

2) $A = \begin{bmatrix} 3 & 4 \\ 2 & 1 \end{bmatrix}, \quad B = \begin{bmatrix} 6 & 8 \\ 4 & 2 \end{bmatrix}$, **B-A=?**

   A) $\begin{bmatrix} 3 & 4 \\ 3 & 1 \end{bmatrix}$　　B) $\begin{bmatrix} 3 & 4 \\ 2 & 1 \end{bmatrix}$　　C) $\begin{bmatrix} 3 & 4 \\ 2 & 2 \end{bmatrix}$　　D) $\begin{bmatrix} 1 & 2 \\ 3 & 4 \end{bmatrix}$　　E) $\begin{bmatrix} 4 & 2 \\ 3 & 1 \end{bmatrix}$

3) **If** $\dfrac{3^x + m}{2^x} = y$ **, then m=?**

   A) $\left(\dfrac{2}{3}\right)^x$　　B) $\left(\dfrac{2}{3}\right)^x y$　　C) $\left(\dfrac{3}{2}\right)^x y$　　D) $\left(\dfrac{3}{2}\right)^x$　　E) $3^x y$

4) **If** $\sqrt{3} + \sqrt{15} + \sqrt{48} = \sqrt{a}(b + \sqrt{b})$ **, then a+b=?**

   A) $\sqrt{5} + 3$　　B) $\sqrt{6} + 3$　　C) $\sqrt{3} + 5$　　D) 8　　E) 11

5) $\left(\dfrac{1}{2} - \dfrac{1}{3}\right) : \left(\dfrac{1}{2} + \dfrac{1}{3}\right) = ?$

   A) 1/2　　　　B) 1/3　　　　C) 3/4　　　　D) 2　　　　E) 1/5

6) $(3^\pi+3^\pi+3^\pi):(2^\pi+2^\pi+2^\pi)=?$

A) 3π 　　B) $\dfrac{1}{2\pi}$ 　　C) $\dfrac{3}{2}$ 　　D) $\left(\dfrac{3}{2}\right)^\pi$ 　　E) $\left(\dfrac{2}{3}\right)^\pi$

7) If a+b=4x, then a^2+b^2=?

A) $16x^2$ 　　B) 16x 　　C) $16x^2+2ab$ 　　D) $16x^2-2ab$ 　　E) $8x^2+ab$

8) Use the given pattern to answer the question:
Utah→8, Kansas→12, Texas→10, Arkansas→?

A) 8 　　B) 9 　　C) 10 　　D) 12 　　E) 16

9) Use the given pattern to answer the question:
Utah→1, Kansas→2, Texas→1, Alabama→4, Arkansas→?

A) 2 　　B) 3 　　C) 4 　　D) 5 　　E) 6

10) Use the given pattern to answer the question:
Kansas△Utah→2, Arkansas△Texas→3,
Texas△Utah→1, Oklahoma△Kansas→?

A) 1 　　B) 2 　　C) 3 　　D) 4 　　E) 5

11)

34	24	41	72
7	6	5	?

    A) 9   B) 8   C) 7   D) 6   E) 5

12)

6	4	1	2	6	6	3	3
8	6	3	18	6	6	3	?

    A) 10   B) 11   C) 12   D) 13   E) 15

13)

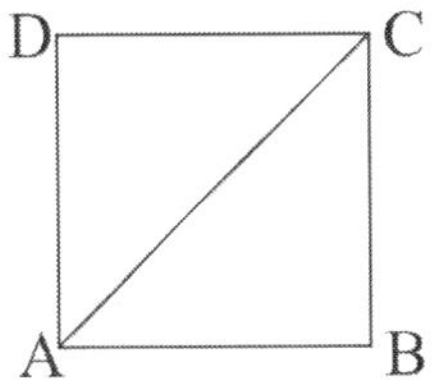

ABCD is a square. $AC = \sqrt{11}$ **if A(ABCD)=?**

    A) 11   B) $\dfrac{11}{3}$ C) $\dfrac{11}{4}$ D) $\dfrac{11}{2}$ E) $\dfrac{11}{5}$

14)

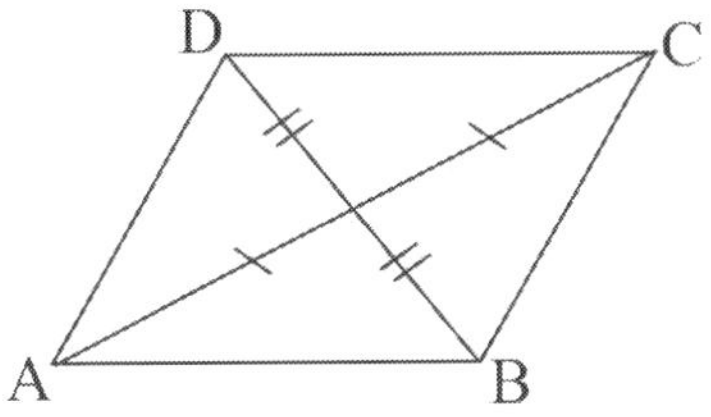

ABCD is parallelogram. A(BCK)= $\sqrt{3}$ **cm^2, A(ABCD)=?**

    A) 3   B) $2\sqrt{3}$ C) $3\sqrt{3}$ D) 4   E) $4\sqrt{3}$

15)

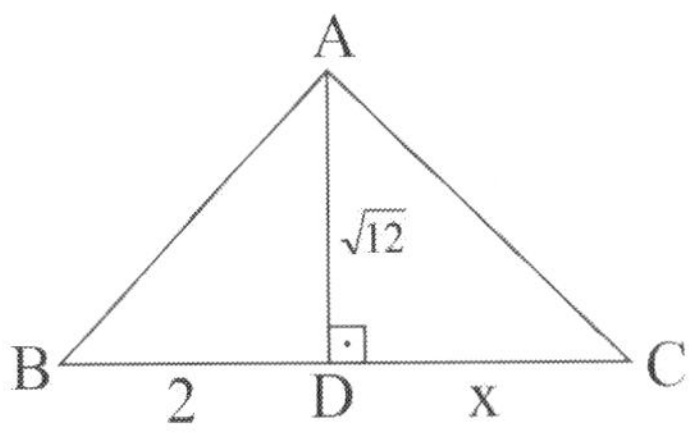

∠A=90°, ∠D=90°, BD=2, DC=x, AD= $\sqrt{12}$ **, x=?**

    A) 8   B) 7   C) 6   D) 5   E) 4

TEST – 1.1
- Solutions -

1) **The correct answer is (D)**
$2(3x+4)+3(2x+4)=2\cdot3x+2\cdot4+3\cdot2x+3\cdot4=6x+8+6x+12=12x+20$

2) **The correct answer is (B)**
$(8 - 4)^2+(4 - 8)^2=4^2+(-4)^2=16+16=32$

3) **The correct answer is (C)**
$x^2+8x+7=0$
$(x+7)\cdot(x+1)=0$
$x+7=0, x=-7$
$x+1=0, x=-1 \qquad \{-7; -1\}$

4) **The correct answer is (A)**

4	5	6	2
2	5	3	2
1	5	3	3
	5		5
	1		

$(4, 5, 6)=2\cdot2\cdot3\cdot5=60$

5) **The correct answer is (A)**
Perimeter of the rectangle is $P=2w+2l$
$36=2\cdot8+2l$, $36=16+2l$, $2l=20$, $l=10$

6) **The correct answer is (D)**
$C=2\pi r$, $24\pi=2\pi r$, $r=12$,
$A=\pi r^2 \Rightarrow A=\pi12^2=144\pi$

7) **The correct answer is (E)**
$2, 7, 22, 67, \_\_\_, 607 \qquad\qquad b=3a+1$
$a, b, c, d, \underline{e}, f \qquad\qquad c=3b+1$
$e=3d+1=3\cdot67+1=202$

8) **The correct answer is (A)**
1, 4, 9, 16, 25,___, 49
1, 2, 3, 4, 5, ___, 7
1^2=1, 2^2=4, 3^2=9, 4^2=16, 5^2=25, **6^2=36**, 7^2=49

9) **The correct answer is (D)**
$|-2\pi|+|2\pi-1|=$
$|-2\pi|=2\pi$, $|2\pi-1|=2\pi-1$,
$2\pi+2\pi-1=4\pi-1$
*$|2\pi-1|=2\pi-1$ because $2\pi-1>0$, $2\pi-1\approx5.3$

10) **The correct answer is (A)**
$5x=7y \Rightarrow x=7, y=5$
$\min(x+y)=7+5=12$

11) **The correct answer is (E)**
abcdef is number $\dfrac{a+b+c+d+e}{3}=3k$

$99981\rightarrow9+9+9+8+1=36$, $\dfrac{36}{3}=12(4k)$

12) **The correct answer is (B)**
List the factors of both numbers
14: 1, <u>7</u>, 14,   21: 1, 3, <u>7</u>, 21
The greatest number that appears in both lists of factors is 7.

13) **The correct answer is (A)**
$x\cdot\%\cdot400=100$, $\dfrac{x}{100}\cdot400=100$, $4x=100$, $x=25$
$x=25$, (25%)

14) **The correct answer is (D)**
A 20% discount is a percent decrease 20%.
100 buy $\rightarrow$ 80 sold
          x $\rightarrow$ 120 sold $x=\dfrac{100\cdot120}{80}=150$

15) The correct answer is (C)
girl students + boy students = 120
40+boys=120, boy students = 80
girl students : boy students → 40:80 → 1:2

16) The correct answer is (A)
$$mean = \frac{5+6+8+10+13+13+15}{7} = \frac{71}{7}$$
medium→10, range=15-5=10

17) The correct answer is (B)
$$mean = \frac{6+6+8+12+16+16}{6} = \frac{32}{3}$$
$$medium = \frac{8+12}{2} = \frac{20}{2} = 10,$$
mode=there are two: 6 & 16, range=16-6=10

18) The correct answer is (D)
x=4, the value of x^2-3x-3
x^2-3x-3=4^2-3·4-3=16-12-3=16-15=1

19) The correct answer is (E)
$$mean = \frac{30 \cdot 80 + 40 \cdot 90}{30+40} = \frac{2400+3600}{70} = 86$$

20) The correct answer is (A)
5, 7, a, b, 17 = 5, 7, 11, 13, 17 ← prime numbers
a=11, b=13   2a+b=2·11+13=22+13=35

21) The correct answer is (B)
$$\frac{3}{4} = \frac{3 \cdot 16}{4 \cdot 16} = \frac{48}{64}, \quad \frac{7}{8} = \frac{7 \cdot 8}{8 \cdot 8} = \frac{56}{64}, \quad \frac{7}{16} = \frac{7 \cdot 4}{16 \cdot 4} = \frac{28}{64},$$
$$\frac{8}{32} = \frac{8 \cdot 2}{32 \cdot 2} = \frac{16}{64}, \frac{17}{64}$$
$$A = \frac{48}{64}, \ B = \frac{56}{64}, \ C = \frac{28}{64}, \ D = \frac{16}{64}, \ E = \frac{17}{64}$$

22) **The correct answer is (D)**

$$\text{mean} = \left(\frac{2}{3} + \frac{1}{5}\right) \cdot \frac{1}{2} = \left(\frac{2 \cdot 5 + 3 \cdot 1}{15}\right) \cdot \frac{1}{2} = \frac{13}{15} \cdot \frac{1}{2} = \frac{13}{30}$$

23) **The correct answer is (A)**

$$2.24 = \frac{224}{100} = \frac{56}{25}, \quad a=56, \ b=25, \ a-b=31$$

24) **The correct answer is (A)**

$$\frac{99}{66} = \frac{99:11}{66:11} = -- = \frac{9}{6} = \frac{3}{2} = 1.5 = a.b$$

$$a=1, \ b=5, \qquad (a+b)=(1+5)=6$$

25) **The correct answer is (C)**

$$64\% = \frac{64}{100} = \frac{16}{25}$$

26) **The correct answer is (A)**

$$x \cdot 14\% = 56, \quad \frac{x \cdot 14}{100} = 56, \ x \cdot 14 = 56 \cdot 100, \ x=400$$

27) **The correct answer is (E)**

$$\left(\frac{17}{15}\right) \cdot 100 = (1.13) \cdot 100 = 113\%$$

28) **The correct answer is (B)**

The actual increase = 28000-24000=4000

The percentage increase is

$$\left(\frac{4000}{2000}\right) \cdot x 100\% = 20\%$$

29) **The correct answer is (E)**

$$300 x 20\% = 300 \cdot \frac{20}{100} = \$60 \ discount$$

$$300-60=240 - cost, \quad 240 x 3\% = 240 \cdot \frac{3}{100} = 7,2 \ box$$

Total price is e=240+7,2=247,2\$

30) **The correct answer is (A)**

$$\left(\frac{7}{32} + \frac{9}{32}\right) \cdot \frac{1}{2} = \frac{16}{32} \cdot \frac{1}{2} = \frac{8}{32} = \frac{1}{4}$$

31) **The correct answer is (D)**

First price is 100$

increase 30%=$100 \cdot \dfrac{30}{100} = 30\$$, 130$ (100+30)

30% decrease = $130 \cdot \dfrac{30}{100} = 39$,

Last price = 130-39=91$ (9% down)

32) **The correct answer is (C)**

$$0.08333... = \frac{1}{12}$$

33) **The correct answer is (A)**

$(3a^2b^3)^3 = (3)^3 \cdot (a^2)^3 \cdot (b^3)^3 = 27a^6b^9$

34) **The correct answer is (D)**

$$\frac{(6x^2)^3}{(3x^3)^2} = \frac{6 \cdot 6 \cdot 6 \cdot x^{2 \cdot 3}}{3 \cdot 3 \cdot x^{3 \cdot 2}} = \frac{24 \cdot x^6}{x^6} = 24$$

35) **The correct answer is (C)**

$3^m + 3^m + 3^m = 3^m(1+1+1) = 3^m \cdot 3 = 3^{m+1}$

36) **The correct answer is (D)**

$$14^m : 7^m = (2 \cdot 7)^m : 7^m = \frac{2^m \cdot 7^m}{7^m} = 2^m$$

37) **The correct answer is (B)**

$-2 \leq x \leq 3$, $x^2 = ?$

$(-2)^2 \leq x^2 \leq 3^2$, $4 \leq x^2 \leq 9$

38) **The correct answer is (A)**

$$\left(\sqrt{5} + \sqrt{2}\right)^2 - 2\sqrt{10} =$$
$$= \left(\sqrt{5}\right)^2 + 2\sqrt{5} \cdot \sqrt{2} + \left(\sqrt{2}\right)^2 - 2\sqrt{10} =$$
$$= \left(5 + 2\sqrt{10} + 2\right) - 2\sqrt{10} = 7 + 2\sqrt{10} - 2\sqrt{10} = 7$$

39) **The correct answer is (B)**
$99^2-90^2=9k$, $(99+90) \cdot (99-90)=9k$, $189 \cdot 9=9k$, $k=189$

40) **The correct answer is (E)**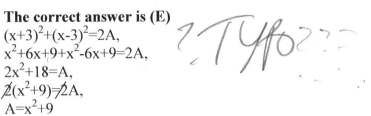
$(x+3)^2+(x-3)^2=2A$,
$x^2+6x+9+x^2-6x+9=2A$,
$2x^2+18=A$,
$\cancel{2}(x^2+9)=\cancel{2}A$,
$A=x^2+9$

41) **The correct answer is (C)**
$$\frac{(24x+6)}{4x+1}=\frac{6 \cdot (4x+1)}{4x+1}=6$$

42) **The correct answer is (A)**
$6x-4=3x+8 \implies 6x-3x=8+4$, $3x=12$, $x=4$

43) **The correct answer is (B)**
$|3x-6|=6$,
I. $3x-6=6$, $3x=12$, $x=4$
II. $3x-6=-6$ $3x=0$, $x=0$

44) **The correct answer is (D)**
$a+b=16$,
$\underline{a-b=2,}$
$2a=18$,
$a=9$, $b=7$

45) **The correct answer is (E)**
$A(6, 2)$, $B(10, 4)$ $AB=\sqrt{(x_2-x_1)^2+(y_2-y_1)^2}$
$AB=\sqrt{(10-6)^2+(4-2)^2}=\sqrt{4^2+2^2}=2\sqrt{5}$

46) **The correct answer is (A)**
$d_1 \| d_2$, $x=70°$, $x+y=180°$, $70°+y=180°$, $y=110°$, $y-x=110°-70°=40°$

47) **The correct answer is (B)**
$AC=12$ if $BA=\dfrac{AC}{2}=\dfrac{12}{2}=6$,
$BC=\dfrac{AC}{2}\sqrt{3}=\dfrac{12}{2}\sqrt{3}=6\sqrt{3}$
Perimeter $(ABC)=AB+AC+BC=12+6+6\sqrt{3}=18+6\sqrt{3}$

48) The correct answer is (C)

Area of the 30° sector $= \dfrac{\pi r^2 \alpha}{360} = \dfrac{\pi \cdot 8^2 \cdot 30}{360} = \dfrac{64\pi}{12} = \dfrac{16\pi}{3}$

49) The correct answer is (D)

$V = a^3 = 4^3 = 64$, $SA = 6a^2 = 6 \cdot 4^2 = 6 \cdot 16 = 96$

$V : SA = 64 : 96 = 2 : 3$

50) The correct answer is (E)

$\log_3 x = -3$, $x = 3^{-3}$, $x = \dfrac{1}{27}$

51) The correct answer is (A)

$|a - bi| = \sqrt{a^2 + b^2}$, $|8 - 4i| = \sqrt{8^2 + (-4)^2} = \sqrt{80} = 4\sqrt{5}$

52) The correct answer is (B)

$|AB|^2 + |BC|^2 = |AC|^2$, $(2x)^2 + |BC|^2 = 3^2$, $|BC|^2 = 9 - 4x^2$, $BC = \sqrt{9 - 4x^2}$

$\tan C = \dfrac{2x}{\sqrt{9 - 4x^2}}$

53) The correct answer is (B)

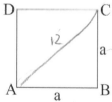

$AC = 12$, $a^2 + a^2 = 12^2$, $2a^2 = 144$, $a = 6\sqrt{2}$

$S(ABCD) = a^2 = \left(6\sqrt{2}\right)^2 = 72\,cm^2$

54) The correct answer is (D)

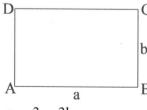

$\dfrac{a}{b} = \dfrac{3}{2} = \dfrac{3k}{2k}$,

Perimeter $= 2(a+b)$, $50 = 2(3k + 2k)$, $50 = 10k$, $k = 5$

Area(ABCD) $= a \cdot b = 3k \cdot 2k = 6k^2 = 6 \cdot 5^2 = 6 \cdot 25 = 150\,cm^2$

55) **The correct answer is (D)**

ax+by+c=0, Slope: $\dfrac{-a}{b}$, Slope$=-\dfrac{7}{9}$

7x+9y=63, 9y=-7x+63, $y=\dfrac{-7x}{9}+\dfrac{63}{9}$, $y=\dfrac{-7x}{9}+7$

60) **The correct answer is (B)**

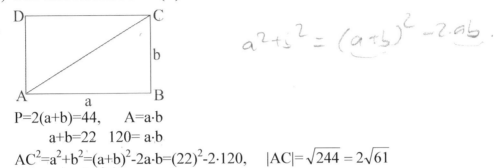

P=2(a+b)=44, A=a·b

a+b=22 120= a·b

$AC^2=a^2+b^2=(a+b)^2-2a\cdot b=(22)^2-2\cdot 120$, $|AC|=\sqrt{244}=2\sqrt{61}$

57) **The correct answer is (A)**

$\dfrac{S(ABD)}{S(ABC)}=\dfrac{BD\cdot H}{BC\cdot H}=\dfrac{8}{18}=\dfrac{4}{9}$

58) **The correct answer is (B)**

$\dfrac{x}{2}+\dfrac{x}{3}=8 \Rightarrow \dfrac{x}{2}+\dfrac{x}{3}=8$, $\dfrac{3x+2x}{6}=8$, 5x=48, x=$\dfrac{48}{5}$

(3) (2)

59) **The correct answer is (C)**

$x^2+y^2+Ax+By+C=0$ $M\left(-\dfrac{A}{2},\ -\dfrac{B}{2}\right)=M(-a,\ b)$

$x^2+y^2+12x+10y+20=0$ A=12, B=10

$M\left(-\dfrac{A}{2},\ -\dfrac{B}{2}\right)=M\left(-\dfrac{12}{2},\ -\dfrac{10}{2}\right)=(-6;\ -5)$

60) **The correct answer is (D)**

$A+B=\begin{bmatrix} 0+4 & 1+5 \\ 2+6 & 3+7 \end{bmatrix}=\begin{bmatrix} 4 & 6 \\ 8 & 10 \end{bmatrix}$

TEST – 1.2
- Solutions -

1) **The correct answer is (A)**
   3x-3y=12, x-y=4, 2x-2y=2(x-y)=2·4=8

2) **The correct answer is (C)**
   2x-6=6-2x,
   $2x+2x=6+6 \Rightarrow 4x=12, x=3, x^2=3^2=9$

3) **The correct answer is (D)**
   a+b=32,
   a-b=2,
   ‾‾‾‾‾‾‾
   2a=34,
   a=17, a-b=2, 17-b=2, b=15

4) **The correct answer is (E)**
   $2x+3y=12, 3y=-2x+12, y=-\dfrac{2x}{3}+4, \text{ slope}=-\dfrac{2}{3}$

5) **The correct answer is (A)**
   The x-intercept of line m: y=0
   2x+3·0=12, 2x=12, x=6,   (6, 0)

6) **The correct answer is (C)**
   The x-intercept of line m: x=0
   2·0+3y=12, 3y=12, y=4,   (0, 4)

7) **The correct answer is (D)**
   $(8)\cdot(0{,}004){:}(0{,}32)=\dfrac{8\cdot4\cdot10^{-3}}{32\cdot10^{-2}}=\dfrac{32\cdot10^{-3}}{32\cdot10^{-2}}=10^{-1}=\dfrac{1}{10}$

8) **The correct answer is (E)**
   $\dfrac{\left(\sqrt{9}+\sqrt{27}\right)}{\sqrt{9}}=\dfrac{3+3\sqrt{3}}{3}=\dfrac{3\left(1+\sqrt{3}\right)}{3}=1+\sqrt{3}$

9) **The correct answer is (B)**
   $\sqrt{5},\ \sqrt{20},\ \sqrt{45},\ \sqrt{80}=\sqrt{5},\ \sqrt{4\cdot5},\ \sqrt{9\cdot5},\ \sqrt{16\cdot5}=\sqrt{5},\ 2\sqrt{5},\ 3\sqrt{5},\ 4\sqrt{5}$
   $\text{Arithmetic mean}=\dfrac{\sqrt{5}+2\sqrt{5}+3\sqrt{5}+4\sqrt{5}}{4}=\dfrac{10\sqrt{5}}{4}=\dfrac{5\sqrt{5}}{2}$

10) **The correct answer is (A)**
Area=a^2, Perimeter=4a
$4a=a^2$ a=4,
Diagonal=$a\sqrt{2}=4\sqrt{2}$

11) **The correct answer is (B)**
$\dfrac{x+y}{x-y}=\dfrac{3}{2}$ $\Rightarrow$ 3(x-y)=2(x+y)

$\dfrac{x}{y}=\dfrac{5y}{y}=5$ 3x-3y=2x+2y

     3x-2x=2y+3y, x=5y

12) **The correct answer is (C)**
$14^x\cdot =7^x\cdot m$, $(14)^x=7^x\cdot m$, $(2\cdot7)^x=7^x\cdot m$,
$2^x\cdot7^x=7^x\cdot m$, $m=2^x$

13) **The correct answer is (A)**
$x^2-y^2=k$, (x+y)=m, (x-y)=?
$(x^2-y^2)=(x+y)(x-y)=k$ $\Rightarrow m\cdot(x-y)=k$, $x-y=\dfrac{k}{m}$

14) **The correct answer is (D)**
$a_1=3$, $a_2=6$
d= $a_2-a_1=6-3=3$
$a_8=a_2+6r=6+6\cdot3=24$

15) **The correct answer is (C)**
$\sqrt{x+3}=3$ $\Rightarrow \left(\sqrt{x+3}\right)^2=3^2$, x+3=9, x=6

16) **The correct answer is (E)**
Jack is 15 $\rightarrow$ after six years $\rightarrow$ 21
Father is 40 $\rightarrow$ after six years $\rightarrow$ 46
46+21=67

17) **The correct answer is (C)**
3x=5y,   4y=7z,
$4\cdot3x=4\cdot5y$, $5\cdot4y=5\cdot7z$
12x=20y   20y=35z

12x=35z $\Rightarrow$ x=35, z=12, $\dfrac{x}{z}=\dfrac{35}{12}$

18) **The correct answer is (C)**

$f(x)=x^2+3x$, $f(3x)=(3x)^2+3 \cdot (3x)=9x^2+9x=9(x^2+1)$

19) **The correct answer is (D)**

$2(2x+4)=(x+5)$,

$4x+8=x+5$, $4x-x=5-8$, $3x=-3$, $x=-1$

20) **The correct answer is (A)**

An arithmetic sequence: 10, 4,-2,-8,-14,-20

$a_1=10$, $a_2=4$, $r=d=a_2-a_1=4-6=-4$,

$a_5+a_6=a_1+4r+a_1+5r=2a_1+9r=2 \cdot 10a+9r=20-54=-34$

21) **The correct answer is (A)**

$$2A = 2 \cdot \begin{bmatrix} 4 & 2 \\ 3 & 1 \end{bmatrix} = \begin{bmatrix} 8 & 4 \\ 6 & 2 \end{bmatrix}, \quad 3B = 3 \cdot \begin{bmatrix} 3 & 6 \\ 9 & 12 \end{bmatrix},$$

$$2A+3B = \begin{bmatrix} 8+3 & 4+6 \\ 6+9 & 2+12 \end{bmatrix} = \begin{bmatrix} 11 & 10 \\ 15 & 14 \end{bmatrix}$$

22) **The correct answer is (B)**

$$A-B = \begin{bmatrix} 9-1 & 8-2 \\ 7-3 & 6-4 \end{bmatrix}, \quad A-B = \begin{bmatrix} 8 & 6 \\ 4 & 2 \end{bmatrix}$$

23) **The correct answer is (E)**

$$\frac{2+\sqrt{5}}{2-\sqrt{5}}+9 \Rightarrow$$

$$\frac{(2+\sqrt{5})(2+\sqrt{5})}{(2-\sqrt{5})(2+\sqrt{5})}+9 = \frac{4+2 \cdot 2\sqrt{5}+5}{4-5}+9 = \frac{9+4\sqrt{5}}{-1}+9 = -4\sqrt{5}$$

24) **The correct answer is (D)**

$f(x)=3x+3$, $g(x)=2x+2$, $f(g(2))=?$

$f(g(x))=3g(x)+3=3 \cdot (2x+2)+3=6x+9$, $f(g(2))=6(2)+9=6 \cdot 2+9=21$

25) **The correct answer is (B)**

$i^8-i^6=(i^2)^4-(i^2)^3=(-1)^4-(-1)^3=1-(-1)=2$

26) **The correct answer is (E)**

Squares have two diagonals, and trapezoids have two diagonals.

27) **The correct answer is (C)**

$$\frac{z_1}{z_2} = \frac{3}{4} = \frac{P_1}{P_2} \Rightarrow \frac{3}{4} = \frac{24}{P_2} \Rightarrow P_2=32$$

28) **The correct answer is (A)**

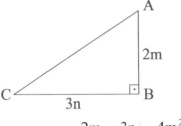

$$\tan C + \cot C = \frac{2m}{3n} + \frac{3n}{2m} = \frac{4m^2 + 9n^2}{6mn}$$

29) **The correct answer is (D)**

$$(x\sqrt{5} + x\sqrt{20}) : \sqrt{5}$$

$$x\sqrt{5} + 2x\sqrt{5} : \sqrt{5} \Rightarrow \frac{3x\sqrt{5}}{\sqrt{5}} = 3x$$

30) **The correct answer is (B)**

$$f(x) = \frac{x^2 + 2x + 3}{9x^2 - 9}, \quad 9x^2 - 9 = 0, \quad 9x^2 = 9, \quad x^2 = 1, \quad x = \pm 1$$

31) **The correct answer is (D)**

$$4\% \cdot 4\% \cdot 4 = 0.0000064$$

32) **The correct answer is (A)**

$$\text{men : women} : \frac{4}{5} = \frac{4k}{5k}$$

$$4k + 5k = 3600 \quad \Rightarrow \quad 9k = 3600, \, k = 400$$

women − men = 5k - 4k = k = 400

33) **The correct answer is (B)**

$$\pi r^2 = 5, \quad r^2 = \frac{5}{\pi}, \quad r = \sqrt{\frac{5}{\pi}}$$

34) **The correct answer is (B)**

$$\frac{14^x}{7^x} = \frac{2^x \cdot 7^x}{7^x} = 2^x$$

35) **The correct answer is (C)**

$$(5^2 - 5) \cdot (4^2 - 4^1) \cdot (3^2 - 3^1) = (25 - 5) \cdot (16 - 4) \cdot (9 - 3) = 20 \cdot 12 \cdot 6 = 1440$$

36) **The correct answer is (E)**

$$(\sqrt{5} + \sqrt{10}) : (1 + \sqrt{2}) = \frac{\sqrt{5} + \sqrt{10}}{1 + \sqrt{2}} = \frac{\sqrt{5}(1 + \sqrt{2})}{1 + \sqrt{2}} = \sqrt{5}$$

37) **The correct answer is (D)**

$$\frac{4}{5} \cdot \frac{9}{9} = \frac{36}{45}$$

38) **The correct answer is (A)**

First number: n

Second number: n+2

$$T_2^2 - T_1^2 = (n + 2)^2 - (n)^2 = 24$$

$$n^2 + 4n + 4 - n^2 = 24, \quad 4n = 20, \quad n = 5$$

First: n=5, Second: n+2=5+2=7

39) **The correct answer is (E)**

$$0.22 = \frac{a}{b} = \frac{22}{99} = \frac{2 \cdot 11}{9 \cdot 11} = \frac{2}{9} = \frac{a}{b}, \quad a+b=2+9=11$$

40) **The correct answer is (A)**

The number at the given digit is 8, and the number right of it is 7, so we add 1 to 8 round from of 0.87 to its tenths place as 0.9.

41) **The correct answer is (A)**

x-6=y $\Rightarrow$ x-y=6

|4x-4y|=4·|x-y|, |6y-6x|=|6x-6y|=6·|x-y|, 4·|x-y|+6·|x-y|=10·|x-y|=10·6=60

42) **The correct answer is (C)**

Geometric means:

43) **The correct answer is (A)**

Original cost=x, x-x·20%=800, $x - \frac{1}{5} = 800$, 4x=800·5, x=$1000

44) **The correct answer is (C)**

$(x-2)^2 - (x-4)^2$, $x^2 - 4x - 4 = x^2 - 8x + 16$, -4x+4=-8x+16, 4x=12, x=3

45) **The correct answer is (E)**

$$\left(\frac{3}{2} - \frac{2}{3}\right) \cdot \left(\frac{3}{2} + \frac{2}{3}\right) = \left(\frac{3}{2}\right)^2 - \left(\frac{2}{3}\right)^2 = \frac{4}{9} - \frac{9}{4} = \frac{9 \cdot 9 - 4 \cdot 4}{36} = \frac{65}{36}$$

46) **The correct answer is (B)**
$\log_9 x^2 = 2$ if $x = ?$
$\log_9 2 = x^2$, $x^2 = 9^2$, $x = 9$, $\sqrt{x} = \sqrt{9} = 3$

47) **The correct answer is (B)**
$r = 9$

48) **The correct answer is (C)**

$6^2 = 5^2 + BC^2$, $36 = 25 + BC^2$, $BC = \sqrt{11}$

$\sin 2x = 2\sin x \cdot \cos x = 2 \cdot \dfrac{5}{6} \cdot \dfrac{\sqrt{11}}{6} = \dfrac{10\sqrt{11}}{36} = \dfrac{5\sqrt{11}}{18}$

49) **The correct answer is (A)**
$2a + 3b = 12$
$3a + 2b = 13$
$+$ _____
$5a + 5b = 25$, $\Rightarrow a + b = 5$

50) **The correct answer is (A)**
$x^2 - x(x_1 + x_2) + (x_1 \cdot x_2) = 0$,
$x_1 = \dfrac{4}{7}$, $x_2 = -\dfrac{2}{7}$

$x^2 - \left(\dfrac{4}{7} - \dfrac{2}{7}\right) + \left(\dfrac{4}{7}\right) \cdot \left(\dfrac{-2}{7}\right) = 0$

$x^2 - \dfrac{2x}{7} - \dfrac{8}{49} \Rightarrow 49x^2 - 14x - 8 = 0$

51) **The correct answer is (D)**
$x^2 + 12x = 0$, $x(x + 12) = 0$,
$x = 0$, $x = -12$, $f(x)$ is undefined.

52) **The correct answer is (A)**
$\sqrt{7 + 2\sqrt{12}} = \sqrt{(3 + 4) + 2\sqrt{3 \cdot 4}} = \sqrt{4} + \sqrt{3} = 2 + \sqrt{3}$

53) **The correct answer is (B)**
$x^2+5x+3m=(x+3)\cdot(x+n)$,
$x^2+(a+b)\cdot x+a\cdot b$, $a+b=5$, $3+b=5$, $b=2$
$x^2+5x+6=(x+3)\cdot(x+2)$, $n=2$

54) **The correct answer is (C)**
$A:B:C=2:4:6=2k:4k:6k$,
$A+B+C=60$, $2k+4k+6k=60$, $12k=60$, $k=5$
$c=6k=6\cdot5=30$

55) **The correct answer is (A)**

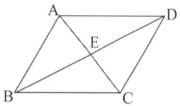

ABE,AED,BCE,CED,ABD,BCD,ADC,ABC

56) **The correct answer is (C)**
$\angle A+\angle B=180^o$, $2x+110^o=180^o$, $2x=70^o$, $x=35^o$

57) **The correct answer is (D)**
$|AD|^2=|BD|\cdot|DC|=4\cdot7$, $AD=2\sqrt{7}$

58) **The correct answer is (E)**

$|AC|^2=12^2+4^2=160$, $AC=4\sqrt{10}$

59) **The correct answer is (A)**
$$\left(\frac{a}{b}+\frac{b}{a}\right)^2-2=\frac{a^2}{b^2}+2\cdot\frac{a}{b}\cdot\frac{b}{a}+\frac{b^2}{a^2}=\frac{a^2}{b^2}+\frac{b^2}{a^2}+2-2=\frac{a^2}{b^2}+\frac{b^2}{a^2}$$

60) **The correct answer is (A)**
d_1: $2x+3y=12$, d_2: $y=3x+4$.
$$m_1=-\frac{2}{3}, \quad m_2=3, \quad m_1+m_2=3-\frac{2}{3}=\frac{7}{3}$$

TEST – 1.3
- Solutions -

1) **The correct answer is (C)**

   A, B, D and E are same: $\dfrac{3}{4} = \dfrac{9}{12} = \dfrac{15}{20} = \dfrac{12}{16}$

2) **The correct answer is (B)**

   $\sqrt{9 + 2\sqrt{18}} = \sqrt{(6+3) + 2(6 \cdot 3)} = \sqrt{6} + \sqrt{3}$

3) **The correct answer is (C)**

   $f(x) = 8x^2 + 4 = 2(x^2 + 2) \Rightarrow f(x) = 2g(x)$
   $g(x) = x^2 + 2$

4) **The correct answer is (A)**

   $g(x) = (x+4)^2 = x^2 + 8x + 16 = x^2 + 16 + 8x = f(x) + 8x$
   $f(x) = x^2 + 16$

5) **The correct answer is (A)**

   1, 4, 16, 36, 64 $\Rightarrow \{1,2,4,6,8\}$ five numbers

6) **The correct answer is (C)**

   $1^3 = 1$, $2^3 = 8$, $3^3 = 27$, $4^3 = 64$

7) **The correct answer is (B)**

   $\dfrac{4^x}{2^{2x}} = \dfrac{4^x}{4^x} = 1,\; \dfrac{14^x}{7^x} = \dfrac{7^x \cdot 2^x}{7^x} = 2^x,\; \dfrac{3^{2x}}{9^x} = \dfrac{9^x}{9^x} = 1,\; \dfrac{5^{2x}}{25^x} = 1,\; \dfrac{6^{2x}}{36^x} = 1$

8) **The correct answer is (D)**

   $800 \cdot x\% = 600,\; 800 \cdot \dfrac{x}{100} = 600,\; 8x = 600,\; x = 75\ (75\%)$

9) **The correct answer is (A)**

   $4x + 4 = 2x + 16,\; 4x - 2x = 16 - 4,\; 2x = 12,\; x = 6$

10) **The correct answer is (B)**

   $4a^2 - 2ab + b^2 = 4 \cdot (2)^2 - 2 \cdot 2 \cdot (-3) + (-3)^2 = 4 \cdot 4 + 12 + 9 = 29$

11) **The correct answer is (B)**

   $4x + 3y + 6xy - x - 6y - 3xy = 3x - 3y + 3xy = 3(x - y + xy)$

12) **The correct answer is (C)**

$a^2-b^2=2x$, $(a+b)\cdot(a-b)=2x$, $(a+b)\cdot y=2x$, $(a+b)=\dfrac{2x}{y}$

13) **The correct answer is (C)**

$\dfrac{6n+3}{4}=\dfrac{2n-5}{5}$ $\Rightarrow$ $5\cdot(6n+3)=4\cdot(2n-5)$, $30n+15=8n-20$, $22n=-35$

14) **The correct answer is (A)**

$\sqrt{3x+12}-4=x$, $\sqrt{3x+12}=x+4$,

$\left(\sqrt{3x+12}\right)^2=(x+4)^2$, $3x+12=x^2+8x+16$,

$\Rightarrow x^2+5x+4=0$, $\Rightarrow (x+4)\cdot(x+1)=0$, $x=-4$, $x=-1$

15) **The correct answer is (A)**

$4(x^2+3)=2(2x^2+2x)$, $4x^2+12=4x^2+4x$ $\Rightarrow$ $12=4x$, $x=3$

16) **The correct answer is (B)**

14, 13, 26, 25, 50, **49, 98**
a, b, c, …
b=a-1, c=2b, x=49, y=98 $\Rightarrow$ x+y=49+98=147

17) **The correct answer is (D)**

ax+by+cx=my, ax+cx=my-by, x(a+c)=y(m-b), $y=\dfrac{x(a+c)}{m-b}$

18) **The correct answer is (E)**

B) $\dfrac{\pi}{4}=\dfrac{\pi}{\sqrt{16}}$; since the numerators are all the same, the fraction with the

largest denominator is the smallest fraction.

19) **The correct answer is (C)**

$\dfrac{5}{9}\cdot\dfrac{12}{12}=\dfrac{60}{108}$

20) **The correct answer is (C)**

$40=8\cdot5=2^3\cdot5^1$, $\qquad$ $(3+1)\cdot(1+1)=8$
40,20,10,8,5,4,2,1

21) **The correct answer is (C)**
GCF (84,105)=21
84:21=4 - first tin, 105:21=5 - second tin, We need (4+5)=9 bottles

22) **The correct answer is (D)**

5!=1·2·3·4·5=120, 4!=1·2·3·4=24,

2!=1·2=2, 1!=1, 5!-4!-2!-1!=120-24-2-1=93

23) **The correct answer is (B)**

$|x-3|=4$	$|x-3|=-4$	$x_1 \cdot x_2 = -7$
$x-3=4$	$x-3=-7$	
$x=7$	$x=-1$	

24) **The correct answer is (C)**

x-4=y, x-y=4,

$|6x-6y|=6 \cdot |x-y|=6 \cdot |4|=6 \cdot 4=24$

25) **The correct answer is (A)**

Geometric mean = $\sqrt{a.b} = \sqrt{100.49} = 10\text{x}7 = 70$

26) **The correct answer is (D)**

$$\frac{30}{(30+70)} = \frac{30}{100} = \frac{3}{10}$$

27) **The correct answer is (B)**

$\dfrac{b}{a} = \dfrac{3}{7} = \dfrac{3k}{7k}$, Perimeter=2(a+b), 80=2(3k+7k), 40=10k, k=4

Shorter side = 3k=3·4=12

28) **The correct answer is (C)**

Direct proportion formula=y=kx,

8=k·4, y=2, y=kx, y=24·2=48

29) **The correct answer is (C)**

$30\% \cdot 40 = \dfrac{30}{100} \cdot 40 = \dfrac{1200}{100} = 12$

30) **The correct answer is (D)**

$\dfrac{x}{3} - \dfrac{x}{4} = 5$, $\dfrac{4x - 3x}{12} = 5$, $\dfrac{x}{12} = 5$, $x = 60$

31) **The correct answer is (D)**

$\angle A + \angle B + \angle C = 180^\circ$, $AB = AC$, $\angle B = \angle C = 3x$
$4x + 3x + 3x = 180^\circ$, $10x = 180^\circ$, $x = 18^\circ$

32) **The correct answer is (A)**

Perimeter: ABC = 6+6+7 = 19,
ABD = 6+4+3 = 13,
ADC = 4+4+6 = 14
Sum = 46

33) **The correct answer is (A)**

$\angle C = \angle E = 45^\circ$, $CF = EF = x$
$\angle E = \angle A = 45^\circ$, $AK = EK = y$
$EF = KB = x$, $EK = FB = y$
Perimeter(KBFE) = $2x + 2y = 2(x+y) =$
$= 2(AB) = 2 \cdot 16 = 32$

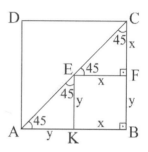

34) **The correct answer is (C)**

$\angle AOC + \alpha = 180^\circ$, $\alpha = 180^\circ - 142^\circ = 38^\circ$

35) **The correct answer is (B)**

Surface Area = $2(ab + ac + bc) = 2(7 \cdot 8 + 7 \cdot 5 + 8 \cdot 5) =$
$a = 7$, $b = 8$, $c = 5$ \qquad $= 2(56 + 35 + 40) = 262 cm^2$

36) **The correct answer is (D)**

Slope = $\dfrac{y_2 - y_1}{x_2 - x_1} = \dfrac{6 - 3}{12 - 9} = \dfrac{3}{3} = 1$

37) **The correct answer is (B)**

The sum of age 4 years ago: $80 - 6 \cdot 4 = 56$

38) **The correct answer is (A)**

Two together = $\dfrac{1}{12} + \dfrac{1}{16} = \dfrac{1}{12_{(4)}} + \dfrac{1}{16_{(3)}} - \dfrac{7}{48}$

39) **The correct answer is (B)**

$\left(\dfrac{1}{t_1} + \dfrac{1}{t_2} \right) = \dfrac{1}{t} \Rightarrow \left(\dfrac{1}{12} + \dfrac{1}{20} \right) = \dfrac{1}{t}$, $\left(\dfrac{1}{12_{(5)}} + \dfrac{1}{20_{(3)}} \right) = \dfrac{1}{t}$, $\dfrac{8}{60} = \dfrac{1}{t} \Rightarrow$

$t = \dfrac{60}{8} = \dfrac{30}{4} = 7.5$

40) **The correct answer is (A)**

(5-1)!=4!=1·2·3·4=24

41) **The correct answer is (C)**

$y=x^2+b$, x=0, y=4, y=b=4

42) **The correct answer is (C)**

2a+b+c=14
a+2b+c=16
a+b+2c=18
+ _____
4a+4b+4c=48, a+b+c=12

43) **The correct answer is (D)**

$$\frac{1}{100}+\frac{1}{60}+\frac{1}{40}=\frac{1}{x}, \quad \frac{1}{100}_{(6)}+\frac{1}{60}_{(10)}+\frac{1}{40}_{(15)}=\frac{1}{x}, \quad x=\frac{600}{31}\cong 19\,days$$

44) **The correct answer is (B)**

246+264+426+462+642+624=2654

45) **The correct answer is (A)**

24 → divisors → 1, 2, 3, 4, 6, 8, 12, 24,   Sum: (1+2+3+4+6+8+12+24)=60

46) **The correct answer is (D)**

A) $\frac{\sqrt{3}}{\sqrt{2}}=\frac{\sqrt{3}\sqrt{2}}{\sqrt{2}\sqrt{2}}=\frac{\sqrt{6}}{2}$ B) $\sqrt{5}$ C) $\sqrt{7}$ E) $\sqrt{13}$ D) $\frac{\sqrt{100}}{\sqrt{289}}=\frac{10}{17}$

47) **The correct answer is (B)**

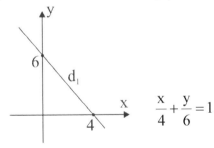

$$\frac{x}{4}+\frac{y}{6}=1$$

48) **The correct answer is (D)**

$\log_3 x=4 \Rightarrow x=3^4$, x=81, $x=3^4$, $x^2=(3^4)^2=3^8$

49) **The correct answer is (B)**

$|AC|^2=|AB|^2+|BC|^2$
$13^2=12^2+|BC|^2$
$|BC|^2=25, BC=5$
$\sin2\alpha=2\sin\alpha\cdot\cos\alpha=2\cdot\dfrac{5}{13}\cdot\dfrac{12}{13}=\dfrac{120}{169}$

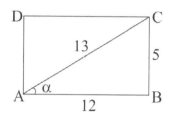

50) **The correct answer is (A)**

$\dfrac{4}{4+2}=\dfrac{6}{6+x}\Rightarrow\dfrac{4}{6}=\dfrac{6}{6+x},\ \dfrac{2}{3}=\dfrac{6}{6+x}$
$3\cdot6=2\cdot(6+x),\ 18=12+2x,\ 6=2x,\ x=3$

51) **The correct answer is (C)**
$x^2+4x=12\Rightarrow x^2+4x-12=0\Rightarrow(x+6)\cdot(x-2)=0$
$\qquad\qquad\qquad\qquad x+6=0,\ x-2=0$
$\qquad\qquad\qquad\qquad x=-6,\quad x=2$

52) **The correct answer is (D)**

The y-intercept of $12x-9y=17$: $x=0,\ 12\cdot0-9\cdot y=17\Rightarrow-9y=17,\ y=-\dfrac{17}{9}$

53) **The correct answer is (B)**
$i^2=-1,\ i^8+i^4+4i^2=(i^2)^4+(i^2)^2+4\cdot(i^2)=(-1)^4+(-1)^2+4\cdot(-1)=1+1-4=-2$

54) **The correct answer is (A)**
$6x-2x-4=12,\ 4x-4=12,\ 4x=16,\ x=4$

55) **The correct answer is (A)**
$P=4x+4,\ 2P=2(4x+4)=8x+8,\ Q=4y+8,$
$2P-Q=(8x+8)-(4y+8)=8x+8-4y-8=8x-4y$

56) **The correct answer is (E)**
$6a+6b-6c+12d=6(a+b-c+2d)$

57) **The correct answer is (D)**
$m=-11,$ if $|2m+20|=|2\cdot(-11)+20|=|-22+20|=|-2|=2$

58) **The correct answer is (B)**

6-3(2x-2)+6x

6-3·2x-3·(-2)+6x

6-6x+6+6x=12

59) **The correct answer is (C)**

$|AC|^2=|AB|^2+|BC|^2$, $|AC|^2=2^2+1^2=\sqrt{5}$

$\sin x=\dfrac{AB}{AC}=\dfrac{2}{\sqrt{5}}=\dfrac{2\sqrt{5}}{5}$

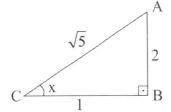

60) **The correct answer is (C)**

7x-6y=15 $\Rightarrow$ -6y=-7x+15 $\Rightarrow$ $y=\dfrac{-7}{-6}x+\dfrac{15}{-6}$, Slope=$\dfrac{-7}{-6}=\dfrac{7}{6}$

TEST – 1.4

- Solutions -

1) **The correct answer is (E)**
Let's name the books the bookseller has: x
The first purchase price: 5x-120
The second purchase price: 4x+100
In this case :   5x-120=4x+100
                             5x-4x=100+120, x=220

2) **The correct answer is (B)**
Let's name the number of married couples: x
Now there are x number of men and x number of women joining the room.
$$\begin{pmatrix} Number \\ of\ Men \end{pmatrix} = 3 \begin{pmatrix} Number \\ of\ Women \end{pmatrix}$$
64+x=3(x+16),
64+x=3x+48,
64-48=3x-x, 16=2x, x=8

3) **The correct answer is (A)**
$$\frac{y^2-9}{y-3} = \frac{(y-3)(y+3)}{y-3} = y+3$$, y=-4, for (y+3)=(-4+3)=-1

4) **The correct answer is (C)**
A>B, 30A=70B, 3A=7B, A=7, B=3
For the sum to be minimum =(A+B)=3+7=10

5) **The correct answer is (C)**
There are 5 yellow, 7 red, 5 green and 4 blue marbles in one box. The probability of the marble to be green $$= \frac{5}{4+7+5+4} = \frac{5}{20} = \frac{1}{4}$$

6) **The correct answer is (C)**

Perimeter ABCD=2(AB+BC)=2(2^x+2^y)=
=$2^{x+1}+2^{y+1}$

7) **The correct answer is (E)**
Clearance made: 160·25%=160·$\frac{1}{4}$=$40
The clearance price: 160-40=$120

8) **The correct answer is (B)**

$$\frac{7}{m}=\frac{28}{5} \Rightarrow \frac{7}{m}=\frac{7 \cdot 4}{5}, \quad 4m=5, \quad 4m+1=5+1=6$$

9) **The correct answer is (E)**

-6(m+n-3)=-6n-18, -6m-6n+18=-6n-18, -6m=-36, m=6

10) **The correct answer is (A)**

$\angle x+\angle y+\angle \alpha=360^{\circ}$,
$120^{\circ}+140^{\circ}+\alpha=360^{\circ}$,
$260^{\circ}+\alpha=360^{\circ}, \alpha=100^{\circ}$

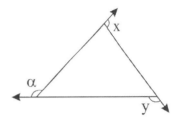

11) **The correct answer is (C)**

$f(x)=3^{x}+x^{3}$ then $f(3)=3^{3}+3^{3}=27+27=54$,
$\qquad f(2)=3^{2}+2^{3}=9+8=17$,
$\qquad f(3)-f(2)=54-17=37$

12) **The correct answer is (E)**

12	18	20	2
6	9	10	2
3	9	5	3
1	3	5	3
	1	5	5
		1	

Least common $=2 \cdot 2 \cdot 3 \cdot 3 \cdot 5=4 \cdot 9 \cdot 5=180$

13) **The correct answer is (D)**

$6^{2}=36, 7^{2}=49, 10^{2}=100, 12^{2}=144, 15^{2}=225$

14) **The correct answer is (B)**

3A+3B-3C=21, 3(A+B-C)=21, A+B-C=7
5A+5B-5C=5(A+B-C)=5·7=35

15) **The correct answer is (C)**

8 triangles

16) **The correct answer is (B)**

$2\alpha+4\alpha=180^{\circ}, 6\alpha=180^{\circ}, \alpha=30^{\circ}$

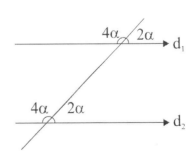

17) **The correct answer is (C)**

$43\triangle\rightarrow71,$ $\qquad ab\triangle\rightarrow xy,$

$62\triangle\rightarrow84$ $\qquad x=a+b$

$94\triangle\rightarrow135$ $\qquad y=a-b$

$75\triangle\rightarrow?$ $\qquad 75\triangle\rightarrow(7+5); (7-5)=12; 2=122$

18) **The correct answer is (B)**

$d_1=\dfrac{x}{a}+\dfrac{y}{b}=1,$

$\dfrac{x}{6}+\dfrac{y}{5}=1,\ 5x+6y=30$

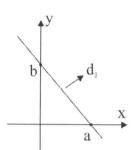

19) **The correct answer is (A)**

The word *difference* means to subtract: $\dfrac{x}{2}-\dfrac{x}{3}=20$

20) **The correct answer is (C)**

$a^2-b^2=(a+b)\cdot(a-b)$

$a^2-b^2=29\cdot1 \Rightarrow (a+b)\cdot(a-b)=29\cdot1$

$a+b=29$

$\underline{a-b=1}$

$2a=30,\ a=15$

$a+b=29,\ 15+b=29,\ b=14,$

$a^2+b^2=15^2+14^2=225+196=421$

21) **The correct answer is (D)**

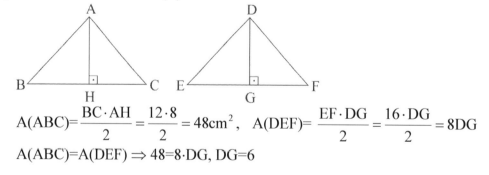

$A(ABC)=\dfrac{BC\cdot AH}{2}=\dfrac{12\cdot8}{2}=48cm^2,\quad A(DEF)=\dfrac{EF\cdot DG}{2}=\dfrac{16\cdot DG}{2}=8DG$

$A(ABC)=A(DEF) \Rightarrow 48=8\cdot DG,\ DG=6$

22) **The correct answer is (D)**

$6(y+4)-4(2y-2)=6y+24-4y+8=6y-8y+24+8=32-2y$

23) **The correct answer is (C)**

$x+2y=3m$

$\underline{x-2y=m}$

$2x=4m,\ x=2m$

24) The correct answer is (E)

$$x^2+6x+9=(x+3)^2=\left(\sqrt{7}-3+3\right)^2=\left(\sqrt{7}\right)^2=7$$

25) The correct answer is (A)

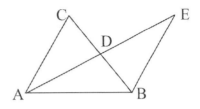

ABD,ADC,ABC,ABE,ADE,

26) The correct answer is (B)

d_1 equation: 8y-6x=12, 8y=6x+12, $m_1=\dfrac{6}{8}=\dfrac{3}{4}$

d_2 equation: 7y+4x=14, 7y=-4x+14, $m_2=-\dfrac{4}{7}$

$m_1+m_2=\dfrac{3}{4}+\left(-\dfrac{4}{7}\right)=\dfrac{21-16}{28}=\dfrac{5}{28}$

27) The correct answer is (C)
$3x^2+19x+20=(3x+4)(x+5)$

3x ⤬ 4
 x ⤬ 5

$3x^2+19x+20=(3x+4)(x+5)=(ax+4)(bx+5)$
a=3, b=1
2a+3b=2·3+3·1=6+3=9

28) The correct answer is (C)

$(AC)^2=5^2+12^2$, $AC^2=169$, AC=13
$\dfrac{P(ABCD)}{P(ABC)}=\dfrac{2(12+5)}{12+5+13}=\dfrac{34}{30}=\dfrac{17}{15}$

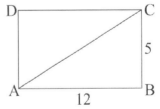

29) The correct answer is (D)

Let us say the number is x,

$x\cdot\dfrac{6}{7}=36$, $\dfrac{6x}{7}=36$, $6x=36\cdot7$, $x=42$

30) The correct answer is (E)
The sum of ages after 7 years:
75+6*7=77+42=119

31) **The correct answer is (A)**

a, 6, 4a, 24, 16a, x

$b_1, b_2, b_3, b_4, b_5, b_6$ ...., is the geometric sequence

$b_2^2 = b_1 \cdot b_3$, $(6)^2 = a \cdot 4a$, $36 = 4a^2$, $9 = a^2$, $a = 3$

a, 6, 4a, 24, 16a, x

3, 6, 12, 24, 48, 96

32) **The correct answer is (D)**

$\dfrac{1}{a} + \dfrac{1}{b} + \dfrac{1}{c} = 3x$ if $\dfrac{3}{a} + \dfrac{3}{b} + \dfrac{3}{c} = 3\left(\dfrac{1}{a} + \dfrac{1}{b} + \dfrac{1}{c}\right) = 3 \cdot 3x = 9x$

33) **The correct answer is (A)**

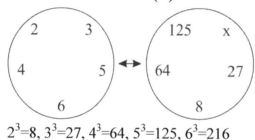

$2^3 = 8$, $3^3 = 27$, $4^3 = 64$, $5^3 = 125$, $6^3 = 216$

34) **The correct answer is (B)**

$$\dfrac{13^n + 13^{n+1}}{13^n + 13^n} = \dfrac{13^n + 13^n \cdot 13^1}{2 \cdot 13^n} = \dfrac{13^n(1+13)}{2 \cdot 13^n} = \dfrac{14}{2} = 7$$

35) **The correct answer is (D)**

$\tan\alpha = 3a$ if $\sin\alpha = ?$

$|AB|^2 + |BC|^2 = |AC|^2$

$(3a)^2 + (1)^2 = (AC)^2$, $AC = \sqrt{9a^2 + 1}$

$\sin\alpha = \dfrac{AB}{AC} = \dfrac{3a}{\sqrt{9a^2 + 1}}$

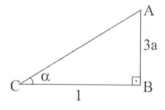

36) **The correct answer is (E)**

$\sqrt{4} + \sqrt{9} + \sqrt{16} + \sqrt{25} = \sqrt{14}x$ if

$2 + 3 + 4 + 5 = \sqrt{14}\sqrt{x} \Rightarrow 14 = \sqrt{14}\sqrt{x}$

$x = \dfrac{14}{\sqrt{14}} = \dfrac{14 \cdot \sqrt{14}}{14} \Rightarrow x = \sqrt{14}$

37) The correct answer is (A)

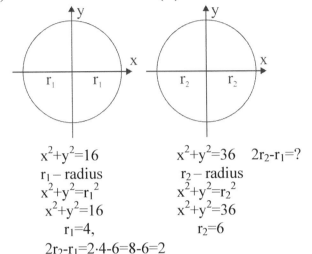

$$x^2+y^2=16 \qquad x^2+y^2=36 \quad 2r_2-r_1=?$$
$$r_1 - \text{radius} \qquad r_2 - \text{radius}$$
$$x^2+y^2=r_1^2 \qquad x^2+y^2=r_2^2$$
$$x^2+y^2=16 \qquad x^2+y^2=36$$
$$r_1=4, \qquad\qquad r_2=6$$
$$2r_2-r_1=2\cdot4-6=8-6=2$$

38) The correct answer is (E)

$$3.175=\frac{3175}{1000}=\frac{3175:25}{1000:25}=\frac{127}{40}=\frac{120+7}{40}=3\frac{7}{40}$$

$$3\frac{7}{40}=a\frac{b}{c} \Rightarrow a=3,\ b=7,\ c=40$$

$$a+b+c=3+7+40=50$$

39) The correct answer is (B)

a+b=16, a+c=14, b+c=12 if a+b+c=?

$$\begin{aligned}a+b&=16\\a+c&=14\\b+c&=12\\+\overline{}\\2a+2b+2c&=42,\end{aligned}$$ 2(a+b+c)=42, a+b+c=21

40) The correct answer is (C)

Numbers that can be created:
123,132,231,213,321,312 defined numbers can be created.
123+132+231+213+321+312=1332

41) The correct answer is (A)

Chemistry=150, Biology=170, $2\cdot150+1\cdot170=300+170=470$
The books are: 2 Chemistry, Biology

42) The correct answer is (C)

$f(x)=(x+3)^2$, $g(x)=2x^2+12x+18$
$f(x)=(x+3)^2=x^2+6x+9$, $g(x)=2x^2+12x+18=2(x^2+6x+9) \Rightarrow g(x)=2f(x)$

43) **The correct answer is (D)**

$V_1 = a^3 = 27 \Rightarrow a^3 = 27 \Rightarrow a^3 = 3^3 \Rightarrow a = 3$

$V_2 = b^3 = 64 \Rightarrow b^3 = 64 \Rightarrow b^3 = 4^3 \Rightarrow b = 4$

$a:b = 3/4$

44) **The correct answer is (D)**

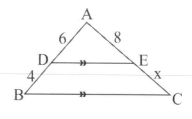

$\dfrac{AD}{AB} = \dfrac{AE}{AC} \Rightarrow \dfrac{6}{6+4} = \dfrac{8}{8+x}$

$\dfrac{6}{10} = \dfrac{8}{8+x} \Rightarrow \dfrac{3}{5} = \dfrac{8}{8+x} \Rightarrow 40 = 24 + 3x$

$\Rightarrow 3x = 16, \ x = \dfrac{16}{3}$

45) **The correct answer is (A)**

For there to be 80 liters in the tank, 320 mile have to be washed.

80 liters gas	320 miles
25 liters gas	x miles

$80 \cdot x = 25 \cdot 320$

$x = \dfrac{25 \cdot 320}{80}, \ x = 100$ miles

46) **The correct answer is (D)**

$\dfrac{17}{3} - 3x = \dfrac{11}{3} + 3y \Rightarrow \dfrac{17}{3} - \dfrac{11}{3} - 3x + 3y \Rightarrow 3(x+y) - \dfrac{6}{3} \Rightarrow x+y = \dfrac{2}{3}$

47) **The correct answer is (A)**

The circle with the radius r and center (h, k) has an equation

$(x-h)^2 + (y-k)^2 = r^2$

$(x-5)^2 + (y-4)^2 = 6^2$

48) **The correct answer is (E)**

$\ln(5e^3) - 3 = \ln 5 + \ln e^3 = \ln 5 + 3\ln e = \ln 5 + 3 - 3 = \ln 5 \quad *\ln e = 1$

49) **The correct answer is (C)**

$3^4 \cdot 4^4 \cdot 5^4 = (ab)^c, \ (3^4 \cdot 4^4 \cdot 5^4) = (3 \cdot 4 \cdot 5)^4 = 60^4$

$a^x \cdot b^x \cdot c^x = (a \cdot b \cdot c)^x$

$(ab)^c = (60)^4 \Rightarrow ab + c = 60 + 4 = 64$

50) **The correct answer is (A)**

A: {2, 3, 4, 5, 6, 7, 8, 9, 10, 11, 12, 13, 14, 15}

Prime numbers: 2, 3, 5, 7, 11, 13

51) **The correct answer is (A)**

v_1=16m/s, v_2=12m/s

x_1=v_1·t, x_2=v_2·t

x_1=16t, x_2=12t

x_1+x_2=280, 16t+12t=280, 28t=280,

t=10, t=10 seconds later they will meet again.

52) **The correct answer is (E)**

14, 16, 18, …, 84

Even number= $\dfrac{\text{last term}-\text{first term}}{\text{increased amount}}+1$ = (84-14)2 +1=36

53) **The correct answer is (E)**

(18a-14b)-(14b-18a)=18a-14b-14b+18a=36a-18b

54) **The correct answer is (D)**

(6!+8!):6!= $\dfrac{6!+8!}{6!} = \dfrac{6!+8\cdot7\cdot6!}{6!} = \dfrac{6!(1+8\cdot7)}{6!} = 57$

55) **The correct answer is (A)**

Let's call this number x, 8x+8=88, 8x=88-8, 8x=80, x=10

The number = 10, Total of its digits is=1+0=1

56) **The correct answer is (C)**

That the number is x, x·14%- x·4%=30, $\dfrac{14x}{100} - \dfrac{4x}{100} = 30$, $\dfrac{10x}{100} = 30$, x=300

57) **The correct answer is (B)**

Because there is no condition, the number of people is 3 teachers and 5 students. Sum=(3+5)=8. There are (8-1)!=7! arrangements.

58) **The correct answer is (C)**

$a^x\cdot a^y\cdot a^z=a^{x+y+z}$, $11^{0.32}\cdot11^{0.26}\cdot11^{0.42}=11^{0.32+0.26+0.42}=11^1=11$

59) **The correct answer is (C)**

|4x-8|=8 ⇒   4x-8=8   4x-8=-8

4x=16   4x=-8+8

x=4   4x=0

x=0   {4, 0}

60) **The correct answer is (D)**

Geometric average= $\sqrt{a\cdot b}$.

Geometric average of 7 and 4 numbers= $\sqrt{7\cdot4} = 2\sqrt{7}$

TEST – 1.5
- Solutions -

1) **The correct answer is (A)**

6x-6=6-6x, 6x+6x=6+6 $\Rightarrow$ 12x=12, x=1

2) **The correct answer is (D)**

3x+3y=9, 3(x+y)=9, x+y=3, 2x+2y=2(x+y)=2·3=6

3) **The correct answer is (D)**

$$\frac{\pi}{\sqrt{25}} < \frac{\pi}{\sqrt{17}} < \frac{\pi}{\sqrt{13}} < \frac{\pi}{\sqrt{10}}$$

4) **The correct answer is (D)**

$$70\sqrt{7} \cdot 70\% = 70\sqrt{7} \cdot \frac{70}{100} = \frac{4900\sqrt{7}}{100} = 49\sqrt{7}$$

5) **The correct answer is (B)**

	Father	Daughter
	34	10
x years later	34+x	10+x

$$\frac{x+34}{x+10} = \frac{5}{2} \Rightarrow 2(x+32)=5(x+10), \ 2x+68=5x+50, \ 3x=18, \ x=6$$

6) **The correct answer is (B)**

First number: n
Second number: n+2
n+n+2=34, 2n+2=34, 2n=32, n=16, First=n=16, Second=n+2=18

Second number : first number = 18:16= $\dfrac{9}{8}$

7) **The correct answer is (C)**

P=3^x-1, Q=3^x+1, P·Q=(3^x-1)(3^x+1)=3^{2x}-1

8) **The correct answer is (D)**

$\angle$A+$\angle$B+$\angle$C=180°,
60°+$\angle$B+70°=180°, $\angle$B=50°,
AB∥KF $\Rightarrow$ $\angle$EKF=$\angle$B=50°,
50°=x+20°, x=30°

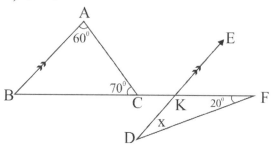

9) **The correct answer is (C)**

If x=4, $x^2 - \sqrt{x} + \dfrac{\sqrt{x}}{2} - 4 = 4^2 - \sqrt{4} + \dfrac{\sqrt{4}}{2} - 4 =$

$= 16 - 2 + \dfrac{4}{2} - 4 = 16 + 2 - 2 - 4 = 12$

10) **The correct answer is (B)**

$a_1 = \sqrt{7}$, $a_2 = \sqrt{28} = 2\sqrt{7}$, $a_3 = 3\sqrt{7}$

Arithmetic mean$= \dfrac{a_1 + a_2 + a_3}{3} = \dfrac{\sqrt{7} + 2\sqrt{7} + 3\sqrt{7}}{3} = \dfrac{6\sqrt{7}}{3} = 2\sqrt{7}$

11) **The correct answer is (B)**

$3^x + x^3 \cdot 3^x = 3^x(1 + x^3)$

12) **The correct answer is (C)**

10kg of fresh apricots $\rightarrow$ 8kg of dried apricots
x kg of fresh apricots $\rightarrow$ 24kg of dried apricots

$\dfrac{10}{x} = \dfrac{8}{24} \Rightarrow \dfrac{10}{x} = \dfrac{1}{3} \Rightarrow x = 30\text{kg}$

13) **The correct answer is (C)**

Let us take squares of each side of the inequality: $(-3)^2 < x^2 \le (7)^2 \Rightarrow 9 < x^2 \le 49$

14) **The correct answer is (B)**

$a\Upsilon b \rightarrow xy$, $x = a + b$, $y = a - b$
$6\Upsilon 2 \rightarrow x = (6+2) = 8$, $y = (6-2) = 4$
$6\Upsilon 2 \rightarrow 84$

15) **The correct answer is (D)**

$\angle A = \angle B = 45^0$, if AC=BC=4

$\dfrac{x}{4} + \dfrac{y}{4} = 1$, $x + y = 4$

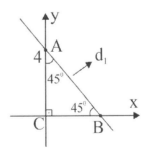

16) **The correct answer is (B)**
$ab + a^2b^2 + a^3b^3 = ab(1 + ab + a^2b^2)$

17) **The correct answer is (E)**

Let us call the number x, $\quad x \cdot \dfrac{4}{11} = 60$, $\Rightarrow$ 4x=60·11, x=15·11, x=165

18) **The correct answer is (A)**

$$x \cdot 10\% = 10^9, \Rightarrow x \cdot \frac{1}{10} = 10^9, \Rightarrow x = 10^9 \cdot 10^1, \; x = 10^{10}$$

19) **The correct answer is (B)**

$$\frac{1}{m} + \frac{1}{n} = \frac{1}{t} \Rightarrow \frac{1}{10} + \frac{1}{12} = \frac{1}{t}, \quad t = \frac{12 \cdot 10}{12 + 10} = \frac{120}{22} = \frac{60}{11}$$

20) **The correct answer is (D)**

$$\frac{3^n + 3^n + 3^n}{2^n + 2^n + 2^n} = \frac{3 \cdot 3^n}{3 \cdot 2^n} = \frac{3^n}{2^n} = \left(\frac{3}{2}\right)^n \qquad * \frac{a^x}{b^x} = \left(\frac{a}{b}\right)^x$$

21) **The correct answer is (B)**
a+b=100 must be
64+x=100, x=36

22) **The correct answer is (C)**

$$\sqrt{88} + \sqrt{66} = \sqrt{11 \cdot 8} + \sqrt{6 \cdot 11} = \sqrt{11}\left(\sqrt{8} + \sqrt{6}\right) = A \cdot \sqrt{11}, \quad A = \sqrt{8} + \sqrt{6}$$

23) **The correct answer is (D)**

In 1 day: Ahmet completes 1/18 of the work and Mehmet complete 1/24 of the same work

$$\left(\frac{1}{18} + \frac{1}{24}\right) \cdot 6 = \left(\frac{1}{18_{(4)}} + \frac{1}{24_{(3)}}\right) \cdot 6 = \frac{7 \cdot 6}{72} = \frac{7}{12}$$

24) **The correct answer is (E)**

A·x%+ B·y%=(A+B) ·c%
A·x+B·y=(A+B) ·c
300·30+500·50=(300+500) ·c
9000+25000=800c ⇒ c=42.5%

25) **The correct answer is (B)**

$$x^2 + 4x = 12 \Rightarrow x^2 + 4x - 12 = 0$$
$$(x+6)(x-2) = 0$$
$$x+6=0, \; x-2=0$$
$$x=-6, \quad x=2$$

26) **The correct answer is (C)**

$$\frac{(a-b)^2+4ab}{(a+b)^2-4ab} = \frac{a^2-2ab+b^2+4ab}{a^2+2ab+b^2-4ab} =$$

$$= \frac{a^2+2ab+b^2}{a^2-2ab+b^2} = \frac{(a+b)^2}{(a-b)^2} = \left(\frac{a+b}{a-b}\right)^2 = \left(\frac{77+33}{77-33}\right)^2 = \left(\frac{110}{44}\right)^2 = \left(\frac{5}{2}\right)^2 = \frac{25}{4}$$

27) **The correct answer is (A)**

$$\frac{a}{7} + \frac{b}{14} + \frac{c}{28} = 12, \quad \frac{a}{7_{(4)}} + \frac{b}{14_{(2)}} + \frac{c}{28_{(1)}} = 12 \Rightarrow$$

$$\Rightarrow \frac{4a+2b+c}{28} = 12 \Rightarrow 4a+2b+c=336$$

28) **The correct answer is (E)**

$i^2+i^4+i^6+i^8=(i)^2+(i^2)^4+(i^2)^3+(i^2)^4=-1+(-1)^4+(-1)^3+(-1)^4=-1+1-1+1=0$

29) **The correct answer is (B)**

$3x+2y=5$ x-intercept $\Rightarrow$ y=0

$3x+2\cdot0=5$

$3x=5, x=\dfrac{5}{3}$

30) **The correct answer is (C)**

$$\frac{3!+4!}{4!-3!} = \frac{3!+4\cdot3!}{4\cdot3!-3!} = \frac{3!(1+4)}{3!(4-1)} = \frac{5}{3}$$

31) **The correct answer is (D)**

$(x+4)^2+(y+5)^2=13$

$x^2+8x+16+y^2+10y+25=13$

$x^2+8x+10y+y^2+41-13=0$

$x^2+8x+10y+y^2+28=0$

$x^2+y^2+Dx+Ey+F=0$

$x^2+y^2+8x+10y+28=0$

$r=\dfrac{\sqrt{D^2+E^2-4F}}{2},$

$r=\dfrac{\sqrt{8^2+10^2-4\cdot28}}{2} = \dfrac{\sqrt{52}}{2} = \dfrac{2\sqrt{13}}{2} = \sqrt{13},$

$r=\sqrt{13}$

32) **The correct answer is (C)**

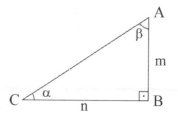

$AC^2=|AB|^2+|BC|^2$

$AC^2=m^2+n^2$

$AC=\sqrt{m^2+n^2}$

$\sin\alpha=\dfrac{m}{\sqrt{m^2+n^2}}$, $\cos\beta=\dfrac{m}{\sqrt{m^2+n^2}}$

$\sin\alpha+\cos\beta=\dfrac{m}{\sqrt{m^2+n^2}}+\dfrac{m}{\sqrt{m^2+n^2}}=\dfrac{2m}{\sqrt{m^2+n^2}}$

33) **The correct answer is (B)**

$\dfrac{(6x^2y)\cdot(-3x^3y^3)^2}{54x^2y^2}=\dfrac{6x^2y\cdot(9x^6y^6)}{54x^2y^2}=\dfrac{54x^8y^7}{54x^2y^2}=x^{8-2}y^{7-2}=x^6y^5$

34) **The correct answer is (E)**

$\dfrac{a+b}{a-b}=\dfrac{11}{7}$ then $7\cdot(a+b)=11\cdot(a-b)$ $\Rightarrow$ $7a+7b=11a-11b$ $\Rightarrow$

$\Rightarrow$ $7b+11b=11a-7a$ $\Rightarrow$ $18b=4a$, $9b=2a$ $\Rightarrow$ $b=2$, $a=9$, $a\cdot b=9\cdot2=18$

35) **The correct answer is (A)**

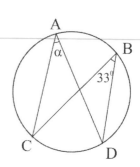

$\alpha=DC=33^o$, $\alpha=33^o$

36) **The correct answer is (B)**

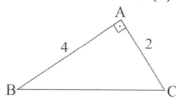

$BC^2=|AB|^2+|AC|^2=4^2+2^2$, $BC^2=20$, $BC=2\sqrt{5}$

Area(ABC)$=\dfrac{4\cdot2}{2}=4$, Perimeter (ABC) $=4+2+2\sqrt{5}=6+2\sqrt{5}$

$\dfrac{A(ABC)}{P(ABC)}=\dfrac{4}{6+2\sqrt{5}}$

37) **The correct answer is (C)**

$V_{cylinder}=\pi\cdot r^2\cdot h=\pi\cdot4^2\cdot6=\pi\cdot16\cdot6=96\pi$ cm^3

38) The correct answer is (C)

$$\frac{11x}{2}+\frac{7x}{3}=\frac{11x}{2_{(3)}}+\frac{7x}{3_{(2)}}=\frac{33x}{6}+\frac{14x}{6}=\frac{47x}{6}, \text{ Maximum value = 47}$$

39) The correct answer is (B)

$6x+4y=24$, $4y=-6x+24$ slope=$m_1=-\dfrac{6}{4}$

$3x+ay=18$, $ay=-3x+18$ slope=$m_2=-\dfrac{3}{a}$

$d_1\|d_2$, if $m_1=m_2$, $-\dfrac{6}{4}=-\dfrac{3}{a} \Rightarrow$ -12=-6a,   a=2

40) The correct answer is (D)

$3x+2y=12$
$x=0$, $2y=12$, $y=6$
$y=0$, $3x=12$, $x=4$

$$A(ABC)=\frac{AB\cdot BC}{2}=\frac{y\cdot x}{2}=\frac{6\cdot 4}{2}=12cm^2$$

41) The correct answer is (B)

42) The correct answer is (C)

43) The correct answer is (C)

$$AB=\frac{AC}{2}=\frac{6}{2}=3, \;\; BC=\frac{AC\cdot\sqrt{3}}{2}=\frac{6\sqrt{3}}{2}=3\sqrt{3}$$

Perimeter (ABC)=$6+3+3\sqrt{3}$ =$9+3\sqrt{3}$

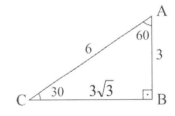

44) The correct answer is (A)

AB=DC, AD=BC

A(ABCD)=|AB|·DH=10·6=60cm²

$$A(ADB)=\frac{AB\cdot DH}{2}=\frac{10\cdot 6}{2}=30cm^2,$$

$$\frac{A(ABCD)}{A(ADB)}=\frac{60}{30}=2$$

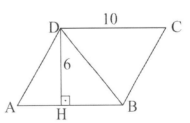

45) The correct answer is (E)

AB=BC=$2r=4\sqrt{2}$, $r=2\sqrt{2}$, A(KMDE)=KM·MD=$2r\cdot MD=2\cdot 2\cdot 2\sqrt{2}=8\sqrt{2}$

46) **The correct answer is (C)**

$$A(DEBF) = \frac{A(ABCD)}{2} = \frac{12\sqrt{2}}{2} = 6\sqrt{2} \text{ cm}^2$$

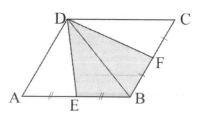

47) **The correct answer is (E)**

A(ABCD)=A(EFKM)

$$\frac{|BC| \cdot |AD|}{2} = EF \cdot FK, \quad \frac{20 \cdot 4}{2} = 10 \cdot FK, \quad 40 = 10 \cdot FK, \quad FK = 4$$

48) **The correct answer is (B)**

a=2+x, x=a-2, $x^2+2=(a-2)^2-4=a^2-4a+4-4= a^2-4a$

49) **The correct answer is (D)**

$\log_2 x=6$, $x=2^6$, x=64   X/2+X/4=64/2+64/4=48

50) **The correct answer is (A)**

7, 11, 13, 17, 19, …. primer number
7,11,13,17,19,23,29,31,…
x=23, y=29, y-x=29-23=6

51) **The correct answer is (B)**

$AC^2-|AB|^2+|BC|^2-3^2+2^2=13$, $AC=\sqrt{13}$

$$\sin 2x = 2\sin x \cdot \cos x = 2\frac{3}{\sqrt{13}} \cdot \frac{2}{\sqrt{13}} = \frac{12}{13}$$

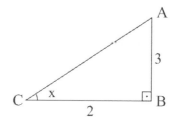

52) **The correct answer is (C)**

$AK=KA'$, A(3, 4), x=3, y=4
$AK=KA'$, $3=KA'$, $KA'=3$, x=6+3=9, $A'=(9, 4)$

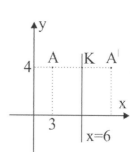

53) **The correct answer is (D)**

|x-y|=|y-x|
|x-7|+|7-x|=10 $\Rightarrow$ |x-7|+|x-7|=10,
2|x-7|=10, |x-7|=5 $\Rightarrow$ x-7=5, x-7=-5
                                    x=12   x=2
x_1+x_2=12+2=14

54) **The correct answer is (A)**

Arithmetic sequence: $a_2+a_6=a_5+a_3$, $20=a_5+a_3$

55) **The correct answer is (D)**

Subset number : 64, $64=2^n$, $2^6=2^n$, $n=6$

56) **The correct answer is (C)**

$A=\{1,2,3,4,5,6,7,8,9,10,11\}$
$B=\{2,3,5,7\}$
$A\cap B=\{2,3,5,7\}$

57) **The correct answer is (B)**

$3^n\cdot 7^n=k$, $3^{2n}\cdot 7^{2n}=(3^n)^2\cdot(7^n)^2=(3^n\cdot 7^n)^2=k^2$

58) **The correct answer is (A)**

$$\boxed{\begin{array}{c} a \\ \hline b \end{array}}$$
$a\cdot b=24$, $x\cdot 24=24$, $x=1$

59) **The correct answer is (E)**

6^3

$6^3=6\cdot 6\cdot 6=216$

60) **The correct answer is (B)**

$\sqrt{m}+\sqrt{n}=a$ if
$\sqrt{m}=a-\sqrt{n}$
$\left(\sqrt{m}\right)^2=\left(a-\sqrt{n}\right)^2$
$m=a^2-2a\sqrt{n}+n$

TEST – 1.6
- Solutions -

1) **The correct answer is (A)**
   $3x+3=6x-6$, $3+6=6x-3x$, $9=3x$, $x=3$

2) **The correct answer is (B)**
   $\square\Delta\rightarrow12$ $\square\square\rightarrow16$ $\Delta\Delta\rightarrow$
   $4\cdot3=12$ $4\cdot4=16$ $3\cdot3\rightarrow9$

3) **The correct answer is (E)**
   $x=2a+b$ and $y=2b+a$
   $x-y=(2a+b)-(2b+a)=2a+b-2b-a=2a-a+b-2b=a-b$

4) **The correct answer is (A)**

	Ahmet	Mehmet
Now	14	12
After 6 years	14+6=20	10+4=14

   Sum ages: $20+18=38$

5) **The correct answer is (B)**
   Perimeter(ABCD)$=2(a+b)=2(6+4)=20$
   Perimeter(EFKL)$=4a=4\cdot4=16$
   $$\frac{\text{Perimeter(ABCD)}}{\text{Perimeter(EFKL)}}=\frac{20}{16}=\frac{5}{4}=125\%$$

6) **The correct answer is (C)**
   $a^2=289 \Rightarrow a=17$, $b^2=169 \Rightarrow b=13$
   $$\frac{a+b}{a-b}=\frac{17+13}{17-13}=\frac{30}{4}=\frac{15}{2}$$

7) **The correct answer is (A)**
   $2x+3x=180^o$
   $x=36^o$
   $\alpha=2x=2\cdot36^o=72^o$

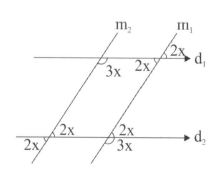

8) **The correct answer is (D)**

$x^3+x^2+x+12=(-2)^3+(-2)^2-2+12=-8+4-2+12=16-10=6$

9) **The correct answer is (B)**

$|2x-2a|=14 \Rightarrow 2|x-a|=14, |x-a|=7$
$|3x-3a|=3|x-a|=3 \cdot 7=21$

10) **The correct answer is (A)**

$ax+bx=m+n$ if $x(a+b)=m+n$, $x=\dfrac{m+n}{a+b}$

11) **The correct answer is (E)**

$(x^4)^{12}=(x^{16m}) \Rightarrow (4 \cdot 12)=16 \cdot m \Rightarrow 48=16m, m=3$

12) **The correct answer is (B)**

$2 \le x \le 12$, $x=2,3,5,7,11$
All sum x number $= 2+3+5+7+11=28$

13) **The correct answer is (D)**

A=6y	A+B+C+D=360	A=6y=6·24=144
B=4y	6y+4y+3y+2y=360	B=4y=4·24=96
C=3y	15y=360	C=3y=3·24=72
D=2y	y=24°	D=2y=2·24=48

14) **The correct answer is (D)**

$(x+\sqrt{3})(x-\sqrt{2})=0$
$x+\sqrt{3}=0, x-\sqrt{2}=0$
$x=-\sqrt{3}, x=\sqrt{2}$

15) **The correct answer is (B)**

Average for five days $= \dfrac{244+240+260+280+300}{5}=264.8$

16) **The correct answer is (A)**

$3(3x+3)-2(2x+2)=3 \cdot 3x+3 \cdot 3-2 \cdot 2x-2 \cdot 2=9x-4x+9-4=5x+5$

17) **The correct answer is (E)**

$x \cdot 4\%=2^{10}$, $x \cdot \dfrac{40}{100}=2^{10} \Rightarrow \dfrac{x \cdot 4}{10}=2^{10} \Rightarrow \dfrac{2x}{5}=2^{10}$, $2x=5 \cdot 2^1 \cdot 2^9$, $x=5 \cdot 2^9$

18) **The correct answer is (B)**

Math book=m, Chemistry book=c

$$2m+c=12$$
$$m+2c=15$$
$$+\overline{}$$
$$3m+3c=27, \Rightarrow 3(m+c)=27, \ m+c=9$$

19) **The correct answer is (E)**

Ahmet paint alone = 8 hours=a
Mehmet paint alone =12 hours =b

$$t = \frac{a \cdot b}{a+b} = \frac{8 \cdot 12}{8+12} = \frac{8 \cdot 12}{20} = 4.8 \text{ hours}$$

20) **The correct answer is (B)**

	x	y	z
m	2	3	6
m^2	4	9	36
m^3	8	27	216

a=3, b=27, c=6, d=36,
a+b+c+d=3+27+6+36=72

21) **The correct answer is (C)**

$$\frac{\pi}{3} + \frac{3}{\pi} = \frac{\pi}{3_{(\pi)}} + \frac{3}{\pi_{(3)}} = \frac{\pi \cdot \pi + 3 \cdot 3}{3 \cdot \pi} = \frac{\pi^2 + 9}{3\pi}$$

22) **The correct answer is (E)**
$A=9+a^2$, $B=18+2a^2$
$B=18+2a^2=2(9+a^2)=B=2A$

23) **The correct answer is (A)**

$$\text{Slope} = \frac{y_2 - y_1}{x_2 - x_1} = \frac{9-3}{3-7} = \frac{6}{-4} = -\frac{3}{2}$$

24) **The correct answer is (B)**

A·B=77	A·C=55	A=11, B=7, C=5
A·B=11·7	11·5=55	B+C=7+5=12

25) **The correct answer is (C)**
$(2^a+3^a)=m$, $(2^a+3^a)^2=m^2$
$$2^{2a}+2 \cdot 2^a \cdot 3^a + 3^{a2}=m^2$$
$$4^a+9^a+2 \cdot 6^a=m^2$$
$$4^a+9^a=m^2-2 \cdot 6^a$$

26) The correct answer is (C)

$$x^{(\sqrt{2})^{\sqrt{3}}} = x^{\sqrt{2}\cdot\sqrt{3}} = x^m \Rightarrow x^{\sqrt{6}} = x^m, \ m = \sqrt{6}$$

$$y^{(\sqrt{3}-1)^{(\sqrt{3}+1)}} = y^n \Rightarrow n = (\sqrt{3}-1)(\sqrt{3}+1) = (3-1) = 2 \ n=2 \Rightarrow m+n = \sqrt{6}+2$$

27) The correct answer is (C)

$\log_3 5 = a$ if $\log_3 125 + \log_3 5 = 3\log_3 5 + 2 \ \log_3 5 = 3a + 2a = 5a$

28) The correct answer is (D)

A(8, 7)   C(6, 4)   B(x, y)

C is the midpoint. $C(6, \ 4) = \left(\dfrac{8+x}{2}, \dfrac{7+y}{2}\right)$

$\dfrac{8+x}{2} = 6 \Rightarrow x = 4, \ \dfrac{y+7}{2} = 4 \Rightarrow y = 1, \ B(x, \ y) = (4, \ 1)$

29) The correct answer is (C)

Standard form of a Circle: $(x-h)^2 + (y-k)^2 = r^2$,

$(x-5)^2 + (y-2)^2 = 15, \ r^2 = 15, \ r = \sqrt{15}$

30) The correct answer is (C)

$AC^2 = 3^2 + 2^2, \ AC = \sqrt{13}, \ \sin\alpha = \dfrac{3}{\sqrt{13}}, \ \cos\alpha = \dfrac{2}{\sqrt{13}}$

$\dfrac{1}{\sin\alpha} + \dfrac{1}{\cos\alpha} = \dfrac{1}{\left(\dfrac{3}{\sqrt{13}}\right)} = \dfrac{1}{\left(\dfrac{2}{\sqrt{13}}\right)} =$

$= \dfrac{\sqrt{13}}{3} + \dfrac{\sqrt{13}}{2} = \dfrac{5\sqrt{13}}{6}$

31) The correct answer is (B)

$$\dfrac{(3a^3b^3)^2 \ 4a^4b^4}{(2a^2b^2)^2} = \dfrac{9\cdot a^6 \cdot b^6 \cdot 4 \cdot a^4 b^4}{4\cdot a^4 \cdot b^4} = 9a^6 b^6$$

32) The correct answer is (E)

AB=AC=BC=6cm,

$A(ABC) = \dfrac{a^2\sqrt{3}}{4} = \dfrac{6^2\sqrt{3}}{4} = \dfrac{36\sqrt{3}}{4} = 9\sqrt{3} \ cm$

$P(ABC) = 3a = 3\cdot 6 = 18, \ \dfrac{A(ABC)}{P(ABC)} = \dfrac{9\sqrt{3}}{18} = \dfrac{\sqrt{3}}{2}$

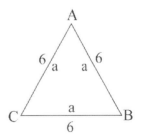

33) **The correct answer is (C)**

$d_1 = \dfrac{x}{-4} + \dfrac{y}{-4} = 1, \quad x + y = -4$

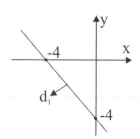

34) **The correct answer is (E)**

P(AHFK)=14
P(HBEF)=14
P(FECD)=14
P(HBCD)=20
P(ABEK)=22
Sum of all rectangles' perimeters=84

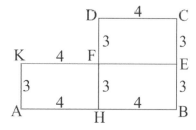

35) **The correct answer is (C)**

$A = \begin{bmatrix} 1+5 & 2+6 \\ 3+7 & 4+8 \end{bmatrix} = \begin{bmatrix} 6 & 8 \\ 10 & 2x \end{bmatrix}, \quad 2x=12, \; x=6$

36) **The correct answer is (A)**

$x^2+y^2=a^2+b$, then $x^2=a^2- y^2+b$, $x = \sqrt{a^2 - y^2 + b}$

37) **The correct answer is (D)**

m_1: 3x+2y=6 $\Rightarrow$ 2y=-3x+6, slope=$-\dfrac{3}{2}$

m_2: 4x+ay=10 $\Rightarrow$ ay=-4x+10, slope=$-\dfrac{4}{a}$

If line m_1 perpendicular to line m_2, $m_1 \cdot m_2$=-1

$\left(-\dfrac{3}{2}\right) \cdot \left(-\dfrac{4}{a}\right) = -1, \quad 3a=-8, \; a=-\dfrac{8}{3}$

38) **The correct answer is (C)**

y=x   slope is 1
y=-2x   slope is -2

39) **The correct answer is (D)**

$AC^2 = AB^2 + BC^2 = 2^2 + 1^2 = 5$, $AC = \sqrt{5}$

$\tan\alpha = \dfrac{2}{1} = 2$, $\cot\alpha = \dfrac{1}{2} = 1/2$, $\sin\alpha = \dfrac{2}{\sqrt{5}}$

$\dfrac{\tan\alpha + \cot\alpha}{\sin\alpha} = \dfrac{2 + \dfrac{1}{2}}{\dfrac{2}{\sqrt{5}}} = \dfrac{\dfrac{5}{2}}{\dfrac{2}{\sqrt{5}}} = \dfrac{5\sqrt{5}}{4}$

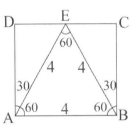

40) **The correct answer is (B)**

3 pages $\rightarrow$ 33 minutes
x pages $\rightarrow$ 77 minutes

$x \cdot 33 = 3 \cdot 77$, $x = \dfrac{3 \cdot 77}{33} = 7$, x=7 pages

41) **The correct answer is (B)**

One gallon = 3.8 liter
2400 gallon = x
$x \cdot 1 = 2400 \cdot 3.8 = 9120$ liters

42) **The correct answer is (A)**

AB=BE=AE=4cm. $\angle EAB = \angle ABE = \angle AEB = 60^{o}$
P(ABCD)=4a=4·4=16

$P(ABE) = \dfrac{a^2\sqrt{3}}{4} = \dfrac{4^2\sqrt{3}}{4} = 4\sqrt{3}$

$\dfrac{P(ABE)}{P(ABCD)} = \dfrac{4\sqrt{3}}{16} = \dfrac{\sqrt{3}}{4}$

43) **The correct answer is (D)**

Let the slope of 3x+4y=12 be m_1,

3x+4y=12, 4y=-3x+12, slope $m_1 = -\dfrac{3}{4}$

The lines are parallel, so $m_1 = m_2$, $\Rightarrow m_2 = -\dfrac{3}{4}$

$A(x_1, y_1) = (2, 4)$
$y - y_1 = m_2(x - x_1)$

$y - 4 = -\dfrac{3}{4}(x - 2)$, $y - 4 = -\dfrac{3x}{4} + \dfrac{3}{2}$, $y = -\dfrac{3x}{4} + \dfrac{11}{2}$

44) The correct answer is (B)

$$4.25 = \frac{425}{100} = \frac{85}{20} = \frac{17}{4} = \frac{a}{b}, \quad a = 17, \ b = 4, \quad (a+b)^2 = (17+4)^2 = 21^2 = 441$$

45) The correct answer is (D)

$$\frac{a}{5} + \frac{b}{7} = 15 \quad \Rightarrow \quad \frac{7a + 5b}{35} = 15, \quad 7a + 5b = 35 \cdot 15 = 525$$

46) The correct answer is (B)

a=874, b=888

875·889−874·888

(a+1)·(b+1)−a·b=ab+a+b+1−ab=a+b+1= =874+888+1=1763

47) The correct answer is (E)

x=a−b, x=6−1=5

72	84	93	61	ab
5	4	6	x	x

48) The correct answer is (B)

5 yellow, 4 red, 6 green, 5 blue marbles.

$$\text{Marble to be green} = \frac{6}{5+4+6+5} = \frac{6}{20} = \frac{3}{10}$$

49) The correct answer is (A)

35's positive divisors: 1, 5, 7, 35. Sum=1+5+7+35=48

50) The correct answer is (C)

The set of football playing students: A
The set of basketball playing students: B
x+8+18=50, x+26=50, x=24

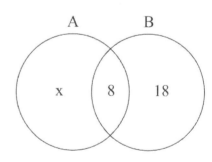

51) The correct answer is (E)

The area of the sector =

$$= \pi r^2 \frac{\alpha}{360} = \pi 4^2 \frac{45}{360} = \frac{16\pi}{8} = 2\pi$$

Area(AOB)=2π

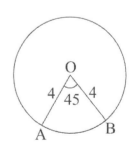

52) **The correct answer is (B)**

The problem wants us to find the LCM of the numbers 30 and 45.
LCM(30, 45)=90
The bus and taxi will meet again after 90 minutes, which is 1.5 hours later.
The time: 10+1.5=11.5 $\Rightarrow$ 11:30 a.m.

53) **The correct answer is (A)**

$\tan x = \dfrac{3}{1}$, then $(AC)^2 = (AB)^2 + (BC)^2 = 3^2 + 1^2$

$AC = \sqrt{10}$

$\sin x + \cos x = \dfrac{3}{\sqrt{10}} + \dfrac{1}{\sqrt{10}} = \dfrac{4}{\sqrt{10}}$

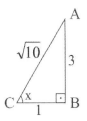

54) **The correct answer is (D)**

$2x-4y+3z=3$
$6x-4y+3z=7$
Multiply the first equation by (-1), then

$\quad -2x+4y-3z=-3$
$\quad 6x-4y+3z=7$
$+$ _____
$\quad 4x=4,$
$\quad\quad x=1$

55) **The correct answer is (E)**

$6a+3=7b+3=x$
$6a-7b=x-3$
LCM(6, 7)=42   x-3=42, x=45

56) **The correct answer is (C)**

If 400 grams $\rightarrow$ \$1.60
   100 grams $\rightarrow$ \$0.40
Therefore: 900 grams $=900 \cdot 0.4 = \$3.60$

57) **The correct answer is (C)**

Ahmet   Mehmet   Mehmet has \$100
  600   x
600-200=4x, 400=4x, x=100.

58) **The correct answer is (D)**

$$\binom{9}{2} = \frac{9!}{2!(9-2)!} = \frac{9!}{2! \cdot 7!} = \frac{9 \cdot 8 \cdot 7!}{2! \cdot 7!} = 36$$

59) **The correct answer is (A)**

P(ABC)=6+4+7=17
P(ABD)=6+4+5=15
P(ADC)=4+4+2=10   Sum=42

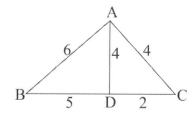

60) **The correct answer is (D)**

Perimeter (ABCD)=4·a=4·8=32

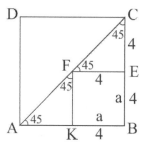

TEST – 1.7
- Solutions -

1) **The correct answer is (A)**

123	324	442	552	abc
6	9	10	?	x

x=a+b+c=5+5+2=12

2) **The correct answer is (B)**
$(888-886)^2+(777-775)^2=(2)^2+(2)^2=8$

3) **The correct answer is (D)**
4(4x+4)=3(3x+3)
16x+16=9x+9, 16x-9x=9-16, 7x=-7, x=-1

4) **The correct answer is (D)**
$$\frac{3^{x-1}}{3^{x+2}}=\frac{3^x\cdot 3^1}{3^x\cdot 3^2}=\frac{3}{9}=\frac{1}{3}=33\%$$

5) **The correct answer is (E)**
The number at the given digit is 6, and the number right of it is 7, so we add 1 to 6 (because 8>5). Rounded form of 0.68 into this tenths digit is 0.7.

6) **The correct answer is (C)**
4-4(x+4)=5-5(x+5)
4-4x-16=5-5x-25, -4x-12=-5x-20, 5x-4x=-20+12, x=-8

7) **The correct answer is (E)**
$$A=\frac{1}{2}, \ B=\frac{14}{28}=\frac{1}{2}, \ C=\frac{\sqrt{50}}{\sqrt{200}}=\frac{5\sqrt{2}}{10\sqrt{2}}=\frac{1}{2}$$
$$D=\frac{\pi}{2\pi}=\frac{1}{2}, \ E=\frac{\sqrt{3}}{\sqrt{6}}=\frac{\sqrt{3}}{\sqrt{3}\sqrt{2}}=\frac{1}{\sqrt{2}}, \ A=B=C=D=\frac{1}{2}, \ E=\frac{1}{\sqrt{2}}$$

8) **The correct answer is (D)**

|DE|·|EB|=|AE|·|EC|, 8·3=|AE|·6, AE=4

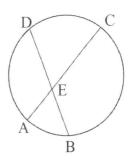

9) **The correct answer is (D)**

$x^3y^3+x^2y^2-xy=(2)^3\cdot(-2)^3+(2)^2\cdot(-2)^2-2\cdot(-2)=$

$=(8)\cdot(-8)+4\cdot4+4=-64+16+4=-64+20=-44$

10) **The correct answer is (A)**

    1) ABCD   6) FBKM
    2) FBCE   7) KMEC
    3) AFED   8) AFKC
    4) LKED   9) ABML
    5) LMCD

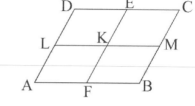

11) **The correct answer is (D)**

$$\sqrt[3]{ab}\sqrt[3]{a^2b^2}\sqrt[3]{a^3b^3}=\sqrt[3]{ab\cdot a^2b^2\cdot a^3b^3}=$$

$$=\sqrt[3]{a^{1+2+3}\cdot b^{1+2+3}}=\sqrt[3]{a^6b^6}=(ab)^{\frac{6}{3}}=(ab)^2$$

12) **The correct answer is (D)**

$A=\sqrt{289}=17$ $C=\sqrt{400}=20$ $E=100$

$B=\sqrt{900}=30$ $D=\sqrt{200}=10\sqrt{2}$

13) **The correct answer is (C)**

$(3^x+3)^2=(3^x)^2+2\cdot3^x\cdot3+3^2$ $^*(a+b)^2=a^2+2ab+b^2$

$=3^{2x}+2\cdot3^{x+1}+9=9^x+2\cdot3^{x+1}+9$

14) **The correct answer is (B)**

3!+4!=6A   3!+4!=6·A

3!=1·2·3=6   6+24=6A

4!=1·2·3·4=24   6A=30,   A=5

15) **The correct answer is (A)**

$$EF=\frac{AB+DC}{2}=\frac{12+8}{2}=10$$

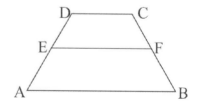

16) **The correct answer is (E)**

$|\pi-4|+|4-\pi|=-(\pi-4)+(4-\pi)=-\pi+4+4-\pi=8-2\pi$,
$\pi-4<0$, $4-\pi>0$

17) **The correct answer is (B)**

ADE,AFE,ABE,FEB,BCE

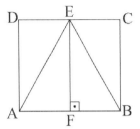

18) **The correct answer is (E)**

$2x+3y=24$
$x=0$, $3y=24$, $y=8$
$y=0$, $2x=24$, $x=12$
$$A(ABC)=\frac{AB\cdot BC}{2}=\frac{y\cdot x}{2}=\frac{8.12}{2}=48$$

19) **The correct answer is (B)**

AB=7, AC=10, x=?
AC-AB<x<AB+AC, 10-7<x<10+7,   3<x<17

20) **The correct answer is (B)**

ED∥BC, E,D,F are midpoint
A(AED)=A(BEF)=A(EFD)=A(FDC)=6
$$A(AED)=\frac{A(ABC)}{4},$$
A(ABC)=4·A(AED)=4·6=24cm^2

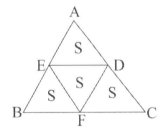

21) **The correct answer is (C)**

△□→3/4, □△→4/5, △△→3/5
3,4   4,5   3,5

22) **The correct answer is (B)**

$$\frac{8}{3}+\frac{7}{5}+\frac{9}{7}-\left(\frac{9}{7}+\frac{7}{5}-\frac{8}{3}\right)$$

$$=\frac{8}{3}+\frac{7}{5}+\frac{9}{7}-\frac{9}{7}-\frac{7}{5}+\frac{8}{3}=\frac{8}{3}+\frac{8}{3}=\frac{16}{3}$$

$$\frac{16}{3}=\frac{15+1}{3}=5\frac{1}{3}=a\frac{b}{c} \Rightarrow a+b+c=5+1+3=9$$

23) **The correct answer is (C)**

$\log_2 256 = \log_2 2^8 = 8\log_2 2 = 8$

24) **The correct answer is (C)**

$|AC|^2 = |AB|^2 + |BC|^2$, $3^2 = 2^2 + |BC|^2$, $9 + 4 + |BC|^2$, $BC = \sqrt{5}$,

$\tan\alpha - \cot\alpha = \dfrac{2}{\sqrt{5}} - \dfrac{\sqrt{5}}{2} = \dfrac{4-5}{2\sqrt{5}} = -\dfrac{1}{2\sqrt{5}}$

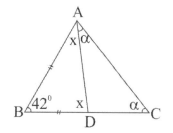

25) **The correct answer is (D)**

$42^\circ + x + x = 180^\circ$
$2x = 138^\circ$
$x = 69^\circ$
$x = \alpha + \alpha$
$69 = 2\alpha$

26) **The correct answer is (B)**

$\angle C = 90^\circ$

$\dfrac{\angle ACD}{\angle COB} = \dfrac{x}{4x} = \dfrac{1}{4}$

$\angle x + \angle 4x = 90^\circ$
$5x = 90^\circ$, $x = 18^\circ$

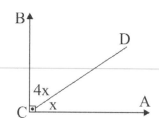

27) **The correct answer is (E)**

A) $\sin 30^\circ = \dfrac{1}{2}$
B) $\dfrac{\pi\sqrt{12}}{2\pi 2\sqrt{3}} = \dfrac{\pi 2\sqrt{3}}{2\pi 2\sqrt{3}} = \dfrac{1}{2}$

C) $\dfrac{0!}{2!} = \dfrac{1}{1\cdot 2} = \dfrac{1}{2}$
D) $\cos 60^\circ = \dfrac{1}{2}$

28) **The correct answer is (A)**

In total there are 5 letters. $5! = 1\cdot 2\cdot 3\cdot 4\cdot 5 = 120$ different words can be made.

29) **The correct answer is (E)**

Does not pass the vertical line test.

30) **The correct answer is (D)**

$\boxed{\dfrac{a}{b}}$

$b=a^3$, $x^3=5^3$, $x=125$

31) **The correct answer is (B)**

$2x+3y=12$ $\rightarrow 2x+2y+y=12$ $x+y=5$
$x+y=5$ $2(x+y)+y=12$ $x+2=5$
                    $2\cdot 5+y=12$ $x=3$
                    $y=2$ $(3, 2)$

32) **The correct answer is (B)**

$x^2y+y^2x=6$, $xy(x+y)=6$, $xy(3)=6$, $xy=2$

33) **The correct answer is (D)**

$a<3$, $\dfrac{|a-3|+|a+3|}{a+3}=\dfrac{-(a-3)+a+3}{a+3}=\dfrac{-a+3+a+3}{a+3}=\dfrac{6}{a+3}$

34) **The correct answer is (B)**

$145=5\cdot 29 \rightarrow \{5, 29\}$

35) **The correct answer is (C)**

$35^o +35^o +\alpha=180^o$,
$70^o +\alpha=180^o$, $\alpha=110^o$

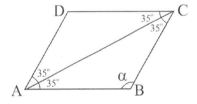

36) **The correct answer is (D)**

$\dfrac{3}{a}+\dfrac{3}{b}+\dfrac{3}{c}=3\left(\dfrac{1}{a}+\dfrac{1}{b}+\dfrac{1}{c}\right)=3\cdot 4=12$

37) **The correct answer is (A)**

$(3xy)^2+4x^4y^3+3xy \rightarrow 9x^2y^2+4x^4y^3+3xy$
Polynomial degree$=4x^4y^3=4+3=7$

38) **The correct answer is (C)**

$\left(\sqrt{3}-1\right)\left(\sqrt{3}+1\right)=3-1=2,$ then $\left(\sqrt{3}\right)^2=3$

39) **The correct answer is (C)**

$x^2+9x+20=0$, $ax^2+bx+c=0$, $x_1+x_2=-\dfrac{b}{a}$, $x_1+x_2=-\dfrac{b}{a}=-\dfrac{9}{1}=-9$

40) The correct answer is (D)

$81^{1/4} = \left(3^4\right)^{\frac{1}{4}} = 3^{4 \cdot \frac{1}{4}} = 3$, $9^{1/2} = \left(3^2\right)^{\frac{1}{2}} = 3^{2 \cdot \frac{1}{2}} = 3$, $3^{1/2} = \sqrt{3}$

Sum $= 3 + 3 + \sqrt{3} = 6 + \sqrt{3}$

41) The correct answer is (E)

$\sin 40^\circ \neq \cos 40^\circ$

42) The correct answer is (B)

$-4^{-4} + 3^{-3} - 3^{-3} = -\dfrac{1}{4^4} + \dfrac{1}{3^3} - \dfrac{1}{3^3} = -\dfrac{1}{64} + \dfrac{1}{27} - \dfrac{1}{27} = -\dfrac{1}{64}$

43) The correct answer is (C)

AK=KB=3cm=r

$|OC|^2 = 3^2 + 3^2 = 3\sqrt{2}$

OE=3cm=r

OC=OE+EC

$3\sqrt{2} = 3 + EC$, $EC = 3\sqrt{2} - 3$

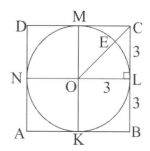

44) The correct answer is (A)

$x^2 + y^2 + Ax + By + c = 0$, The center of circle $= \left(-\dfrac{A}{2}; -\dfrac{B}{2}\right)$

$x^2 + y^2 + 6x - 12y + 64 = 0$, center $= \left(-\dfrac{A}{2}, -\dfrac{B}{2}\right) = \left(-\dfrac{6}{2}, -\dfrac{(-12)}{2}\right) = (-3, 6)$

45) The correct answer is (C)

$A(x_1, y_1)$, $B(x_2, y_2)$ $A(6, 2)$, $B(8, 4)$

$|AB| = \sqrt{(x_2 - x_1)^2 + (y_2 - y_1)^2}$

$AB = \sqrt{(8-6)^2 + (4-2)^2} = \sqrt{2^2 + 2^2} = \sqrt{8} = 2\sqrt{2}$

46) The correct answer is (C)

$A(ABCD) = \dfrac{BD \cdot AC}{2} = \dfrac{10 \cdot 6}{2} = 30cm^2$

47) The correct answer is (E)

$(5)^2 + (3x)^2 = 13^2$,

$25 + 9x^2 = 169$, $9x^2 = 144$, $3x = 12$, $x = 4$

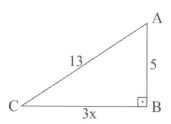

48) **The correct answer is (B)**

$|AB|^2=|BC|\cdot|BD|=4\cdot(4+3)=4\cdot7=28,$ $AB=2\sqrt{7}$

49) **The correct answer is (E)**

$\angle B=\dfrac{AD-EC}{2}=\dfrac{80-20}{2}=30°$

50) **The correct answer is (B)**

If $\dfrac{ax+b}{cx+d}$ yield to $\dfrac{a}{b}=\dfrac{c}{d}$ the fraction $\dfrac{8}{m}=\dfrac{16}{-4}$

$\Rightarrow 16\cdot m=8\cdot(-4)\Rightarrow 16m=-32\Rightarrow m=-2$

51) **The correct answer is 11**

$0.\overline{6}-0.\overline{4}=\dfrac{6}{9}-\dfrac{4}{9}=\dfrac{2}{9}=\dfrac{a}{b}$

$a=2, b=9, (a+b)=(2+9)=11$

52) **The correct answer is (A)**

$|x-3|=5$

$x-3=5$ $x-3=-5$

$x=8$ $x=-2$ $x_1\cdot x_2=8\cdot(-2)=-16$

53) **The correct answer is (A)**

$|A|+|B|+|C|=0$ $|a-3|+|b-4|+|c-6|=0$

$A=0, B=0, C=0$ $a-3=0, b-4=0, c-6=0$

$a=3, b=4, c=6,$ $\dfrac{a+b}{c}=\dfrac{3+4}{6}=\dfrac{7}{6}$

54) **The correct answer is (E)**

$\left(\dfrac{1}{a}+\dfrac{1}{b}\right)=\dfrac{1}{t},$ $a=12, b=18,$ $t=\dfrac{a\cdot b}{a+b}=\dfrac{12\cdot18}{12+18}=\dfrac{12\cdot18_{(3)}}{30_{(5)}}=\dfrac{36}{5}$

55) **The correct answer is (A)**

The question asks: P(12, 2)

P(12, 2)=12·11=132

56) The correct answer is (D)

The numbers that can be created 125, 152, 251, 215, 521, 512 six different numbers can be created. 125+152+251+215+521+512=1776

57) The correct answer is (B)

$3x+3x+3x=360^o$, $9x=360^o$, $x=40^o$

58) The correct answer is (D)

$0<x<1$ let $x=\dfrac{1}{2}$

$a=x=\dfrac{1}{2}$, $b=x^2=\left(\dfrac{1}{2}\right)^2=\dfrac{1}{4}$, $c=2x=2\cdot\dfrac{1}{2}=1$

$a=\dfrac{1}{2}$, $b=\dfrac{1}{4}$, $c=1 \Rightarrow c>a>b$

59) The correct answer is (B)

The number$=\left(\dfrac{1}{3}+\dfrac{3}{7}\right)\dfrac{1}{2}=\left(\dfrac{7\cdot1+3\cdot3}{21}\right)\cdot\dfrac{1}{2}=\left(\dfrac{16}{21}\right)\cdot\dfrac{1}{2}=\dfrac{8}{21}$

60) The correct answer is (A)

$x+y=22$, $x-y=6$
$\qquad x+y=22$
$\qquad x-y=6$
$+$ ‾‾‾‾‾‾‾‾
$\qquad 2x=28$, $x=14$

$x+y=22$
$14+y=22$
$y=8$

$\dfrac{x}{y}=\dfrac{8}{14}=\dfrac{4}{7}$

TEST – 1.8
- Solutions -

1) **The correct answer is (B)**

$$0.2\overline{1} = \frac{21-2}{90} = \frac{19}{90} \qquad * \ 0.a\overline{b} = \frac{ab-a}{90}$$

2) **The correct answer is (D)**

If it is x then x·8%=16, $x \cdot \frac{8}{100} = 16$, 8x=16·100, x=200

3) **The correct answer is (D)**

Geometric mean= $\sqrt{AB} = \sqrt{9x^2 \cdot 4y^2} = \sqrt{36x^2y^2} = 6xy$

4) **The correct answer is (B)**

x^2+8x-33=(x+11)·(x-3)
x^2+8x-33=A·(x-3), A=(x-11)

5) **The correct answer is (B)**

$6x^2y^4+5x^4y^6+3x^2y^2+10$, Polynomials degree =4+6=10

6) **The correct answer is (C)**

$a^m=b^m \Rightarrow \begin{cases} a = b \quad m \text{ is odd} \\ a = b \quad m \text{ is even} \end{cases}$

$(4x-4)^9=(3x+8)^9$, 4x-4=3x+8, $\Rightarrow$ 4x-3x=8+4, x=12

7) **The correct answer is (C)**

equation form: $x^2-(x_1+x_2)x-x_1 \cdot x_2=0$, $x^2-(1+3)x+1 \cdot 3=0$, $x^2-4x+3=0$

8) **The correct answer is (E)**

x=v·t, $t = \frac{x}{v} = \frac{x}{v_1 + v_2}$

9) **The correct answer is (C)**

a_1=4, a_8=25
$a_8=a_1+7$ d $\Rightarrow$ 25=4+7 d $\Rightarrow$ 21=7 d $\Rightarrow$ d=3

10) The correct answer is (E)

$\tan^m(kx+b)$ period is $T = \dfrac{\pi}{|k|}$

$\cot^m(kx+b)$ period is

$f(x)=\tan 5x$ period$=\dfrac{\pi}{5}$

11) The correct answer is (D)

$\log_3 30=\log_3(3\cdot 10)=\log_3 3+\log_3 10=1+\log_3 10$

12) The correct answer is (D)

$3^0+3^1+3^2+4\cdot 3^3=1+3+9+4\cdot 27=121$

13) The correct answer is (A)

$9x^2-4y^2=\left(\sqrt{2}x+3y\right)\cdot\left(\sqrt{2}x-3y\right)$

14) The correct answer is (A)

$\dfrac{(a-b)^2+2ab}{(a+b)^2-2ab}=\dfrac{a^2-2ab+b^2+2ab}{a^2+b^2+2ab-2ab}=\dfrac{a^2+b^2}{a^2+b^2}=1$

15) The correct answer is (D)

Common difference = 6

16) The correct answer is (A)

$6x-(5x+5)=-7x-(6x-6)$,

$6x-5x-5=-7x-6x+6$, $x-5=-13x+6$, $x+13x=6+5$, $14x=11$, $x=\dfrac{11}{14}$

17) The correct answer is (E)

$\angle AOC+\angle COB=180°$
$82°+\angle COB=180°$
$\angle COB=98°$

$\angle CDB=\dfrac{\angle COB}{2}=\dfrac{98}{2}=49°$

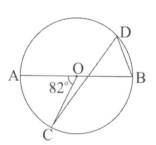

18) The correct answer is (E)
If $\pi\approx 3$ then

A) $2\pi=2\cdot 3=6$ B) $\sqrt{72}=6\sqrt{2}$ C) $(\pi)^2=(3)^2=9$

D) $3\cdot 3-3=6$ E) $2\pi-4=2\cdot 3-4=2$

19) The correct answer is (B)

$$C(6, 3)=\frac{6!}{(6-3)!3!}=\frac{6!}{3!3!}=\frac{6\cdot5\cdot4\cdot3\cdot2\cdot1}{3\cdot2\cdot1\cdot3\cdot2\cdot1}=20$$

20) The correct answer is (A)

$(7-1)!=6!=6\cdot5\cdot4\cdot3\cdot2\cdot1=240$

21) The correct answer is (C)

$P(7, 3)+P(6, 3)=7\cdot6\cdot5+6\cdot5\cdot4=210+120=330$

22) The correct answer is (C)

$$\frac{3x+1}{3_{(4)}}+\frac{4x+1}{4_{(3)}}=\frac{1}{8}, \ \frac{4(3x+1)+3(4x+1)}{3\cdot4}=\frac{1}{8}$$

$$\frac{12x+4+12x+3}{12}=\frac{1}{8} \Rightarrow \frac{24x+7}{12}=\frac{1}{8}, \ 8(24x+7)=12$$

$2(24x+7)=3, \ 48x+14=3, \ 48x=-11, \ x=-\dfrac{11}{48}$

23) The correct answer is (E)

AD∥BE, ∠D=α=∠E=α
∠E=∠B=α, EC=BC=16
DC=12+16=28

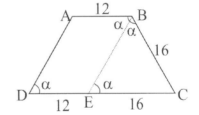

24) The correct answer is (B)

$(2xy^2+xy+4x)^3 \Rightarrow (2xy^2)^3=8x^3y^6$
$8x^3y^6 \rightarrow$ degree is $(3+6)=9$

25) The correct answer is (D)

$ax^2+bx+c=0 \quad x^2+13x+42=0$
$x_1\cdot x_2=\dfrac{c}{a} \quad x_1\cdot x_2=\dfrac{42}{1}=42$

26) The correct answer is (A)

$2\cdot10^4+3\cdot10^3+5\cdot10^2+6\cdot10=2\cdot10000+3\cdot1000+$
$+5\cdot100+6\cdot10=20000+3000+500+60=23560$

27) **The correct answer is (C)**

12	18	2	LCM(12, 18)=$2^2 \cdot 3^2$=36
6	9	2	
3	3	3	
1	3	3	
	1		

28) **The correct answer is (B)**

$$\sqrt{2}, 4\sqrt{2}, \sqrt{8}, \sqrt{50} \rightarrow \sqrt{2}, 4\sqrt{2}, 2\sqrt{2}, 5\sqrt{2}$$

$$\text{Average}= \frac{\sqrt{2}, +4\sqrt{2}+2\sqrt{2}+5\sqrt{2}}{4} = \frac{12\sqrt{2}}{4} = 3\sqrt{2}$$

29) **The correct answer is (C)**

$$\text{ratio}= \frac{45}{25+45} = \frac{45}{70} = \frac{9}{14}$$

30) **The correct answer is (D)**

$$\frac{\dfrac{1}{3^x}+\dfrac{1}{2^x}}{\dfrac{1}{3^x}-\dfrac{1}{2^x}} = \frac{\dfrac{2^x+3^x}{3^x \cdot 2^x}}{\dfrac{2^x-3^x}{3^x \cdot 2^x}} = \frac{2^x+3^x}{3^x \cdot 2^x} \cdot \frac{3^x \cdot 2^x}{2^x-3^x} = \frac{2^x+3^x}{2^x-3^x}$$

31) **The correct answer is (E)**

$$36^{2x+3}=1 \Rightarrow 36^{2x+3}=36^0, 2x+3=0, x=-\frac{3}{2}$$

32) **The correct answer is (C)**

$$\frac{144 \cdot 10^{-8}}{24 \cdot 10^{-4}} = \frac{12 \cdot 12 \cdot 10^{-8}}{12 \cdot 2 \cdot 10^{-4}} = 6 \cdot 10^{-8} \cdot 10^{+4} = 6 \cdot 10^{-4}$$

33) **The correct answer is (A)**

A(8, 2), B(-3, -4)   A(x_1, y_1), B(x_2, y_2)

$$\text{Slope}= \frac{y_2-y_1}{x_2-x_1} = \frac{-4-2}{-3-8} = \frac{-6}{-11} = \frac{6}{11}$$

34) **The correct answer is (B)**

GCF(18, 24, 16)=2

Number of cubes:

$$\frac{Volume \ of \ prism}{Volume \ of \ cube} = \frac{18 \cdot 24 \cdot 16}{2 \cdot 2 \cdot 2} = 864$$

35) **The correct answer is (A)**

5 squares and 4 rectangles

36) **The correct answer is (D)**

$a^2+b^2=c$, $3^2+4^2=c$, $c=25$

a	b	c
3	4	25

37) **The correct answer is (B)**

AB∥DC, if ∠A=∠D, ∠B=∠C,

$\dfrac{BE}{CE}=\dfrac{AE}{DE}$, $\dfrac{9}{x}=\dfrac{7}{3}$, $x=\dfrac{27}{7}$

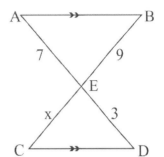

38) **The correct answer is (B)**

$$y-x=22$$
$$y+x=180$$
$$+\overline{}$$
$$2y=202, \quad y=101$$

39) **The correct answer is (E)**

$y=x^2-9$

$x=0$, $y=-9=L$

$y=0$, $x^2-9=0$, $x=\pm3$, $B=-3$, $A=3$

$\dfrac{|AK|}{|KL|}=\dfrac{3}{9}=\dfrac{1}{3}$

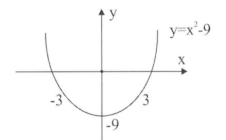

40) **The correct answer is (B)**

$A(ABC)=\dfrac{BC\cdot AH}{2}=\dfrac{6\cdot\left(6+6\sqrt{3}\right)}{2}=18+18\sqrt{3}\,cm^2$

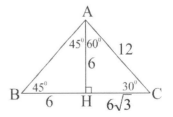

41) **The correct answer is (C)**

$\dfrac{4-3i}{4+3i}=\dfrac{(4-3i)(4-3i)}{(4+3i)(4-3i)}=\dfrac{16-24i+9i^2}{16+9}=\dfrac{16-24i-9}{25}=\dfrac{7-24i}{25}$

42) **The correct answer is (D)**

S(E)=16, A=blue=6, B=red=7

S(E)=16,   S(A)=6   S(B)=7 $P(A\cup B)=P(A)+P(B)=\dfrac{6}{16}+\dfrac{7}{16}=\dfrac{13}{16}$

43) **The correct answer is (E)**

$\log_4 64=\log_4 4^3=3\log_4 4=3$
$\log_5 25=\log_5 5^2=2\log_5 5=2$

44) **The correct answer is (C)**

P(ABCD)=4·4k=16k
P(EFKL)=4·9k=36k

$\dfrac{P(ABCD)}{P(EFKL)}=\dfrac{4}{9}=\dfrac{4k}{9k},\ \dfrac{P_1}{P_2}=\dfrac{16k}{36k}=\dfrac{4}{9}$

$\dfrac{A(ABCD)}{A(EFKL)}=k^2=\left(\dfrac{4}{9}\right)^2=\dfrac{16}{81}$

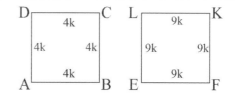

45) **The correct answer is (E)**

$\sin 10^o=\cos(90^o-10^o)=\cos x,\ x=80^o$

46) **The correct answer is (C)**

$y=-6\sin(5x+\pi)$, Period of function $P=\dfrac{\pi}{a}=\dfrac{\pi}{5}$

47) **The correct answer is (C)**

$\angle C=\dfrac{AB}{2}=\dfrac{78}{2}=39^o,\ \angle C=2\alpha=39^o,\ \alpha=\dfrac{39}{2}$

48) **The correct answer is (C)**

$P_1(ABC)=2a+2b$
$P_2(ABD)=a+b+c$
$P_3(ADC)=a+b+c$
$P_1+P_2+P_3=4a+4b+2c$

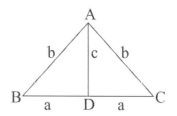

49) **The correct answer is (D)**

A(ABCD)=2a AB=2a·2a=4aa
A(ALMK)=P(LBEM)=P(KMFD)=P(MECF)=4aa
All area=4aa+4a=8aa

50) The correct answer is (B)

$$A(ABCD)=a \cdot b \cdot \sin A=10 \cdot 6 \cdot \sin 30^0=60 \cdot \frac{1}{2}=30 cm^2$$

$$A(EFK)=\frac{KE \cdot LF}{2}=\frac{8LF}{2}=30, \quad 4LF=30, \quad LF=\frac{15}{2}$$

51) The correct answer is (C)

$4^2+4^1+4^0=16+4+1=21$
$3^2+3^1+3^0=9+3+1=13$
$(4^2+4^1+4^0)-(3^2+3^1+3^0)=21-13=8$

52) The correct answer is (C)

53) The correct answer is (D)

$$\frac{7^x+7^x+7^x+7^x}{14^x}=\frac{4 \cdot 7^x}{(2 \cdot 7)^x}=\frac{4 \cdot 7^x}{2^x \cdot 7^x}=\frac{4}{2^x}$$

54) The correct answer is (E)

$3x+2y-z=9, \quad 6x+4y-2z=?$
$6x+4y-2z=2 \cdot (3x+2y-z)=2 \cdot 9=18$

55) The correct answer is (A)

$$\left(x+\sqrt{x}\right)^2=(x)^2+2x\sqrt{x}+\left(\sqrt{x}\right)^2=x^2+2x\sqrt{x}+x=x(x+2\sqrt{x}+1)$$

56) The correct answer is (C)

Prime numbers: 2, 3, 5, 7, 11, 13, 23, 29, 37, 47, 61

57) The correct answer is (D)

$ab \leftrightarrow ba, \Rightarrow 79 \leftrightarrow 97, \quad x=97$

58) The correct answer is (D)

$d_1=4, d_2=2, d_3=5, d_1+d_2+d_3=11$

59) The correct answer is (D)

$$\sqrt{2}+\sqrt{6}+\sqrt{18}+\sqrt{32}=\sqrt{2}+\sqrt{3}\sqrt{2}+\sqrt{2 \cdot 9}+\sqrt{16 \cdot 2}=$$
$$=\sqrt{2}+\sqrt{3}\sqrt{2}+3\sqrt{2}+4\sqrt{2}=\sqrt{2}(1+\sqrt{3}+3+4)=\sqrt{2}\left(8+\sqrt{3}\right), \quad A=8+\sqrt{3}$$

60) The correct answer is (B)

$x+y=a, (x+y)^2=a^2, x^2+2xy+y^2=a^2, x^2+y^2=a^2-2xy$

TEST – 1.9

- Solutions -

1) **The correct answer is (D)**

   $A^2-5=B$, $A^2=B+5$, $A=\sqrt{B+5}$

2) **The correct answer is (B)**

   $3^x+3^x+3^x=9$, $3^x(1+1+1)=9$, $3^x3^1=9$, $3^x=3^1$, $x=1$

3) **The correct answer is (C)**

   $$\frac{99^2-88^2}{11^2}=\frac{(9\cdot 11)^2-(8\cdot 11)^2}{11^2}=\frac{11^2(9^2-8^2)}{11^2}=81\text{-}64=17$$

4) **The correct answer is (A)**

   92 page $\rightarrow$ 22

   100 page $\rightarrow$ x $x=\dfrac{2200}{92}=23.9\%$

5) **The correct answer is (B)**

   $$\frac{1}{\pi_{(12)}}+\frac{1}{2\pi_{(6)}}+\frac{1}{3\pi_{(4)}}+\frac{1}{4\pi_{(3)}}=\frac{12+6+4+3}{12\pi}=\frac{25}{12\pi}$$

6) **The correct answer is (D)**

   $ab\Delta ba$, $75\Delta 57$

7) **The correct answer is (E)**

   $?=\dfrac{42}{2}=21$

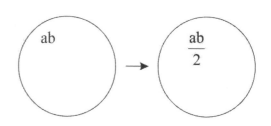

8) **The correct answer is (D)**

   $$\begin{array}{r}3<x<5\\6<y<8\\+\underline{}\\9<x+y<13\end{array}$$

9) **The correct answer is (D)**

   $3x^2+12xy+24x=3x(x+4y+8)$

10) **The correct answer is (A)**

$ab^2+(a+2b)-(2b+a)=ab^2+a-a+2b-2b=ab^2=4\cdot3^2=36$

11) **The correct answer is (B)**

$$\sqrt{12\pi x^2}\sqrt{24\pi4x^3y^3}=\sqrt{12\cdot24\cdot\pi\cdot\pi\cdot x^5\cdot4\cdot y^3}=$$
$$=\sqrt{12\cdot12\cdot4\cdot2\pi^2\cdot\pi\cdot x^4\cdot x\cdot y^2\cdot y}=12\cdot2\cdot\pi x^2y\sqrt{2xy}=24\pi x^2y\sqrt{2xy}$$

12) **The correct answer is (E)**

$\sin 2^o=\cos(90^o-2^o)=\cos x$, $x=88^o$

13) **The correct answer is (C)**

$$\sqrt{1-\sin x}\cdot\sqrt{1+\sin x}+\cos x=\sqrt{(1-\sin x)(1+\sin x)}+\cos x=$$
$$=\sqrt{1-\sin^2 x}+\cos x=\cos x+\cos x=2\cos x$$

14) **The correct answer is (B)**

$$\frac{1}{a}_{(bc)}+\frac{2}{b}_{(ac)}+\frac{3}{c}_{(b)}=\frac{bc+2ac+3ab}{abc}$$

15) **The correct answer is (A)**

$$\frac{3\cdot3^x+9\cdot3^{2x}}{3\cdot3^x}=\frac{3\cdot3^x(1+3\cdot3^x)}{3\cdot3^x}=1+3\cdot3^x=1+3^{x+1}$$

16) **The correct answer is (D)**

$$A=0.\overline{3}+0.\overline{2}=\frac{3}{9}+\frac{2}{9}=\frac{5}{9},\ 9A+9=9\cdot\frac{5}{9}+9=5+9=14$$

17) **The correct answer is (A)**

$90=2\cdot3\cdot3\cdot5=2^1\cdot3^2\cdot5^1$
90 has three prime factors which are 2,3,5
The sum of three prime factors: $(2+3+5)=10$

18) **The correct answer is (C)**

$17=17^1\cdot1^1$ Then the prime factors of 17 are 17 and 1.

19) **The correct answer is (C)**

The divisors of 40: 1, 2, 4, 5, 8, 10, 20, 40

20) **The correct answer is (E)**

GCF=(6, 8, 10)=2

The number wooden cube pieces=

$$\frac{Volume\ of\ rec\tan gular\ solid}{Volume\ of\ wooden\ cube} = \frac{6\cdot 8\cdot 10}{2\cdot 2\cdot 2} = \frac{6\cdot 8\cdot 10}{8} = 60$$

21) **The correct answer is (D)**

Geometric mean$= = \sqrt{A\cdot B} = \sqrt{\left(\sqrt{7}+2\right)\left(\sqrt{7}-2\right)} = \sqrt{7-4} = \sqrt{3}$

22) **The correct answer is (B)**

$\dfrac{a+b}{a} = 9,\ \ a+b = 9a,\ \ b = 8a,\ \dfrac{a+b}{b} = \dfrac{a+8a}{8a} = \dfrac{9a}{8a} = \dfrac{9}{8}$

23) **The correct answer is (A)**

Let us say number x,

$\dfrac{1}{3}\cdot x - \dfrac{1}{7}\cdot x = 8,\ \ \dfrac{x}{3} - \dfrac{x}{7} = 8,\ \ \dfrac{7x-3x}{21} = 8,\ \ \dfrac{4x}{21} = 8,\ $ x=42

24) **The correct answer is (D)**

x=v·t, 780=130·t, t$=\dfrac{780}{130} = 6$

25) **The correct answer is (B)**

$$
\begin{aligned}
2x+3y&=28\\
+\ \ 3x+2y&=27\\
\hline
5x+5y&=55 \Rightarrow 5(x+y)=55,\ x+y=11
\end{aligned}
$$

26) **The correct answer is (E)**

f(x)=x^2+2x+a, f(2)=10, f(2)=2^2+2·2+a=10, 4+4+a=10, 8+a=10, a=2

27) **The correct answer is (B)**

$$\frac{a}{\sqrt{900}} + \frac{b}{\sqrt{400}} + \frac{c}{\sqrt{100}} = \frac{a}{30} + \frac{b}{20} + \frac{c}{10} \Rightarrow$$

$$\frac{a}{30}_{(2)} + \frac{b}{20}_{(3)} + \frac{c}{10}_{(6)} = \frac{2a+3b+6c}{60}$$

28) **The correct answer is (A)**

$5^2+5^1+5^0$=25+5+1=31, $4^2+4^1+4^0$=16+4+1=21

29) **The correct answer is (D)**

GCF=(25, 35, 45)=5, Number of bags=$\dfrac{25}{5}+\dfrac{35}{5}+\dfrac{45}{5}=5+7+9=21$

30) **The correct answer is (D)**

1st number=n, 2nd number=n+1, 3rd number=n+2

Arithmetic mean=$\dfrac{n+n+1+n+2}{3}=16$

$\dfrac{3n+3}{3}=16,\ \dfrac{3(n+1)}{3}=16,\ n+1=16,\ n=15$

31) **The correct answer is (D)**

Let's say Ahmet's working speed is v, and Mehmet's working speed is 4v.

$\dfrac{1}{v}+\dfrac{1}{4v}=\dfrac{1}{20},\ \dfrac{1}{v_{(4)}}+\dfrac{1}{4v_{(1)}}=\dfrac{1}{20},\ \dfrac{5}{4v}=\dfrac{1}{20},\ v=25$

Mehmet can finish the job in 4v=4·25=100days

32) **The correct answer is (C)**

$\dfrac{girls}{boys}=\dfrac{7}{4}=\dfrac{7k}{4k}$

girls+boys=7k+4k=55, 55=11k, k=5, girls=7k=7·5=35

33) **The correct answer is (C)**

$4x^2-4x=4x,\ 4x^2=8x,\ x^2=2x,\ x=2$

34) **The correct answer is (C)**

$|AD|^2=|BD|\cdot|DC|,\ |AD|^2=3\cdot8=24,\ AD=2\sqrt{6}$

35) **The correct answer is (D)**

4x-3y=24, when x=0, -3y=24, y=-8

36) **The correct answer is (D)**

$3^{2a}-3^{2b}=(3^a)^2-(3^b)^2=(3^a+3^b)\cdot(3^a-3^b)=xy$

37) **The correct answer is (A)**

$7^2=5^2+m^2,\ 49=25+m^2,\ m^2=49-25,\ m^2=24,\ m=2\sqrt{6}$

$\cos^2x=(\cos x)^2=\left(\dfrac{2\sqrt{6}}{7}\right)^2=\dfrac{24}{49}$

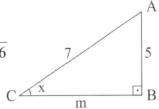

38) **The correct answer is (E)**

$$\frac{\dfrac{3}{4}+\dfrac{4}{3}}{\dfrac{3}{4}-\dfrac{4}{3}}=\frac{\dfrac{3\cdot 3+4\cdot 4}{3\cdot 4}}{\dfrac{3\cdot 3-4\cdot 4}{4\cdot 3}}=\frac{\dfrac{9+16}{12}}{\dfrac{9-16}{12}}=\frac{9+16}{12}\cdot\frac{12}{9-16}=\frac{25}{-7}$$

39) **The correct answer is (C)**

$$A(ABCD)=\frac{(AB+DC)\cdot DH}{2}=\frac{(4x+2x)\cdot x}{2}=\frac{6x\cdot x}{2}=3x^2$$

40) **The correct answer is (A)**

ax+by=cx+dy

ax-cx=dy-by

$$x(a-c)=y(d-b),\quad x=\frac{y(d-b)}{a-c}$$

41) **The correct answer is (C)**

$$\frac{x^2-x-30}{x-6}=\frac{(x-6)(x+5)}{x-6}=x+5$$

42) **The correct answer is (E)**

$(AC)^2=AB^2+BC^2,\quad 7^2=AB^2+2^2$

$AB^2=49-4=45\quad\Rightarrow\quad AB=3\sqrt{5}$

$$\sin^2 x=(\sin x)^2=\left(\frac{3\sqrt{5}}{7}\right)^2=\frac{45}{49}$$

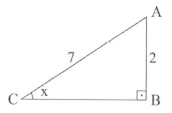

43) **The correct answer is (C)**

$$-3-5x\leq-7x,\ -3\leq-7x+5x,\ -3\leq-2x,\ 3\geq 2x,\ x\leq\frac{3}{2}$$

44) **The correct answer is (B)**

New price=60-60·30%=60-18=42

45) **The correct answer is (E)**

$3x^2+3x-9=3\cdot 3^2+3\cdot 3-9=3\cdot 9+9-9=27$

46) **The correct answer is (E)**

$2x\cdot 3x^2\cdot 8x^3=2\cdot 3\cdot 8\cdot x^1\cdot x^2\cdot x^3=48x^6$

47) **The correct answer is (A)**

-6<6x-12, -6x<-12+6, -6x<-6, -x<-1, x>1

48) **The correct answer is (A)**

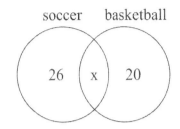

$x+26+20=60$

$x+46=60$

$x=14$

49) **The correct answer is (C)**

First car: $x_1=v_1 \cdot t$ $300=v_1 \cdot 5$ $v_1=60$

Second car: $x_2=v_2 \cdot t$ $500=v_1 \cdot 5$ $v_2=100$

$$\frac{v_1}{v_2}=\frac{60}{100}=\frac{3}{5}$$

50) **The correct answer is (A)**

$f(x)=x^2-2x-2$, $f(-2)=(-2)^2-2 \cdot (-2)-2=4+4-2=6$

51) **The correct answer is (E)**

Volume cylinder$=\pi r^2 h=\pi \cdot 6^2 \cdot 8=\pi \cdot 36 \cdot 8=288\pi cm^3$

52) **The correct answer is (C)**

Volume cylinder$=\pi(2\pi)^2 \cdot 3\pi=\pi \cdot 4\pi^2 \cdot 3\pi=12\pi^4 cm^3$

53) **The correct answer is (A)**

$f(x)=4x+4$, $f(x+4)=4(x+4)+4=4x+16+4=4x+20$

54) **The correct answer is (D)**

Center(-3, 4), Radius=10, General form: $(x-h)^2+(y-k)^2=r^2$,

$(x+3)^2+(y-4)^2=10^2$

55) **The correct answer is (A)**

$(2+i)^2+(2-i)^2=4+2\cdot2\cdot i+(i)^2+4-2\cdot2\cdot i+(i)^2=4+4i-1+4-4i-1=6$

56) **The correct answer is (C)**

Perimeter: $2\pi r_1 = 2\pi(4) = 8\pi$
Perimeter: $2\pi r_2 = 2\pi(11) = 22\pi$

$\dfrac{r}{R} = \dfrac{4}{11}, \quad \dfrac{P_1}{P_2} = \dfrac{8\pi}{22\pi} = \dfrac{4}{11}$

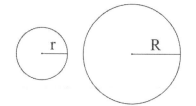

57) **The correct answer is (B)**

$x^2 - 10x + 24 = 0,$
$(x-4)(x-6) = 0$
$x-4 = 0, \ x-6 = 0$
$x = 4 \quad x = 6$

58) **The correct answer is (E)**

$AB = \sqrt{(x_2 - x_1)^2 + (y_2 - y_1)^2} = \sqrt{(8-3)^2 + (11-4)^2} = \sqrt{5^2 + 7^2} = \sqrt{74}$

59) **The correct answer is (C)**

$ax + by = mx,$ then

$by = mx - ax = x(m-a) \Rightarrow b = \dfrac{x(m-a)}{y}$

60) **The correct answer is (C)**

$2A = 2 \cdot \begin{bmatrix} 3 & 4 \\ 5 & 6 \end{bmatrix} = \begin{bmatrix} 6 & 8 \\ 10 & 12 \end{bmatrix}$

$3B = 3 \cdot \begin{bmatrix} 1 & 3 \\ 4 & 2 \end{bmatrix} = \begin{bmatrix} 3 & 9 \\ 12 & 6 \end{bmatrix}$

$2A + 3B = \begin{bmatrix} 6+3 & 8+9 \\ 10+12 & 12+6 \end{bmatrix} = \begin{bmatrix} 9 & 17 \\ 22 & 18 \end{bmatrix}$

TEST – 1.10
- Solutions -

1) **The correct answer is (D)**
   f(x)=x+1, q(x)=x^2+2x+1=(x+1)^2
   q(x)=(x+1)^2=[f(x)]^2

2) **The correct answer is (A)**
   $$B-A=\begin{bmatrix} 6-3 & 8-4 \\ 4-1 & 2-1 \end{bmatrix}=\begin{bmatrix} 3 & 4 \\ 3 & 1 \end{bmatrix}$$

3) **The correct answer is (B)**
   $$\frac{3^x+m}{2x}=y, \ 3^x+m=y\cdot2x, \ m=\frac{y\cdot2^x}{3^x}=y\left(\frac{2}{3}\right)^x$$

4) **The correct answer is (D)**
   $$\sqrt{3}+\sqrt{15}+\sqrt{48}=\sqrt{a}(b+\sqrt{b})$$
   $$\sqrt{3}\left(1+\sqrt{5}+4\right)=\sqrt{a}(b+\sqrt{b})$$
   $$\sqrt{3}\left(5+\sqrt{5}\right)=\sqrt{a}(b+\sqrt{b})$$
   $$\sqrt{a}=\sqrt{3}, \ a=3$$
   $$5=b, \ a+b=8$$

5) **The correct answer is (D)**
   $$\left(\frac{1}{2}-\frac{1}{3}\right):\left(\frac{1}{2}+\frac{1}{3}\right)=\left(\frac{1}{6}\right):\left(\frac{5}{6}\right)=\frac{1}{6}\cdot\frac{6}{5}=\frac{1}{5}$$

6) **The correct answer is (D)**
   $$(3^{\pi}+3^{\pi}+3^{\pi}):(2^{\pi}+2^{\pi}+2^{\pi})=\frac{3\cdot3^{\pi}}{3\cdot2^{\pi}}=\left(\frac{3}{2}\right)^{\pi}$$

7) **The correct answer is (D)**
   a+b=4x, (a+b)^2=(4x)^2,
   a^2+2ab+b^2=16x^2, a^2+b^2=16x^2-2ab

8) **The correct answer is (E)**
   Arkansas=8 letters

9) **The correct answer is (B)**

Utah has one "a"
Texas has one "a"
Kansas has two "a"
Alabama has four "a"
Arkansas has three "a"

10) **The correct answer is (B)**

Oklahoma△Kansas → (8 letters - 6 letters)=2

11) **The correct answer is (A)**

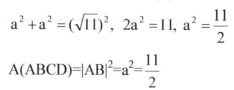

$\dfrac{ab}{c}$ c=(a+b), $\dfrac{72}{9}$

12) **The correct answer is (E)**

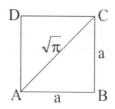

a	b
c	d

a+b+c+d=24,
3+3+3+?=24, ?=15

13) **The correct answer is (D)**

$a^2 + a^2 = (\sqrt{11})^2$, $2a^2 = 11$, $a^2 = \dfrac{11}{2}$

$A(ABCD)=|AB|^2=a^2=\dfrac{11}{2}$

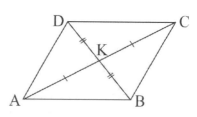

14) **The correct answer is (E)**

$A_1 + A_2 + A_3 + A_4 = \dfrac{A(ABCD)}{4} = \sqrt{3}$

$A(ABCD) = 4\sqrt{3}$

15) **The correct answer is (C)**

$|AD|^2=|BD|\cdot|DC|$
$\left(\sqrt{2}\right)^2 = 2 \cdot x$
$12 = 2x$, $x = 6cm$

555 ACT MATH
1110 Questions with Solutions

- Second Edition -

LEVEL 2: 555 Questions with Solutions

TEST – 2.1

- Questions -

1) If $\dfrac{2x-4}{3}=4m$, find the value of 3x.

   A) 18m   B) 18m+3   C) 18m+6   D) 6m+18   E)7m+12

2) $\log_2 8 + \log_3 81 + \log_5 25 = ?$

   A) 9   B) 10   C) 11   D) 12   E) 13

3) Pencils in a box are distributed to 15 people equally. If these pencils had been distributed to 20 people equally, each person would have 10 pencils less than the first situation. What is the solution equation of this problem?

   A) 15x=20(x–10)   B) 16x=(20–x)10   C) 15x=20(x+10)
   D) 20x=15(x–10)   E)14x=(20-x)12

4) Formula to calculate the wage of an employee working for a computer company is $m_1 = 30 + 10n_1$ for Saturday and $m_2 = 40 + 9n_2$ for Sunday, where n is the number of working hours for the given day. If an employee has earned 150\$ on Saturday and 130\$ on Sunday, how many hours has he worked throughout the weekend?

   A) 18   B) 19   C) 20   D) 22   E)23

5) $x(x+y)+y(x+y)+(x+y)^2=?$

   A) $x^2+6xy+y^2$ B) $2(x+y)^2$ C) $4(x+y)^2$ D) $3(x^2+y^3)$ E) $6(x+y)^2$

6) Pricing formula of a window company is $p=6a+4b$, where a is the long edge and b is the short edge of the window in terms of cm. A customer orders a window with 60cm and 40 cm edges. How much does he need to pay?

   A) 320   B) 420   C) 520   D) 620   E) 655

7) $h = V_0 \cdot t - \dfrac{1}{2}gt^2$ is the formula used to calculate the height of an object in vertical motion, where V_0 is the initial velocity, and t is the time. What is the height of an object thrown upwards vertically with an initial velocity of 2V after 4 seconds?

    A) 8V+8g   B) 8V–8g   C) 6V+6g   D) 6V–6g   E)7V+4g

8) If $\dfrac{a-2}{b-2} = \dfrac{1}{3}$, $\dfrac{3a}{2b+8} = ?$

    A) $\dfrac{1}{2}$ B) $\dfrac{1}{3}$ C) $\dfrac{2}{3}$ D)2   E) $\dfrac{3}{2}$

9) Find out (x, y) in the following system of equations.
$$2x + 3y = 21$$
$$3y - x = 12$$

    A) (5, 3)   B) (3, 5)   C) (2, 3)   D)5,6   E) (4, 3)

10) If $f(x)=ax^2+4$ and $\dfrac{f(2)}{f(1)} = \dfrac{1}{3}$, a=?

    A) $\dfrac{11}{8}$ B)3   C) $\dfrac{-11}{8}$ D) $\dfrac{-8}{11}$ E) $\dfrac{-8}{7}$

11) One of two parallel trees has a height of *m*, while its shadow's length is *m+4*. If the height of the second tree is *n*, what is the length of its shadow?

    A) m+1   B) $\dfrac{m+4}{2m}$ C) m+4   D) $\dfrac{n(m+4)}{m}$ E) $\dfrac{m(n+4)}{n}$

12) $\dfrac{\dfrac{1}{3^x} - \dfrac{1}{2^x}}{\dfrac{1}{3^x} + \dfrac{1}{2^x}} = ?$

    A) $\dfrac{2^x - 3^x}{2^x + 3^x}$ B) $\dfrac{3^x - 2^x}{3^x + 2^x}$ C) $\dfrac{6^x - 3^x}{6^x + 3^x}$ D) $\dfrac{6^x - 2^x}{6^x + 2^x}$ E) 1

13) $\dfrac{3^x + 3^{x+1} + 3^{x+2}}{3^{x+1} + 3^{x+2} + 3^{x+3}} = ?$

A) $\dfrac{3^x}{3}$　　　　B) $\dfrac{1}{3}$　　　　C) $\dfrac{1}{8}$　　　　D) 3^{x+1}　　　　3) 3^{x-2}

14) **Line d_1 in the figure passes through the origin. Find out the equation of the line d_1.**

A) y=9x　　　B) y=4x　　　C) y=$\dfrac{x}{3}$

D) y=3x　　　E)y=6x

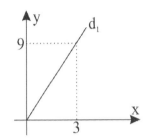

15) **If $(x+4)-(x+5)=x^2+3ax+5b$, $\left(\dfrac{a+b}{b-a}\right)=?$**

A) 2　　　　B) 3　　　　C) 7　　　　D) 4　　　　E) $\dfrac{1}{7}$

16) **If $a>0$ and $3a^2-9a=0$, $a=?$**

A) 3　　　　B) 4　　　　C) 5　　　　D) 6　　　　E) 7

17) **If [BD]=x and [EC]=y in the figure what is x?**

A) 9　　　B) 8　　　C) 6

D) 5　　　E) 4

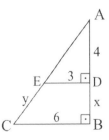

18) **If $\left.\begin{array}{l}2a+3b=18\\6b+7a=27\end{array}\right\}$, a+b=?**

A) 10　　　　B) 9　　　　C) 8　　　　D) 6　　　　E) 5

19) x is an angle, If 0<x<90 and sin14=cosx, x=?

    A) 60   B) 65   C) 68   D) 70   E) 76

20) If $\sqrt{(a+b)+2\sqrt{ab}} = \sqrt{a}+\sqrt{b}$, $\dfrac{\sqrt{(5)+2\sqrt{6}}}{\sqrt{3}+\sqrt{2}} = ?$

    A) 1   B) 2   C) 3   D) 4   E) 5

21) Figure shows the number of books sold by a publisher in a month. How many physics - biology books are sold more than history - chemistry books?

	History	Math	Physics	Chemistry	Biology
History				300	
Math				360	400
Physics					400
Chemistry	300	360			
Biology			700	440	

    A) 300   B) 350   C) 400   D) 500   E) 600

22) $2400 of money is divided between four siblings in a way to be directly proportional to 2, 4, 6 and 8. How much money is given to the one who gets the most?

    A) 960   B) 860   C) 760   D) 660   E) 670

23) If $d_1 \| d_2 \| d_3$ and $m_1 \| m_2$, $\angle y - \angle x = ?$

    A) 100   B) 102   C) 106
    D) 108   E) 110

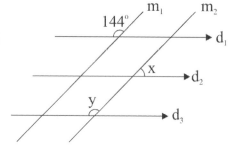

24) What is the difference between *8a+6b–3c* and *6a+8b–3c*?

    A) 2a   B) 2c   C) 6c   D) 2a–2b   E) 3c

25) $\log x = \log_{10} x$, $\log 1000 + \log \dfrac{1}{100} = ?$

  A) 1   B) 2   C) 3   D) 4   E) -2

26) Find the median of -4, 20, -6, 2, 11

  A) -4   B) 20   C) -6   D) 2   E) 11

27) Following table shows the number of students and the amount of charities collected by the students in four schools.

School	Number of students	Amount of Charity
A	40	1600$
B	50	1500$
C	60	1800$
D	30	600$

What is the ratio of the charity collected by school B to the entire charity collected?

  A) $\dfrac{3}{11}$ B) $\dfrac{3}{10}$ C) $\dfrac{11}{3}$ D) $\dfrac{4}{11}$ E) 5.3

28) $|\pi-4| + |\pi-3| + |\pi-2| = ?$

  A) $\pi-1$ B) π_1 C) $\pi-2$ D) $\pi+2$ E) 3

29) The potential energy (E_p) between charges q_1 and q_2 is calculated by the formula $E_p = k \cdot \dfrac{q_1 \cdot q_2}{d}$, where the distance between the two charges is d. Find k in terms of E_p, q_1, q_2 and d.

  A) $\dfrac{E_p}{q_1 \cdot q_2}$ B) $\dfrac{E_p \cdot d}{q_1 \cdot q_2}$ C) $\dfrac{d}{E_p \cdot q_1 \cdot q_2}$ D) $\dfrac{q_1 \cdot q_2}{E_p \cdot d}$ E) $\dfrac{E_p}{d \cdot q_1 \cdot q_2}$

30) If the distance between the two charges is decreased by 50%, how much would the potential energy between the two charges increase?

   A) 50% B) 100% C) 150% D) 200% E) 220%

31) What value of x will give the term |3x–12| its smallest value?

   A) 3 B) 4 C) 5 D) 0 E) 6

32) The table shows the number of students studying at schools A, B, C and D in years 2014 and 2015. Which school's number of students has increased about 23%?

School	2014 Year	2015 Year
A	300	364
B	400	404
C	420	440
D	325	400

   A) A B) B C) C D) D E) B, C

33) Table below shows the ratio of salary expenses to the school budget for schools A, B, C, D and E in years 2014 and 2015. Which school's salary expense ratio has increased the least in 2015 with respect to 2014?

School	Ratio of salary expenses to school budget in 2014 (%)	Ratio of salary expenses to school budget in 2015 (%)
A	24	32
B	31	39
C	30	33
D	20	26
E	25	32

   A) A B) B C) C D) E E) A,B

34) Which of the following could NOT be found by using the data in the table above?

   A) Average budget of the five schools
   B) Average salary expenses ratio of the five schools
   C) Average increase in salary expenses for the five schools
   D) Increase of salary expenses for each school

35) **The given linear graph shows the total amount of water consumed by a family since week How much water have they used by the end of week 3?**

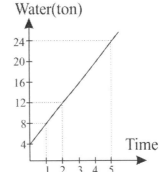

A) 11
B) 12
C) 13
D) 14
E) 15

36) **Find the relationship between the consumed water (w) and time (t)**

A) w=4t   B) w=4t+4   C) w=4t+6   D) $w = \dfrac{t}{4} + 4$ E) w=6t

37) **According to the y=f(x) graph given, calculate f(–6)+f(4)+f(6)=?**

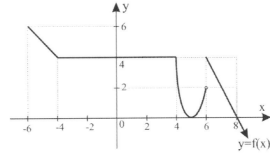

A) 14   B) 13   C) 12   D) 11   E) 15

38) **If –8<a<4, |a–4|+|a+8|=?**

A) 12   B) 10   C) 4   D) 2a+4   E) 3a+3

39) **Some of the 30 houses on a street have 5 rooms, while the rest have 4 rooms. If there are totally 132 rooms in these houses, how many of them have 5 rooms?**

A) 16   B) 14   C) 12   D) 10   E) 13

40) **Price of a TV set increases by 40%, reaching up to $308. What is the original price of this TV set?**

A) 222   B) 230   C) 240   D) 250   E) 220

41) Below table shows the sports activities in a summer school and the number of students who attend these activities in years 2014 and 2015. Which sport has attracted the greatest number of new students in 2015?

Sport Activity	Number of students	
	2014	2015
Basketball	300	410
Football	300	370
Tennis	200	290
Swimming	320	500
Volleyball	130	160

A) Basketball   B) Football   C) tennis   D) swimming   E) Volleyball

42) What is the Ratio of attendees of the sport with the least number of increase in students in 2015 to the entire number of students for?

A) $\frac{16}{173}$ B) $\frac{19}{174}$ C) $\frac{18}{174}$ D) $\frac{19}{173}$ E) $\frac{17}{174}$

43) The center of the following circle is A(4, 8), while B(5, 9) is any point on the circle. Find out the equation of this circle.

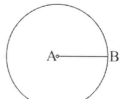

A) $(x-4)^2+(y+8)^2=\sqrt{2}$
B) $(x-4)^2+(y-8)^2=\sqrt{2}$
C) $(x-4)^2+(y+8)^2=2$
D) $(x+4)^2+(y+4)^2=2$
E) $(x+5)^2+(y+4)^2=2$

44) The velocity of an object in vertical motion is calculated by $V=V_0-gt$. Find the velocity of an object thrown with an initial velocity of 50m/s after 2 seconds ($g\approx10m/s^2$).

A) 20m/s   B) 34m/s   C) 36m/s   D) 40m/s   E) 30m/s

45) Students in a classroom are to be selected either for a basketball or a football team. The probability of a student being selected to the football team is 3/7. If 24 students are selected for the basketball team from this classroom, how many students are selected for the football team?

A) 26   B) 22   C) 21   D) 18   E) 20

46) The given graph shows the number of guests in a hotel according to their professions. If this graph was to be shown as a pie chart, what would the angle of the engineers be? (A: teachers, B: engineers, C: nurses, D: doctors)

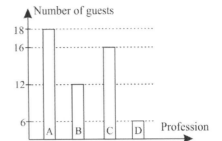

A) 83.1°   B) 86.2°   C) 89.3°
D) 92.3°   E) 94.3

47) Find the sum of the slopes of lines y=3x+√2 and y=$x\sqrt{2}$+3

A) 3+√2   B) √3+2   C) √3–2   D) 2–√3   E) 3

48) What is the remainder when the polynomial $P(x)=x^3+4x^2+4x-8$ is divided by the polynomial $Q(x)=x^2+2x$?

A) 6   B) –6   C) –8   D) –9   E) 7

49) Figure shows the parabola y=f(x).
Find the value of f(4)

A) $\dfrac{5}{3}$ B) $\dfrac{4}{3}$ C) $-\dfrac{3}{5}$

D) $-\dfrac{5}{3}$ E) $\dfrac{7}{3}$

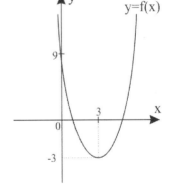

50) Numbers from 1 to 80 are written on cards separately and put into a box. One of the cards is selected randomly. What is the probability of selecting either an even number or an odd number under 10?

A) $\dfrac{9}{16}$ B) $\dfrac{9}{17}$ C) $\dfrac{8}{17}$ D) $\dfrac{8}{19}$ E) $\dfrac{9}{19}$

51) Each team plays with another only once in a football league consisting of 16 teams. How many combinations are there for the first match?

A) 80   B) 90   C) 100   D) 110   E) 120

52) One piece of chocolate is left when chocolates in a box are packed by four, six and nine. What is the minimum number of chocolates in this box?

  A) 120   B) 124   C) 128   D) 130   E) 37

53) Following table shows the number of students who have visited a science museum from a school. How many percent has the number of visiting students in May 2015 has increased with respect to May 2014?

Months	2014	2015
February	240	180
March	290	240
April	390	440
May	440	490

  A) 16%   B) 15%   C) 13%   D) 12%   E) 11.4%

54) Let A be the sum of all the even numbers between 1 and 11

Let B be the sum of all the odd numbers between 2 and 12

Let C be the sum of all the prime numbers between 4 and 14

$$\frac{(A+B)}{(A+B+C)} = ?$$

  A) $\dfrac{65}{101}$ B) $\dfrac{65}{102}$ C) $\dfrac{75}{101}$ D) $\dfrac{85}{102}$ E) 8

55) If |AB|=2cm and |BD|=3 cm in the given cylinder, find out the volume of the cylinder in cm ($\pi \approx 3$)

  A) 24   B) 30   C) 36

  D) 40   E) 48

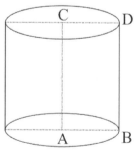

56) Which value(s) of x make(s) the function $f(x) = \dfrac{x^3 + 8}{x^2 - 9x}$ undefined?

  A) 0; 9   B) 0; 7   C) 9; 8   D) 3; 4   E) 9; 5

57) How much does a person who buys 1800 grams of a nut sold for $16 per kilogram needs to pay?

    A) 18   B) 18.8   C) 22   D) 28   E) 28.8

58) What is the result when numbers 663 and 986 are rounded to the nearest tens and then summed?

    A) 1650   B) 1666   C) 1679   D) 1680   E) 1700

59) If $x^2+8x+7=0$ which of the following show all of the possible value(s) of x?

    A) 7, 1   B) 1, 8   C) -7, -1   D) 8   E) 9

60) $|-2\pi| + |2\pi-1|=?$

    A) 1   B) 4π C) $4\pi-1$ D) $4\pi+1$ E) 4

TEST – 2.2
- Questions -

1) If $6x+6=16$ find out $9x^2+3x+4=$?

   A) 30　　　　B) 31　　　　C) 32　　　　D) 34　　　　E) 36

2) Find out (x, y) in $\begin{cases} x+y=5 \\ 2x+4y=18 \end{cases}$ equation system.

   A) $(2, 3)$　　B) $(2, 1)$　　C) $(-2, 1)$　　D) $(1, 4)$　E)$(2,7)$

3) The price of a new TV set is x while a second hand TV set costs (x–m). How many second hand TV sets can be bought with the cost of 20 new TV sets?

   A) $\dfrac{20x}{x-m}$　　B) $\dfrac{20x}{x+m}$　　C) $\dfrac{40x}{x-m}$　　D) $\dfrac{40x}{x+m}$　　E) $20x+m$

4) Which of the following is equal to $8x^2+12xy+9y^2-4x^2$?

   A) $(x+3y)$　　B) $(2x+3y)^2$　　C) $(2x+4y)^2$　　D) $(x-2y)^2$　　E) $(5x+4y)^2$

5) If $\sqrt{2x^2+2m-12}-\sqrt{2x^2}=0$, then $6m+6=$?

   A) 44　　　　B) 42　　　　C) 41　　　　D) 40　　　　E) 45

6) What are the equations of the lines given in the figure?

   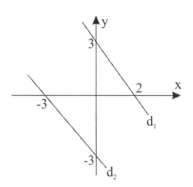

   A) $\dfrac{x}{3}+\dfrac{y}{2}-1,\ x+y=3$

   B) $\dfrac{x}{2}+\dfrac{y}{3}=1,\ x+y=-3$

   C) $\dfrac{x}{4}+\dfrac{y}{3}=1,\ x+y=3$

   D) $2x+3y=1,\ x+y=3$

   E) $2x+3y=12,\ 5x+3y=14$

7) If $m=7^2+7$, then find 7^3+7^2 in terms of m.

    A) 15m   B) 49m   C) 28m   D) 7m   E) 14m

8) The formula $180(n-2)=n\cdot m$ is used to calculate the interior angle of a regular polygon, where n is the number of edges. If the internal angles of a regular polygon are 140, find out its number of edges.

    A) 9   B) 10   C) 11   D) 12   E) 13

9) The equation of the line d_1 in the figure is $y=ax+b$. Find out $a+b$.

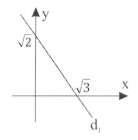

A) $\dfrac{\sqrt{6}+\sqrt{2}}{\sqrt{3}}$ B) $\dfrac{\sqrt{6}-\sqrt{2}}{\sqrt{3}}$ C) $\dfrac{\sqrt{3}+\sqrt{2}}{\sqrt{6}}$

D) $\dfrac{\sqrt{3}-\sqrt{2}}{\sqrt{6}}$ E) $\dfrac{\sqrt{3}+\sqrt{2}}{\sqrt{7}}$

10) What are the equations of lines d_1, d_2, and d_3 in the figure?

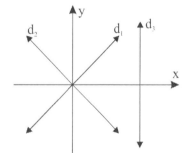

	d_1	d_2	d_3
A)	y=x	y=−x	y=3
B)	y=−x	y=x	y=3
C)	y=x	y=−x	x=3
D)	y=−x	y=x	x=−3

11) Find the mode of 12, 19, 32, 19, -4, 12, 19 31, 30.

    A) 12   B) 19   C) 32   D) 31   E) 30

12) $4a^2=m^2+n^2$ is the formula to calculate the edge of a rhombus, where a is the edge, and m and n are the diagonals of the rhombus. What is the perimeter of the rhombus in terms of m and n?

A) $\sqrt{m^2+n^2}$ B) $2\sqrt{m^2+n^2}$ C) $3\sqrt{m^2+n^2}$

D) $4\sqrt{m^2+n^2}$ E) $4\sqrt{2m^2+n^2}$

13) Given the equation $n^2-9n+20=0$, what is the ratio of sum of the roots to the multiplication of the roots?

   A) $\frac{9}{11}$ B) $\frac{-9}{20}$ C) $\frac{9}{20}$ D) $\frac{20}{9}$ E) $\frac{9}{17}$

14) Find the range of numbers 13, 21, 28, 17, 16, -6, 0, 9, 16.

   A) 30   B) 32   C) 34   D) 35   E) 36

15) $\dfrac{4+4\pi+\pi^2}{\pi+2}+\dfrac{9-6\pi+\pi^2}{3-\pi}+\dfrac{\pi^2+2\pi}{\pi+2}=?$

   A) $5+\pi$ B) $5-\pi$ C) 5   D) π E) 6

16) Trucks need to pay $5 more than the cars for a tollway. If $600 of toll is collected when 80 trucks and 20 cars use the tollway, what is the toll fee for a truck?

   A) 7   B) 8   C) 9   D) 10   E) 11

17) If $(\pi+k)^2+(\pi^2+3k\pi+k^2)=a\pi^2+bk\pi+ck^2$ then a+b+c=?

   A) 10   B) 9   C) 8   D) 7   E) 6

18) Three shapes given in the figure are a rectangle, a square, and a rhombus. How many diagonals are there in the figure?

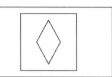

   A) 1   B) 3   C) 4
   D) 5   E) 6

19) If $\angle B=90^{\circ}$, $|AC|=4$ and $|AB|=2$ in the figure, find out $\dfrac{\angle A}{\angle C}$

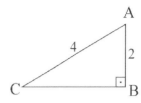

A) 8   B) 7   C) 6

D) 4   E) 2

20) if of $\begin{cases} 4x+6y=10 \\ mx+12y=16 \end{cases}$, which value of m makes the solution set an empty set?

A) 12   B) 11   C) 10   D) 9   E) 8

21) Entrance fee to a science museum is \$3 for children and \$7 for adults. If a of total \$440 of fee is collected when 80 people visit in a day, which of the following represents the pair of solution equation for this problem ,where x is the number of children ,and y is the number of adults.

A) $\begin{cases} x+y=80 \\ 3x+7y=440 \end{cases}$ B) $\begin{cases} x+y=80 \\ 7x+3y=440 \end{cases}$ C) $\begin{cases} x-y=80 \\ 3x+7y=440 \end{cases}$

D) $\begin{cases} x+y=440 \\ 3x+7y=80 \end{cases}$ E) $\begin{cases} 2x+y=440 \\ 3x+7y=80 \end{cases}$

22) 60% of the students in a university are female, and 20% of the female are blonde. How many percent of the total students consist of non–blonde females?

A) 40%   B) 48%   C) 50%   D) 52%   E) 54%

23) Unit price of water sold in a market is calculated by the formula m=1.25+0.25n, where n is the number of liters and m is the total price. How many liters can a customer buy when she pays \$9.25

A) 24   B) 26   C) 28   D) 32   E) 34

24) What time would it be 1446 hours after 8:30 a.m.?

A) 1:450 a.m.   B) 2:00 p.m.   C) 2:30 p.m.   D) 3.30 p.m.   E) 1:30 a.m

25) A petrol station that sells equal amount of fuel per day has an initial stock of 120 tons. If 84 tons of fuel is sold in 4 days, how many tons of fuel were left three days after the initial stock?

A) 63　　　　B) 61　　　　C) 60　　　　D) 57　　　　E) 62

26) Find the difference between the greatest odd number and smallest even number that can be written by using each numerals 3, 4, 5, 6 and 9.

A) 61394　　　B) 61947　　　C) 62949　　　D) 63942　　　E) 62943

27) If f(x)=ax^2+bx+c in the given graph, find a+b+c.

A) $\dfrac{3}{2}$　　　　B) $\dfrac{5}{3}$　　　　C) 4

D) 5　　　　E) $\dfrac{4}{3}$

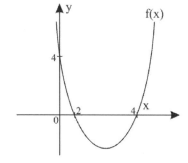

28) Ahmet is 2n and Mehmet is 3m years old. Ahmet's current age is three times of Mehmet's current age. What is the sum of their age after two years from today?

A) 9m+2　　　B) 9m+3　　　C) 9m+4　　　D) 9m+6　　　E) 9m+5

29) If apricots are sold for \$14 per kilogram in a market, \$110　profit is made. If they are sold for \$10 per kilogram, loss is \$40　"A" being the total purchasing price and "x" being the selling price per kilogram, which of the following is the equation system for the solution of this problem?

A) $\begin{cases} 14x = A + 110 \\ 10x = A - 40 \end{cases}$　　B) $\begin{cases} 14x = A - 110 \\ 10x = A + 40 \end{cases}$　　C) $\begin{cases} 14x = A + 110 \\ 10x = 40 - A \end{cases}$

D) $\begin{cases} 10x = A + 110 \\ 14x = A - 40 \end{cases}$　　E) $\begin{cases} 14x = A + 110 \\ 10x = 40 - A \end{cases}$

30) Which of the following is f(x) according to the data given in the table?

N	0	1	2	3
f(n)	2	6	18	54

A) f(x)=3^x+2　　　　　B) f(x)=2·3^x　　　　　C) f(x)=3^x+3

D) f(x)=2^x+3^x　　　　E) f(x)=5^x+3^x

31) Table below shows the price of books in a bookstore. The books are either sold separately, or in packs of 3, while 3–pack books are sold with 60% discount. How much does a person need to pay if he buys 1 math, 3 physics and 6 chemistry books?

Books	Price
Math	15
Physics	20
Chemistry	30
Biology	40
History	10

A) 47   B) 48   C) 50   D) 111   E) 52

32) 3% and 4% of the eggs collected from two separate chicken farms get broken during collecting. If 120 eggs get broken when collecting 4000 eggs from these two farms, find the solution equation of the problem which is used to find how many eggs are collected from each farm.

A) $\begin{cases} 4x + 3y = 100 \\ 100x + 100y = 600 \end{cases}$ B) $\begin{cases} 100x + 100y = 6000 \\ 3x + 4y = 120 \end{cases}$

C) $\begin{cases} 3x + 2y = 120 \\ 100x + 100y = 600 \end{cases}$ D) $\begin{cases} 100x + 100y = 4000 \\ 3x + 4y = 120 \end{cases}$

E) $\begin{cases} 3x + 2y = 120 \\ 100x + 100y = 3000 \end{cases}$

33) A 44–page book is numbered. How many "4" numerals are used in the book?

A) 12   B) 13   C) 10   D) 9   E) 11

34) Let a linear model represent the number of passengers landing to an airport in each separate hour. How many passengers have landed after the first 90 minutes, based on the graph?

A) 4000   B) 4200   C) 4400
D) 6000   E) 4500

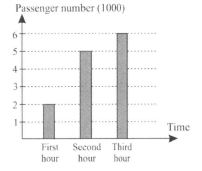

35) Center of gravity of a homogeneous wire shifts 9 cm when $\frac{3}{11}$ of the wire is cut off. What is the original length of the wire?

A) 66cm   B) 61cm   C) 55cm
D) 50cm   E) 60

36) If |AN|=|NB|=2cm and |BE|=|EC|=1cm, find the sum of perimeters of all non-square rectangles in the figure.

A) 50cm   B) 47cm   C) 46cm
D) 56cm   E) 48

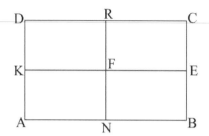

37) The price of a product is $90 without taxes What would its price be when 9% tax is added?

A) $94   B) $96   C) $98.1   D) $99.1   E) $94

38) How many triangles are there in the figure?

A) 7   B) 8   C) 9
D) 10   E) 11

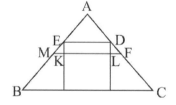

39) The pie chart in the figure shows a student's scores in Algebra I, Algebra II and Algebra III exams. Which of the following shows the Algebra I : Algebra II : Algebra III ratio?

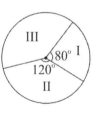

A) 3:2:4   B) 4:3:2   C) 2:3:4
D) 3:4:4   E) 1:2:3

40) The distance between cities A and B is 900km. Following graph shows the time–distance graph for two vehicles. How many hours does it take for these two vehicles to meet each other?

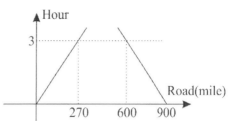

A) $\dfrac{90}{19}$ B) $\dfrac{80}{19}$ C) $\dfrac{90}{17}$

D) $\dfrac{90}{16}$ E) $\dfrac{90}{23}$

41) Students in a classroom collect money to buy a birthday gift for one of their friends. When they collect $30 per person, they need $60 more, and when they collect $45 per person, they have $65 extra cash in hand. What is the solution equation for this problem, where x is the number of people ?

A) 45x–65=30x+60   B) 65x–45=30x+60
C) 30x–60=45x–65   D) 45x+65=30x+60
E) 30x-55+35x-65

42) $\log_7 \sqrt{7} = a$ if $a^2 = ?$

A) 1   B) $\dfrac{1}{2}$ C) $\dfrac{1}{4}$ D) 2   E) 4

43) $E_P = \dfrac{kx^2}{2}$ is the formula to calculate the potential energy stored in a spring, where k is a constant depending on the spring and x is the difference between the initial and final length of the spring. Calculate the potential energy stored on a spring if k=10 and x=20

A) 4000   B) 3000   C) 2500   D) 2000   E) 2200

44) Which of the following is the equation for a circle passing through points A(6, 0), B(0, 8) and the origin?

A) (x-3)^2+(y+4)^2=25   B) (x-3)^2+(y-4)^2=25
C) (x-3)^2+(y-4)^2=50   D) (x-3)^2+(y+4)^2=50
E) (x-3)^2+(y+4)^2=55

45) Find the sum of the slopes of following three lines:

d_1: y=2x, d_2: y=−2x and d_3:y=$x\sqrt{3}$+3

A) 4+ $\sqrt{3}$ B) 4− $\sqrt{3}$ C) $\sqrt{3}$ D) $\sqrt{3}$−2 E) 3

46) What is the sum of x values that satisfies f(x+3)=0 condition in the given graph?

A) –6 B) –5 C) 6
D) 5 E) 7

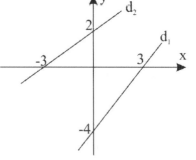

47) Given table shows the number of employees of a company who come late to work for a month. Which of the following statement is wrong according to the table?

Late days	Late-coming employee	
	Male	Female
2–4	10	6
5–7	11	8
8–10	13	8
11–13	8	4
14–16	6	10

A) Number of male employees who has ever come late is 48.
B) Number of female employees who has ever come late is 36.
C) Ratio of late–coming females to late–coming males is ¾
D) The company has 84 employees in total.
E) The company has 64 employees in total.

48) Find out the equations of the lines given in the figure.

A) $\begin{cases} -4x + 3y = -12 \\ 2x - 3y = -6 \end{cases}$ B) $\begin{cases} -4x - 3y = -12 \\ -2x + 3y = -6 \end{cases}$

C) $\begin{cases} 3x - 4y = -12 \\ 3y - 2x = -6 \end{cases}$ D) $\begin{cases} 2x + 3y = 6 \\ 3x - 4y = 12 \end{cases}$

E) $\begin{cases} -3x - 4y = -12 \\ 3y + 2x = -6 \end{cases}$

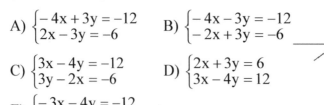
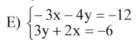

49) Find out the points where the function $f(x) = -x^2 + 25$ cuts x and y axes.

A) (0, 25), (0, 5), (–5, 0)   B) (–5, 0), (5, 0), (0, 25)
C) (5, 0), (–5, 0), (25, 0)   D) (–5, 0), (0, 25), (0, –5)
E) (–6, 0), (0, 25), (0, –5)

50) ABCD and FELK in the figure are squares and the shaded region is x cm^2. If $a^2 + b^2 = y^2$, then find out a^2 in terms of x and y. (y where a is the side of the larger square and b is the side of the smaller square)

A) x+y   B) x–y   C) $x^2 + y^2$
D) (x+y)/2   E) 2x+y

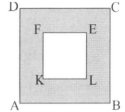

51) A group of athletes consists of 44 people. The number of male athletes in this group is 5 more than twice of the female athletes. How many female athletes are there in this group?

A) 17   B) 16   C) 15   D) 14   E) 13

52) Four students have $120, $140, $80 and $60 in their wallets. They all buy the same products and spend all of their money. What is the minimum number of products they could buy?

A) 20   B) 18   C) 22   D) 23   E) 24

53) If $f(x) = ax^2 + bx + 2$, $f(1) = 7$ and $f(2) = 16$, then find out a/b.

A) 1/3   B) 1/4   C) 2/3   D) 2/5   E) 2/7

54) A student pays $60 for 8 notebooks and 6 pencils, and $80 for 6 notebooks and 8 pencils. What is the price of a notebook and a pencil together?

A) 12   B) 11   C) 10   D) 9   E) 8

55) For an exam of 100 questions, Scoring formula for an exam is S=0.25A+25, where S is the score of the student and A is the number of his/her correct answers. If one of the students answers all of the 100 questions, correctly and the other one did not answer 60 questions, while getting the rest right, what is the sum of their scores?

A) 80   B) 82   C) 83   D) 85   E) 86

56) If |AB|=6cm and |BC|=4cm in the figure, find out the radius of the circle.

A) 5   B) 4   C) 3
D) 2.5   E) 1.5

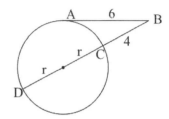

57) The centripetal acceleration of an object in circular motion is calculated by the formula a=v^2/r, where v is the linear velocity and r is the radius. Find out the acceleration of the object moving with 20m/s of velocity and 2m of radius.

A) 150   B) 180   C) 200   D) 220   E) 250

58) Using the same formula, find out the velocity of the object with 18m/s^2 of acceleration and 2m of radius.

A) 1   B) 2   C) 4   D) 5   E) 6

59) The number of people who visited a museum increased from about 20000 in 2011 to about 24000 in 2012. Find the actual increase and the percent increase.

A) 22%   B) 20%   C) 19%`   D) 16%   E) 18%

60) If (x+3)^2+(x-3)^2=2A, then A=?

A) 2x^2+9   B) 2x+6   C) 2x   D) x^2+9   E) 3x+6

TEST – 2.3
- Questions –

1) A water filling facility has two machines to fill empty bottles. While machine A can fill up to 360 bottles per hours, machine B can fill up to 220 bottles. What is the maximum number of bottles that can be filled within 150 minutes by using both of the machines?

A) 1400　　　　B) 1450　　　　C) 1600　　　　D) 1650　　　　E) 1770

2) If $\dfrac{1}{a} + \dfrac{1}{b} + \dfrac{1}{c} = \sqrt{3}$ then $\dfrac{\sqrt{3}}{a} + \dfrac{\sqrt{3}}{b} + \dfrac{\sqrt{3}}{c} = ?$

A) 1　　　　B) 3　　　　C) $3\sqrt{3}$　　　　D) $\dfrac{1}{\sqrt{3}}$　　　　E) 4

3) $a^{\frac{1}{3} + \frac{1}{2} - \left(\frac{1}{2} + \frac{1}{3} \right)} = ?$

A) a　　　　B) a^{-1}　　　　C) $3a$　　　　D) $\dfrac{1}{2a}$　　　　E) $2a$

4) A school has classrooms for either 10 or 13 students. If there are 20 classrooms and 224 students in this school, which of the following is the equation system for the problem?

A) $\begin{cases} x + y = 20 \\ 13x + 13y = 224 \end{cases}$　　　B) $\begin{cases} x + y = 10 \\ 10x + 13y = 224 \end{cases}$　　　C) $\begin{cases} x + y = 20 \\ 10x + 10y = 2240 \end{cases}$

D) $\begin{cases} x + y = 20 \\ 10x + 13y = 224 \end{cases}$　　　E) $\begin{cases} 3x + y = 10 \\ 11x + 13y = 224 \end{cases}$

5) If $\dfrac{6}{\pi} = \dfrac{14}{\pi + x}$ then x=?

A) $\dfrac{4\pi}{5}$　　　　B) $\dfrac{4\pi}{3}$　　　　C) $\dfrac{5\pi}{4}$　　　　D) $\dfrac{4}{5\pi}$　　　　E) 4

6) If 3x–4y=6π and 6x–5y=12π then x–y=?

A) π　　　　B) 3π　　　　C) - π　　　　D) $\dfrac{1}{2\pi}$　　　　E) 2π

7) Find the function f(x) according to the given data.

x	f(x)
-1	-1
0	1
1	3
2	5

A) f(x)=2x+1   B) f(x)=2x   C) f(x)=2x-1
D) f(x)=1+x   E) f(x)=3x+6

8) The equation of line d_1 is n·y=mx+n. while the equation of line d_2 is m·y=nx+m, what is the ratio of slope of d_1 to d_2?

A) $\dfrac{n}{m}$ B) $\dfrac{m}{n}$ C) $\dfrac{m^2}{n^2}$ D) $\dfrac{n^2}{m^2}$ E) 1

9) Which value of m makes the solution set of $\begin{cases} 9x - 6y = 15 \\ mx + 12y = 6 \end{cases}$ equation system an empty set?

A) -18   B) 19   C) 9   D) -9   E) 18

10) What is the distance between points A and B in the figure?

A) 8
B) 6
C) 2
D) –1
E) 7

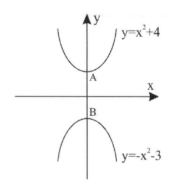

11) ABC is an equilateral triangle, while DEFG is a square.
If ∠ABC=x and ∠FDE=y,
find out $\dfrac{x+y}{x-y}$.

A) 11   B) 9   C) 8   D) 7   E) 10

12) If the roots of the equation $y=x^2-8x+7$ are x_1 and x_2, find out the $\dfrac{x_1 + x_2}{x_1 \cdot x_2}$ ratio.

A) -8   B) 7   C) $\dfrac{7}{8}$ D) $\dfrac{8}{7}$ E) 8

13) $\dfrac{\dfrac{3}{a} + \dfrac{3}{b}}{\dfrac{a}{3} + \dfrac{b}{3}} = ?$

A) $\dfrac{9}{a+b}$ B) $\dfrac{9}{a \cdot b}$ C) $\dfrac{3}{a+b}$ D) $3a$ E) $\dfrac{3}{a \cdot b}$

14) Which are the roots of the equation $x^2-2x-12=0$?

A) $x = \sqrt{13} - 1$ B) $x = \sqrt{13} + 1$ C) $x = 1 \pm \sqrt{13}$
D) $x = \sqrt{13} \mp 2$ E) $x=12$

15) Centripetal acceleration is calculated by $a = \dfrac{v^2}{r}$, where v is the velocity of the object and r is the radius of motion. Which of the following information is/are correct?

I. When the velocity is doubled, the acceleration doubles too.
II. When the radius is halved, the acceleration doubles.
III. When the velocity is halved, the acceleration decreases to its quarter.

A) I, II and III   B) I and III   C) II and III
D) Only III   E) Only I

16) What is one of the roots of the equation $x(x^4-25)=600x$?

A) ± 5 B) ± 6 C) ± 7 D) ± 8 E) 5

17) If $\dfrac{1}{3x} - \dfrac{1}{4x} = \dfrac{1}{3} + \dfrac{1}{4}$, then x=?

A) $\dfrac{1}{7}$ B) $\dfrac{2}{7}$ C) $\dfrac{3}{7}$ D) $\dfrac{1}{6}$ E) $\dfrac{5}{6}$

18) If $d_1 \| d_2$ and $d_3 \| d_4$ and $\alpha=60^0$ in the figure, x=?

A) 100   B) 110   C) 120

D) 130   E) 140

19) There are three copy machines in a stationery shop. Cost of copy with machine A, B and C are 4, 6 and 12 cents per page respectively. A customer gets 24 pages copied in machine C. If machine A were used for this job, how many pages could have been copied?

A) 62   B) 66   C) 72   D) 74   E) 75

20) If |AB|=5, |BD|=3, |DC|=6 and $\angle ADC=90^o$ in the figure, sinx+tany=?

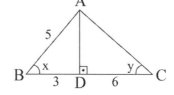

A) $\frac{22}{13}$ B) $\frac{22}{17}$ C) $\frac{22}{15}$

D) $\frac{22}{19}$ E) $\frac{22}{23}$

21) The following graph shows the number of female and male students in four classes in a school. Which of the following information is false according to the graph?

A) The total number of students is 72.

B) The ratio of total female students to total male students is 19/17

C) The ratio of female students to male students in class A is 1.

D) The highest percentage of female students is in class A.

E) The total number of students is 82.

22) If there are 12 American, 18 French and 8 German passengers in a plane, what is the probability of first two passengers disembarking both being American?

A) $\frac{66}{703}$ B) $\frac{55}{603}$ C) $\frac{44}{501}$ D) $\frac{22}{509}$ E) $\frac{33}{405}$

23) The following table shows the costs and profit ratios of some books. If selling some physics books brings $702 of revenue, how many physics books have been sold?

Book Type	Cost	Income Ratio
Math	60	25
Physics	90	30
Chemistry	40	10
Biology	80	80

A) 6   B) 5   C) 8   D) 9   E) 7

24) The following table shows the values of a non–linear function. Find out this function.

N	0	1	3	-1	-2
f(n)	3	6	30	$-1\frac{1}{3}$	$3\frac{1}{9}$

A) $f(n)=2^n+2$ B) $f(n)=3^n+3$ C) $f(n)=3^n+2$

D) $f(n)=2^{2n}+4$ E) $f(n)=3^n+5$

25) A summer sports school consists of football and basketball activities. While 30% of the students attend football activities and 50% of the students attend basketball activities only, 60 students attend both activities. How many students attend football activities only?

A) 30   B) 46   C) 60   D) 90   E) 45

26) What is the sum of two polynomials $4x^3+2x^2+3x+4$ and $4x^2-3x-4$?

A) $4x^3+6x^2$ B) $4x^3+7x+6x$ C) $4x^3+6x^2+4x-3$

D) $4x^3+5x^2+4x$ E) $4x^3+14x$

27) If $\dfrac{2\pi+x}{3}=\dfrac{7}{2}$ then x=?

A) $\dfrac{21-4\pi}{2}$ B) $\dfrac{21+4\pi}{2}$ C) $\dfrac{22+3\pi}{3}$ D) $\dfrac{22-3\pi}{5}$ E) $\dfrac{21+4\pi}{7}$

28) 10 notebooks and 5 pencils cost $9, while 5 notebooks and 10 pencils cost $6. How much does a pencil and a notebook cost?

A) 4   B) 3   C) 2   D) 1   E) 5

29) 27 workers who paint at equal speeds finish painting a school's walls in 86 hours. If 14 workers were hired for this job, about how many hours would it take them to complete?

A) 142   B) 152   C) 166   D) 172   E) 165

30) The condition of staying on course for vehicles on sloping roads is given by $v^2 = g \cdot R \cdot \tan\alpha$, where v is the velocity of the vehicle, R is the radius and α is the slope angle of the road. If the radius of a road is 10m and the slope angle is 45, what is the velocity of the vehicle? (g=10)

A) 14   B) 13   C) 12   D) 10   E) 13

31) What time would it be 1840 minutes after 8:00 am?

A) 2.00 pm   B) 2.40pm   C) 3.00 pm   D) 3.40 pm   E) 2.00pm.

32) How many functions are there in the given graph?

A) 2   B) 3   C) 4
D) 5   E) 1

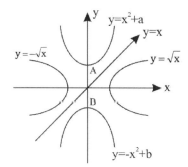

33) $\log_3 3^7 + \log_4 4^8 + 7^{\log_7 4} = ?$

A) 18   B) 19   C) 20   D) 21   E) 22

34) A car park charges 25 cents for an hour. If "h" shows the park hours, which of the following shows the amount of money (m) to be paid by the car owner?

A) 0.25xh   B) 0.75x2h   C) 0.20x4h   D) 0.25x24h   E) 0.34xh

35) log2=a, log3=b, log18=?

A) a+b   B) 2a+b   C) a+2b   D) a-2b   E) a+3b

36) According to the given graph, (m+b)=?

A) 6   B) –6   C) 7
D) –7   E) 8

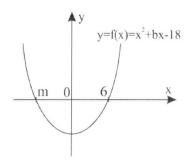

$y=f(x)=x^2+bx-18$

37) All pages in a book are being numbered. During this numbering, the numeral 7 has been used for 21 times. What is the minimum number of pages in this book?

A) 100   B) 102   C) 103   D) 107   E) 104

38) Find $5/14^{th}$ of a number whose $3/7^{th}$ is equal to 6m.

A) 10m   B) 8m   C) 5m   D) 7m   E) 9m

39) A rectangle land of 110m wide and 160m long is to be divided into equal square plots. What is the minimum number of plots?

A) 156   B) 169   C) 176   D) 180   E) 160

40) The given graph shows the number of visitors to a museum between January and May. What is the average number of visitors in January, March and May?

A) 1800   B) 1900   C) 2300
D) 2100   E) 2000

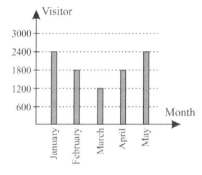

41) The given graph shows the number and models of the cars that a car dealer has sold in a week. Which of the following is wrong according to the graph?

A) Models A and B are the least sold models
B) Average number of cars sold per model is 11
C) Sum of model A and E cars sold is equal to the model C cars sold.
D) Models B and C are the most popular ones.
E) Models A and C are the most popular ones

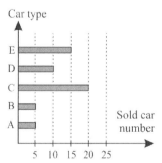

42) Jack wants to put a wire fence around his triangle shaped garden. If two edges of his garden are 14 and 20 m long, what is the maximum possible length of wire fence that could be used?

    A) 60   B) 61   C) 67   D) 68   E) 62

43) Exterior angles of the triangle ABC in the figure are 110 and 134 degrees. Find x=?

    A) 116   B) 118   C) 119

    D) 120   E) 125

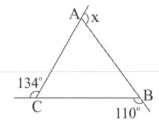

44) Two vehicles with velocities 4v and 3v are to rotate around a 140m–long circular track. How many seconds does it take for them to meet for the first time?

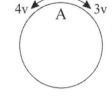

    A) $\dfrac{10}{v}$ B) $\dfrac{20}{v}$ C) 12v

    D) 20v   E) 10v

45) Find the volume of the cylinder which has a radius of 2π cm and height of 3π cm.

    A) $6\pi^2$ B) $12\pi^4$ E) 36

    C) $6\pi^4$ D) $12\pi^2$

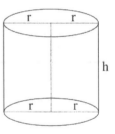

46) Find the area between the line 2x+3y=18, x axis and y axis.

    A) 34   B) 32   C) 34   D) 27   E) 30

47) A rectangle has edges of 20 and 30cm long. If the edges are decreased by 10%, how many cm^2 does the area decrease?

    A) 100   B) 115   C) 120   D) 134   E) 114

48) If x workers finish painting a house within b days, how long would it take for x+y workers to finish the same job?

    A) $\dfrac{x}{x+y}$ B) $\dfrac{xb}{x+y}$ C) $\dfrac{x+y}{xb}$ D) 2x+y   E) $\dfrac{x+y}{2xb}$

49) The given graph shows the number of residents in an apartment building according to their professions. A: doctors, B: teachers, C: engineers, D: faculty members. Which of the following would be the pie chart of this graph?

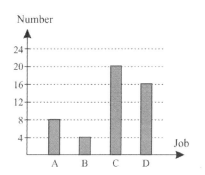

A)  B) 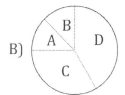 C) 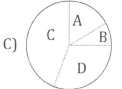 C)

50) Find x in $\begin{cases} \dfrac{1}{x}+\dfrac{3}{y}=4 \\ \dfrac{4}{x}-\dfrac{3}{y}=3 \end{cases}$ equation system.

A) 1/2 B) 1/3 C) 3/7 D) 3/9 E) 5/7

51) How many even numbers are there in [10,125) interval?

A) 44 B) 46 C) 48 D) 50 E) 58

52) The graph given in the figure shows the amount of paper used in five schools. What is the average of least paper consuming three schools? (y axis: school, x axis: packs of paper consumed)

A) 12 B) 13 C) 14
D) 18 E) 20

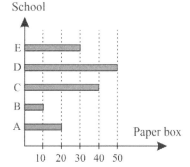

53) O is the center of the circle in the figure, if ∠AOB=64, ∠ACB=?

A) 21 B) 34 C) 33
D) 35 E) 32

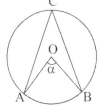

54) Ticket prices of a basketball match are $3 for high school students, $5 for university students and $4 for senior citizens. If 5 high school students, 6 university students and 10 senior citizens go to watch this game, how much do they need to pay?

A) 45   B) 55   C) 55   D) 65   E) 85

55) If $2x^3+3x^2+6x+4-(4x^3-x^2+2x-6)=ax^3+bx^2+cx+d$, then $a+b+c+d=?$

A) 11   B) 12   C) 13   D) 14   E) 16

56) What is the solution (x) for the system of equation $\begin{cases} y \leq -4 \cdot 5^x + 625 \\ y \leq 5^x \end{cases}$

A) 1   B) 2   C) 3   D) 4   E) 5

* Total number of diagonals in a polygon is calculated by the formula $n(n-3)=2D$, where n is the number of edges and D is the number of diagonals.

57) How many diagonals does a heptagon (a polygon with 7 edges) have?

A) 14   B) 12   C) 11   D) 10   E) 9

58) Edges of a regular polygon that has 35 diagonals are 2cm each. What is the perimeter of this polygon?

A) 16   B) 18   C) 20   D) 21   E) 22

59) Given $\angle B=90^0$ and AC=12cm.
The perimeter ABC=?

A) $18\sqrt{3}$ B) $18+6\sqrt{3}$ C) $17+6\sqrt{3}$
D) $8+8\sqrt{3}$ E) 20

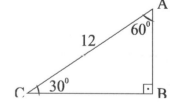

60) The perimeter of a small rectangular garden is 44 feet and its area is 120 square feet. Find the length of the diagonal.

A) $\sqrt{61}$ B) $2\sqrt{61}$ C) $3\sqrt{61}$ D) $\sqrt{5}$ E) 8

TEST – 2.4
- Questions -

1) **If ∠ABD–∠DBC=58⁰, ∠ABD=?**

   A) 119   B) 129   C) 139

   D) 149   E) 159

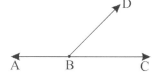

2) $\left(\sqrt{3x} + \sqrt{2x}\right)^2 = ?$

   A) $5x + 2\sqrt{6x}$ B) $4x + 2x\sqrt{6}$ C) $5x + 2x\sqrt{6}$

   D) $6x + 2\sqrt{6x}$ E) $6x + 2\sqrt{3x}$

3) **If f(x)=x²+2x and g(x)=x–2, f(g(2a))=?**

   A) a^2-4a B) a^2+4a C) $3a^2-3a$ D) $4a^2-4a$ E) $4a-4$

4) **Simplify (x+y)²–(y–x)²+(2xy)²**

   A) $5xy+4x^2y^2$ B) $4xy(1+xy)$ C) $3xy(1+2xy)$

   D) $5xy(1+2xy)$ E) $5xy(2+3xy)$

5) $\dfrac{(x + y)^2}{x + y} + \dfrac{(x - y)^2}{x - y} = ?$

   A) 4x   B) 4y+1   C) 2x   D) x+y   E) 4y

6) **Which of the following complex numbers is equivalent to (4+4i)·(3–3i)=?**

   A) 24   B) 24+12i   C) 12+12i   D) 8–8i   E) 8+8i

7) **If (x+2y)²+(y–2x)²=A(x²+y²), which of the following is equivalent to A?**

   A) 3   B) 2   C) 5   D) 6   E) 4

8) Following are the pricing variables of a publishing company.

I. C: Cover in color (vs. black/white)

II. n: More pages (vs. less)

III. v: Pages in color (vs. black/white)

IV. Book in print (vs. e-book)

While anything in color (as opposed to black and white) will increase the price 25%, and e-books cost twice as much as printed books, the number of pages does not change the price of the books. Which of the following should NOT be done by an author who wants his book to be inexpensive?

A) I and II   B) I, II and III   C) I and III   D) III and IV   E) II and IV

9) According to the figure, A^B+B^A=?

A) 80   B) 99   C) 100

D) 120   E) 90

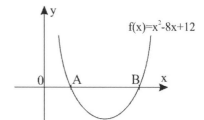

$f(x)=x^2-8x+12$

10) Ticket pricing for a history museum is designated as \$a for children and \$(a+3) for adults. If 160 tickets have been sold and \$880 of revenue has been made in a day, which of the following is the system of solution equations of this problem?

A) $\begin{cases} x+y=160 \\ ax+ay=880 \end{cases}$ B) $\begin{cases} x+y=160 \\ ax+(a+3)y=880 \end{cases}$

C) $\begin{cases} x+y=880 \\ ax+(a+3)y=160 \end{cases}$ D) $\begin{cases} x+y=880 \\ ax+ay=160 \end{cases}$

E) $\begin{cases} 2x+y=880 \\ ax+ay=160 \end{cases}$

11) $\log_3 21$=?

A) 1   B) $\log_3 7$ C) $\log_3 7+2$ D) $\log_3 7+1$ E) 3

12) If $\left.\begin{array}{l}\dfrac{1}{a}+\dfrac{1}{b}=\dfrac{1}{2}\\[2mm]\dfrac{1}{a}-\dfrac{1}{b}=\dfrac{1}{4}\end{array}\right\}$, then $\dfrac{4}{a}=?$

A) $\dfrac{3}{2}$ 　　　　B) $\dfrac{2}{3}$ 　　　　C) $\dfrac{3}{4}$ 　　　　D) $\dfrac{4}{3}$ 　　　　E) 3

13) What is the equation of the line that is parallel to $y = x\sqrt{3} + 3$ and contains the point (3, 4)?

A) y=3x–5 　　　　　　B) $y = x\sqrt{3} + 4$ 　　　　C) $y = x\sqrt{3} - 5$

D) $y = x\sqrt{3} - 3\sqrt{3} + 4$ 　　　　E) y=4x-7

14) An airport charges $200 for planes who use land services for 4 hours, and $300 for 6 hours. Which of the following functions express this linear function ?

A) y=40x+30 　　　　　B) y=50x+33 　　　　　C) y=50x

D) y=20x+50 　　　　　E) y=50x+30

15) Find the solution of the equation 4(x+4)=3(x–3)+3(3–x)

A) 2 　　　　B) -3 　　　　C) 4 　　　　D) –4 　　　　E) 3

16) How many degrees is $\left(\dfrac{\pi}{2}+\dfrac{\pi}{3}+\dfrac{\pi}{4}\right)$ radians equal to?

A) 195 　　　　B) 196 　　　　C) 190 　　　　D) 210 　　　　E) 220

17) If $\dfrac{5}{x} - \dfrac{5}{9} = \dfrac{2}{x}$, x=?

A) 27/5 　　　　B) 27/7 　　　　C)17/5 　　　　D) 17/4 　　　　E) 18/5

18) Which of the following is a member of the solution set of the equation x^2–2x+2=3x–4?

A) 1 　　　　B) 2 　　　　C) 3 　　　　D) 4 　　　　E) 5

19) What is the y intercept of the graph of y–6=6(x–2)?

A) -6   B) 7   C) 8   D) 9   E) 11

20) If $\sqrt{3x+2} = \sqrt{2x+3}$ then $4x^2+4x=?$

A) 2   B) 4   C) 5   D) 6   E) 8

21) How many hours does it take ring together again for three alarms that ring every $\frac{1}{3}$, $\frac{1}{4}$ and $\frac{1}{6}$ hours after the first time they ring together?

A) 1   B) 2   C) 3   D) 4   E) 5

22) $\log_5 125 + \log_3 27 - \log_4 64 = ?$

A) 1   B) 2   C) 9   D) 4   E) 5

23) There are 11 red balls numbered from 5 to 15 and 11 green balls numbered from 7 to 17 in a bag. What is the probability of drawing a ball with an even number on it?

A) $\frac{11}{5}$ B) $\frac{6}{11}$ C) $\frac{5}{9}$ D) $\frac{5}{11}$ E) $\frac{11}{7}$

24) What is the fifteenth term of the arithmetic sequence that begins: 0, 4, 8, 12, ….?

A) 44   B) 48   C) 50   D) 56   B) 60

25) 6% of the eggs collected by each machine in a chicken farm get broken. If there are 2400 starting eggs and m machines in this farm that all eggs have to go through , which of the following functions show the number of good eggs after going through all m machine ?

A) $f(x)=2400+0.94m$ B) $f(x)=2400-0.94m$

C) $f(x)=2400 \cdot (0,6)^m$ D) $f(x)=2400 \cdot (0.94)^m$

E) $f(x)=2400 \cdot (0.094)^m$

26) The function f(x)=0.84x+0.60 shows the height of a newly planted maple tree, where x is the number of years. How many years does it take for a maple tree to reach 5.64m of height?

    A) 6   B) 5   C) 4   D) 3   E) 7

27) How many percent is an equilateral triangle's interior angle of its exterior angle?

    A) 44%   B) 50%   C) 60%   D) 80%   E) %40

28) If $2 \cdot 3^x + 3 \cdot 3^y = 33$ and $3 \cdot 3^x + 2 \cdot 3^y = 27$, then $3^x + 3^y = ?$

    A) 16   B) 15   C) 12   D) 10   E) 14

29) Following graph shows the number of people who go for shopping to a mall in a week. What is the ratio of weekend shoppers to weekday shoppers?

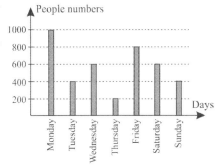

    A) $\dfrac{5}{13}$ B) $\dfrac{5}{14}$ C) $\dfrac{6}{13}$

    D) $\dfrac{1}{3}$ E) $\dfrac{1}{13}$

30) 20 trucks with *8m* of length and *3m* of width can park in a lot. How many cars of *2m* width and *3m* length can park in the same lot?

    A) 60   B) 77   C) 80   D) 90   E) 70

31) Ahmet finishes reading a book within 6 days by increasing the speed pages that he reads by 20 pages per day every day. (second day 20 more than the, third 20 more than the second) If he has read 1/8th of the book in the first day, how many pages is this book?

    A) 1200   B) 1300   C) 1200   D) 1600   E) 1700

32) If |BC|=6 and |DC|=4, |AB|=?

A) $2\sqrt{3}$ B) $2\sqrt{15}$ C) $2\sqrt{14}$

D) $2\sqrt{17}$ E) 14

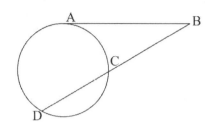

33) Following table shows the number of books and faulty books printed by a publishing company within 3 months. What is the probability of a randomly selected book being a faulty book printed in February?

	January	February	March
Number of published books.	900	1200	1500
Number of faulty books	18	20	30

A) $\dfrac{1}{90}$ B) $\dfrac{11}{190}$ C) $\dfrac{5}{180}$ D) $\dfrac{1}{180}$ E) $\dfrac{11}{180}$

34) Following information about the number of students studying at a school:

- The number of male students who play basketball is equal to the number of female students who play basketball.
- 20% of male students and 30% of female students play basketball.
- There are a total of 300 students studying at this school

What is the number of female students who do not play basketball at this school?

A) 80   B) 85   C) 90   D) 94   E) 84

35) If parabolas $y=x^2-6x+13$ and $y=a(x-b)^2+c$ are identical, then $(a+b+c)=?$

A) 0   B) 1   C) 8   D) 22   E) 24

36) Following graph shows the number of students who have graduated from four

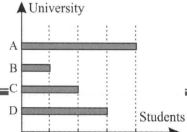

different universities in 2015. Which of the following information is wrong according to the graph?

A) The average number of graduated students is 550.
B) The ratio of greatest number of graduates to least number of graduates is 4/7.
C) The university which is closest to the average is C and D
D) The university with the least number of graduates is B.
E) C) The university which is closest to the average is A and D

Please refer to the following graph for questions 37–39

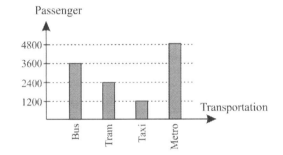

37) The graph shows the four most popular forms of transportation and the daily number of passengers using them in a city. Which of the following is wrong according to the graph? (Bus–Tram–Taxi–Metro)

A) Passengers use metro and tram the most.
B) There are four times more passengers using metro than taxi.
C) The number of bus passengers is 3 times the number of taxi passengers.
D) Tram is the most expensive form of transportation, and bus have the least number of passengers.
E) Passengers use metro and Taxi the most.

38) What is the weekly number of passengers?
    A) 74000   B) 84000   C) 840000   D) 940000   E) 96000

39) What is the average number of passengers for 4 days?
    A) 88000   B) 90000   C) 100000   D) 110000   E) 80000

40) A painting job is completed by x workers within 2^m days. If this job were given to (x+a) workers, how long would it take them to complete?

A) $\dfrac{2^m}{(x+a)}$ B) $\dfrac{2^m}{x-a}$ C) $\dfrac{m \cdot 2^x}{x}$ D) $\dfrac{2^m \cdot x}{(x+a)}$ E) $2x+3a$

41) If A= 40% more of 80 and B=40% less of 80, A/B=?

   A) $\dfrac{7}{3}$ B) $\dfrac{7}{4}$ C) $\dfrac{8}{5}$ D) $\dfrac{8}{7}$ E) $\dfrac{7}{5}$

42) Following graph shows the number of book pages that a student reads in 5 days. How many pages does he read daily on average?

   A) 320 B) 345 C) 360
   D) 380 E) 340

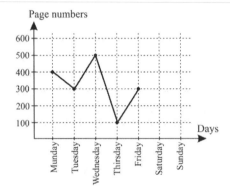

43) Following graph shows the amount of water in a pool with respect to time while it is being emptied. How long does it take to empty this pool?

   A) 1 hour and 23 minutes
   B) 1 hour and 30 minutes
   C) 3 hour and 6 minutes
   D) 2 hours and 30 minutes
   E) 3 hours and 25 minutes

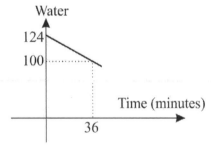

44) x_1 and x_2 being the roots of equation $x^2-5x+6=0$, $|x_1-\pi|+|x_2-\pi|=$?

   A) 2π B) 5 C) $5-2\pi$ D) $2\pi-5$ E) 6

45) 10 notebooks and 6 pencils are sold together for $57 in a stationery shop. If 4 notebooks could be bought for the price of 9 pencils in this shop, how much does a notebook cost?

   A) 4.5 B) 4.8 C) 3.5 D) 3 E) 4

46) Which of the following graphs have a constant function?

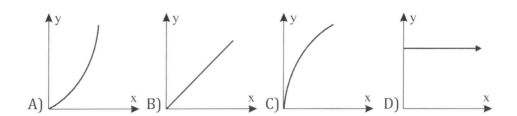

47) Which of the following is the equation of the line perpendicular to 4x+5y+20=0 line?

A) y=2x+5

B) $y = \dfrac{5x}{4} + 5$

C) y=6x+13

D) $y = \dfrac{-5x}{4} + 6$

E) y=4x+6

48) Which of the following graphs show the solution set of 3x+2y≥12 equation?

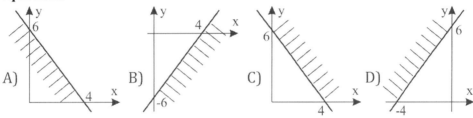

49) According to the graph,

$\dfrac{f(-6) + f(-4)}{f^{-1}(6)} = ?$

A) $\dfrac{5}{9}$

B) $\dfrac{7}{3}$

C) $\dfrac{-3}{7}$

D) $\dfrac{-7}{3}$

E) $\dfrac{3}{7}$

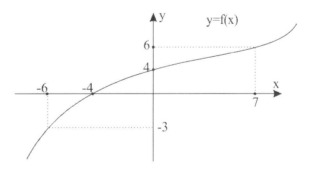

50) The edges of the diameter of a circle are located at (–8, 4) and (8, 4). Which of the following is the equation of this circle?

A) x²+y²=32

B) x²+(y+4)²=32

C) x²+(y+8)²=32

D) x²+(y-4)²=64

E) x²+(y-6)²=64

51) A father is 32 years old and a mother is 28 years old, while their children are 8, 6 and 4 years old. What will the ratio of the sum of parents' age to the children's age be in 6 years?

A) 2   B) -2   C) 3   D) -3   E) 5

52) If $d_1 \parallel d_2$ in the following figure, $\dfrac{x}{2} + 2y = ?$

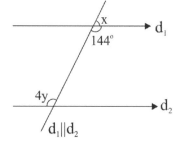

A) 75   B) 80   C) 85

D) 90   E) 95

53) What is the ratio of the sum of first four positive even numbers to the sum of first four prime numbers?

A) $\dfrac{20}{13}$ B) $\dfrac{20}{19}$ C) $\dfrac{21}{17}$ D) $\dfrac{17}{23}$ E) $\dfrac{20}{17}$

54) A publishing company publishes 48000 books in 2004 and 50000 books in 2005. If this company uses $P(b) = m \cdot n^b$ function as model, where m is the number of books published in 2004 and b is the number of years after 2004, find the closest value of n to the nearest hundredth.

A) 1.2   B) 1.3   C) 1.7   D) 1.09   E) 1.04

55) Jack reads 200 pages of books daily. Since he wants to read books more, he increases his daily pages for 10% every day, rounded to the nearest whole number. How many pages would he read in 4 days?

A) 428   B) 525   C) 645   D) 745   E) 928

56) What is the x value that satisfies $2x(2x+6) - 2 = (2x-6) \cdot 2x + 2 = ?$

A) $\dfrac{1}{2}$ B) $\dfrac{1}{3}$ C) $\dfrac{1}{4}$ D) $\dfrac{1}{5}$ E) $\dfrac{1}{6}$

57) If $\begin{cases} 4x - 3y = 14 \\ 2x - y = 10 \end{cases}$, **x−y=?**

    A) -1   B) -2   C) 1   D) 2   E) 3

58) If f(x)=(x+2)^2 and g(x)=4x^2+16x+16, $\dfrac{g(x)}{f(x)} = ?$

    A) 4   B) -4   C) 3   `D) -3   E)5

59) Find the center of circle x^2+y^2+12x+10y+20=0

    A) (6, 5)   B) (-6, 5)   C) (-6, -5)   D) (3, 5)   E) (6,9)

60) If $\dfrac{x+y}{x-y} = \dfrac{3}{2}$**, then** $\dfrac{x}{y} = ?$

    A) 6   B) 5   C) 4   D) 3   E) 7

TEST – 2.5
- Questions -

1) **Simplify the expression: $(6a^2+6a+6)-(4a^2-4a-4)$.**
   A) $a^2-10a+10$ B) $2(a^2+5a+5)$ C) $2a^2-5a+10$
   D) $3a^2-5a+10$ E) $3a^2-5a+12$

2) **Which of the following expressions is equivalent to $x^{\frac{2}{3}} \cdot x^{\frac{3}{2}} \cdot x^{\frac{-14}{6}}$?**

   A) $x^{\frac{1}{6}}$ B) $x^{\frac{2}{7}}$ C) $\dfrac{1}{x^{1/6}}$ D) $x^{\frac{1}{7}}$ E) $2x$

3) **Which of the following expressions is equivalent to**
   $$\frac{3}{2}\left(\frac{1}{a}+\frac{1}{b}+\frac{1}{c}\right) - \frac{6}{4}\left(-\frac{1}{a}+\frac{1}{b}+\frac{1}{c}\right) = ?$$

   A) a B) $2a$ C) $\dfrac{3}{a}$ D) $\dfrac{3}{a+b+c}$ E) $3a$

4) **If parabola $y=x^2-6x+5$ intercepts x axis at x_1 and x_2, then $\dfrac{\sqrt{x_1}+\sqrt{x_2}}{\sqrt{5}-1}=?$**

   A) $\sqrt{5}-2$ B) $2-\sqrt{5}$ C) $\dfrac{3-\sqrt{5}}{2}$ D) $\dfrac{3+\sqrt{5}}{2}$ E)
   $2-\sqrt{26}$

5) **If $6a+4b+8c=24$, what is the value of $15a+10b+20c$?**
   A) 60   B) 62   C) 70   D) 80   E) 65

6) **Formula $A = \pi r^2 \dfrac{\alpha}{360°}$ is used to calculate the partial area of a circle.**
   Express α in terms of A, π and r.

A) $\dfrac{360\pi}{Ar^2}$ B) $\dfrac{A \cdot 360}{\pi r^2}$ C) $\dfrac{\pi r^2}{A \cdot 360}$ D) $\dfrac{180 \cdot A}{\pi r^2}$ C)   E)

$\dfrac{180 \cdot 3A}{\pi r^3}$

7) **Which of the following is not a real number?**

   A) $\dfrac{0}{\sqrt{9}}$ B) 6-4   C) $\sqrt{121}$ D) $-\sqrt{12}$ E) $\sqrt{-14}$

8) **f(x)=ax+b being a linear function, if f(2)=8 and f(3)=4, then 5a+2b=?**
   A) 12   B) 11   C) 10   D) 9   E) 13

9) **Find the area between x and y axes and the line d_1.**

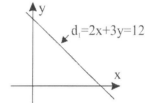

   A) 18   B) 16   C) 15
   D) 12   E) 14

10) **6 notebooks, 4 pencils and 2 erasers cost \$20, while 3 notebooks, 5 pencils and 7 erasers cost \$16. How much does a notebook, a pencil and an eraser cost together?**
   A) 4   B) 3   C) 6   D) 7   E) 5

11) **If DE$\parallel$BC, BC=6x+4 and AD=DB and AE=EC find BC-DE=?**

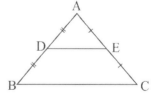

   A) 3x+4   B) 4x+3   C) 3x+2
   D) 2x+3   E) 2x+6

12) $S_n = \dfrac{2a_1 + (n-1)d \cdot n}{2}$ **is the formula for the sum of the numbers in an arithmetic series. What does "d" express in this formula?**

   A) The number of terms in the series
   B) The difference between the terms of the series
   C) Last term of the series
   D) First term of the series

E) Second term of the series

13) "A" is being a real number, if $(3a-4)^7=(a+10)^7$, then a=?

A) 9　　　　B) 10　　　　C) 7　　　　D) 6　　　　E) 8

14) Points B and C are tangent to the circle in the figure. If AB=5, what is the equation of the circle?

A) $(x-5)^2+(y-5)^2=5$
B) $(x-5)^2+(y-5)^2=25$
C) $(x-5)^2+(y+5)^2=5$
D) $(x-5)^2+(y+5)^2=25$
E) $(x-6)^2+(y+5)^2=25$

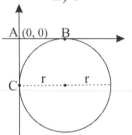

15) If the equation of line d_1 is $y = \sqrt{3}x + 4$ and the equation of line d_2 is y=ax+6 and these two lines are perpendicular to each other, then a=?

A) $\dfrac{\sqrt{3}}{3}$　　　　B) $-\dfrac{\sqrt{3}}{3}$　　　　C) $\sqrt{3}$　　　　D) $-\sqrt{3}$　　　　E) 3

16) What is the smallest number between 230 and 270 which is divisible to both 5 and 13?

A) 139　　　　B) 150　　　　C) 241　　　　D) 255　　　　E) 260

17) ABCDEF is a regular hexagon. If AD=10cm, find out the perimeter of this hexagon.

A) 21　　　　B) 22　　　　C) 25
D) 29　　　　E) 30

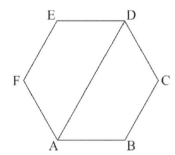

18) If $\dfrac{3+\dfrac{1}{x}}{3-\dfrac{1}{x}} = 3$, find out x.

A) 1/2　　　　B) 1/3　　　　C) 1/4　　　　D) 1/5　　　　E) 2/3

19) If $\begin{cases} \dfrac{3}{x} + \dfrac{3}{y} = 6 \\ 3x - 6y = 0 \end{cases}$, find out x.

   A) 3   B) 4   C) 3/2   D) 3/5   E) 4/5

20) What is the value of "a" in the equation system of $\begin{cases} 3x + 4y = 12 \\ 6x + ay = 24 \end{cases}$, which makes the solution set have infinitely many solutions?

   A) 12   B) 13   C) 15   D) 8   E) 19

21) Sum of a group of friends' ages is 150. If their sum of age will be 250 in 10 years, how many friends are there in this group?

   A) 10   B) 13   C) 12   D) 13   E) 11

22) If $4(x-\pi)+3(\pi-x)=2(\pi+x)$, what is the value of x?

   A) π B) 2π C) -2π D) -3π E) 3

23) Which of the following number is composite?

   A) 2   B) 7   C) 17   D) 23   E) 49

24) What is the degree of: $6x^2y^4+3x^2y^5-2xy^4+6xy-16$?

   A) 3   B) 4   C) 5   D) 6   E) 7

25) If $x = \dfrac{4}{10} + \dfrac{5}{12}$, express $\left(\dfrac{6}{10} + \dfrac{7}{12} \right)$ in terms of x.

   A) x   B) 2x   C) 2x-1   D) 2-x   E) 2x+4

26) According to a survey conducted with 11th graders of a school, 40% of the students want to study computer engineering, 20% medicine, 10% mechanical engineering, and 10% nursing, while the rest do not want to go to college. Which of the following statement is wrong?

   A) 50% of the students want to be engineers

   B) The number of students who want to study medicine is greater than the number of students who do not want to go to college.

C) The percentage of the students who do not want to study college is 20%

D) All the students in this classroom knows what they want after high school ,whether or not they want to go to college.

E) 25% of student want to be engineers.

Please answer the questions 27-28 according to the information below.

Age	Computer Engineering	Economy	Medicine	Civil Engineering
18-20	36	32	26	28
20-22	28	30	22	22
22-24	26	24	20	18
24-26	24	22	16	14

27) **Which of the following is the major that the students aged between 20-24 study at the least ?**

A) Civil Engineering
B) Medicine
C) Economy
D) Computer Engineering
E) Economy and Medicine

28) **Which is the major that the students aged around 25 study the most?**

A) Civil Engineering
B) Medicine
C) Economy and medicine
D) Computer Engineering
E) Economy

29) **Following graph shows the number of questions a student has solved within a week. Find out the total questions that this student has solved in the two days that he/she has solve the most and the least questions.**

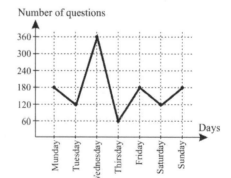

A) 388   B) 390   C) 400
D) 420   E) 380

30) $E_k = \dfrac{mv^2}{2}$ **is the formula for kinetic energy of an object. How much does the kinetic energy of an object change if its velocity is doubled?**

A) increases for 20%
B) increases for 50%
C) increases for 100%
D) increases for 400%
E) increases for 200%

31) **The edges of a triangle are a, b and x. Third edge of a triangle is greater than the difference and smaller than the sum of other two edges. Which of the following inequalities express this term?**

   A) a<x<b   B) b<x<a   C) a-b<x<a+b   D) a-b≤x≤a+b   E) 2b<x<3a

32) **If $\dfrac{\angle ABD}{\angle DBC} = \dfrac{2}{3}$ and ∠B=90° in the figure, z=?**

   A) 34   B) 44   C) 54
   D) 60   E) 66

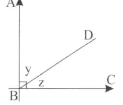

33) **Walls of a school are painted by x workers in b days. If (x+y) workers were to paint these walls, how many days would it take?**

   A) $\dfrac{x \cdot b}{x + y}$ B) $\dfrac{x + b}{x \cdot y}$ C) $\dfrac{x \cdot b}{x - y}$ D) (x+y)·b   E) 2xy

34) **If $\dfrac{1}{3} + \dfrac{1}{4} + \dfrac{1}{12} + \dfrac{1}{x} = \dfrac{1}{6}$ then x=?**

   A) 2   B) -2   C) $\dfrac{1}{2}$ D) $-\dfrac{1}{2}$ E) 3

35) **An electronics shop sells mobile phones for $560. Covers are sold separately to those customers who are interested for $1.85. Which of the following is correct for the equation P=560x+1.85n,**

   A) P shows the number of mobile phones sold.
   B) x shows the number of covers sold
   C) n shows the number of mobile phones sold
   D) n shows the number of covers sold.
   E) n and x shows the number of covers sold

36) If $6 < x \leq 12$ and $4 \leq y < 7$, what is the maximum integer value of x-y?

    A) 10   B) 9   C) 6   D) 7   E) 8

37) Pipe I fills an empty pool within a hours, while pipe II fills within b hours and another pipe at the bottom empties within c hours. Which of the following formula expresses the time to fill this pool when all three pipes are open?

    A) $t = \dfrac{a+b+c}{a \cdot b \cdot c}$ B) $t = \dfrac{a \cdot b \cdot c}{ab + ac + bc}$ C) $t = \dfrac{a \cdot b \cdot c}{bc + ac - ab}$

    D) $t = \dfrac{a \cdot b \cdot c}{a+b+c}$ E) $t = a \cdot b \cdot c$

38) Solve the equation $2\sqrt{2x+3} + 4 = 13$.

    A) $\dfrac{69}{8}$ B) $\dfrac{8}{69}$ C) $\dfrac{79}{9}$ D) $\dfrac{9}{79}$ E) $\dfrac{7}{59}$

39) Which of the following does not a function?

A) 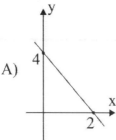   B) 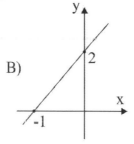   C)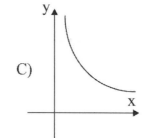

D) 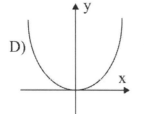   E)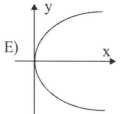

40) Following graph shows the unit price of four of five products and how many of each product has been purchased. If $1600 has been spent

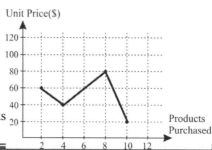

to purchase all these five products, what is the unit price of the last product, knowing that 6 of them were bought?

A) 60   B) 70   C) 88   D) 40   E) 80

41) Following graph shows the number of books published by a publishing company. Which year has this company published 60 000 books?

A) 2002   B) 2004   C) 2005
D) 2008   E) 2006

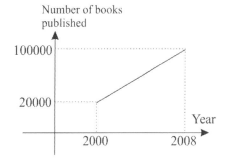

42) What is the complete factorization of the polynomial $144x^4 - 225y^2$?

A) $(14x^2-15y)\cdot(14x^2+15y)$ B) $(12x^2-25y)\cdot(12x^2+25y)$
C) $(24x^2-25y)\cdot(14x^2+15y)$ D) $(12x^2-15y)\cdot(12x+15y)$
E) $(12x^2-15y)\cdot(12x^2+15y)$

43) According to the given graph, $\dfrac{f(-2)+f(3)}{f(5)} = ?$

A) $-\dfrac{4}{5}$ B) 0   C) $-\dfrac{5}{4}$

D) 2   E) 3

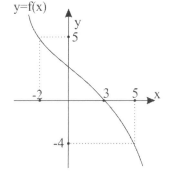

44) Which of the following is the graph for $y \geq x^2-4x-12$?

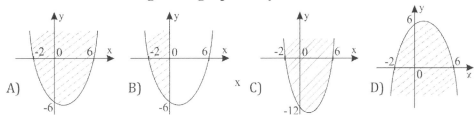

A)   B)   C)   D)

45) How much does the area of a square change if both edges are decreased for 10%?

A) Area decreased for 19%

B) Area decreased for 81%

C) Area decreased for 21%

D) Area decreased for 9%

E) Area decreased for 12%

46) **How many of the following parabolas are concave upwards?**

I) $y=x^2-6x+9$ II) $y=(x-2)^2$ III) $y=(1-x)^2$

IV) $y=-x^2+8x+16$ V) $y=-(x-7)^2$

A) 1   B) 2   C) 3   D) 4   E) 5

Please answer the questions 47-48 according to the information below.

Below table shows the results of a survey about future professions conducted with 11th graders of a school.

	Doctor	Comp. Eng.	Accountant	Teacher
Girl	20	12	18	18
Boy	10	18	16	10
Total	30	30	32	28

47) **What is the probability of a student chosen being a male or a computer engineering wannabe?**

A) $\dfrac{3}{4}$ B) $\dfrac{4}{5}$ C) $\dfrac{5}{4}$ D) $\dfrac{11}{20}$ E) $\dfrac{4}{7}$

48) **What is the probability of a student chosen being a female or a teacher wannabe?**

A) $\dfrac{19}{30}$ B) $\dfrac{37}{60}$ C) $\dfrac{35}{37}$ D) $\dfrac{47}{120}$ E) $\dfrac{57}{120}$

49) **Following graph shows the number of vehicles using 6 different tollways in a city per hour. Which of the following information is wrong?**

A) Maximum number of vehicles in an hour is 2300

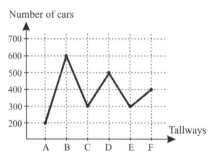

B) B, D and F are the most popular
   tollways
C) Tollways C and E have been used by 600 vehicles in total .
D) Tollways A and B have been used by 2000 vehicles in 2 hours.
E) A,B and F are the most popular tollways

50) What is the slope of the line that passes through A(6, 4) and B(2, 8)?

   A) 1   B) 2   C) -1   D) 2   E) 3

51) 70% of the 6000 spectators who have watched a football game were adult males, where 20% were adult females and the rest were children. What is the ratio of the adult females to children ?

   A) 1   B) 2   C) 3   D) 4   E) 6

52) What is the sum of perimeters of all triangles in the figure?

   A) 32   B) 36   C) 42
   D) 44   E) 46

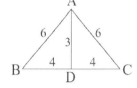

53) A football team plays a match every 2 weeks on average. If a game lasts for 90 minutes, how many hours of football do they play in a year?

   A) 19   B) 22   C) 30   D) 36   E) 39

54) If $ax^2+bx+c=(2x+4)^2$, then a+b+c=?

   A) 32   B) 33   C) 34   D) 35   E) 36

55) The ratio of edges of two cubes is 3:2. What is the ratio of their volumes?

   A) $\dfrac{17}{8}$ B) $\dfrac{17}{9}$ C) $\dfrac{20}{7}$ D) $\dfrac{21}{8}$ E) $\dfrac{27}{8}$

56) If f(x)=4x+3 and g(x)=2x+4, $\dfrac{f(g(2))}{g(f(3))}=?$

   A) $\dfrac{35}{44}$ B) $\dfrac{35}{34}$ C) $\dfrac{38}{43}$ D) $\dfrac{35}{19}$ E) 2

57) What is the sum of x values that satisfy y=3x+2 and y=(x-1)^2+5 conditions?

A) 1   B) 2   C) 3   D) 4   E) 5

58) If the difference between 30% and 24% of a number is 12, find the half of this number.

A) 40   B) 50   C) 60   D) 80   E) 100

59) f(x)=3x+3, g(x)=2x+2, f(g(2))=?

A) 16   B) 19   C) 20   D) 21   E) 18

60) If a circle has an area of $\sqrt{5}$, find its radius.

A) $\dfrac{\pi}{\sqrt{5}}$ B) $\sqrt{\dfrac{5}{\pi}}$ C) $\sqrt{\dfrac{\pi}{5}}$ D) π E) 5

TEST – 2.6
- Questions -

1) 8 workers who are equally powerful work for 24 days to complete a job. Had only 6 workers worked, how long would it take them to complete the same job?

   A) 30 days   B) 32 days   C) 34 days   D) 36 days   E) 38 days

2) If f(x)=2x+3 and g(x)=4x+3, then 2f(2)+3g(3)=?

   A) 59   B) 44   C) 47   D) 46   E) 48

3) The formula for projective motion is given as $S = \dfrac{V_0^2 \cdot \sin 2\alpha \cdot h}{g}$ which expression in this formula is a constant?

   A) V_o B) α C) h   D) g   E) 2h

4) A car moves from point A to point B for 10km, and then to point C for another 24km. What is the shortest distance between A to C?

   A) 26   B) 28   C) 30
   D) 32   E) 36

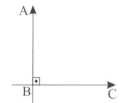

5) y=3(x+4)²–3. Which of the following equations is equivalent to the equation above and shows the x–intercepts as constants?

   A) y=2(x+5)·(x+3)
   B) y=3(x–5)·(x+3)
   C) y=3(x+5)·(x+3)
   D) y=3(x–5)·(x–3)
   E) y=4(x–5)·(x–3)

6) Which of the following is the graph of the equation 4x+3y=24?

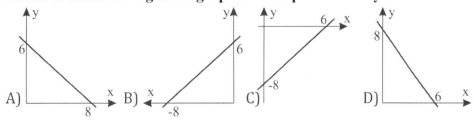

7) **What is the equation of the line whose slope is –2 and passes through (4, 7)?**

A) y=–2x+15   B) y=–2x–15   C) y=3x+14   D) y=–3x–15   E) y=3x+15

8) $\dfrac{4}{7}(x-1)\cdot(x+1)\cdot(x^2+1) = ?$

A) $\dfrac{7}{4}(x^4-1)$ B) $\dfrac{4}{7}(x^4-1)$ C) $\dfrac{4}{7}(x^4+1)$ D) $\dfrac{7}{4}(x^3+1)$ E) $\dfrac{7}{4}(x^5+1)$

9) **If** $\dfrac{a^{5/4}}{a^{4/5}} = a^{\frac{x}{mn}}$, **where m is the tens digit and n is the ones digit, what is** **m+n+x=?**

A) 8   B) 9   C) 10   D) 11   E) 8

10) **Which of the following is the graph of the parabola y=–x²+10?**

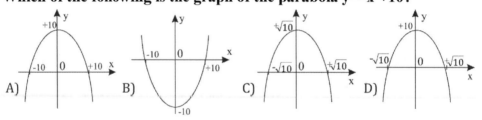

11) **What is the degree of the expression** $(4x^3+5x^2-6)^3+7$?

A) 7   B) 8   C) 9   D) 10   E) 11

12) $\dfrac{2a+1}{5} + \dfrac{2a-1}{3} = \dfrac{3}{15}$ **if** **a = ?**

A) $\dfrac{1}{3}$ B) $\dfrac{2}{3}$ C) $\dfrac{5}{11}$ D) $\dfrac{5}{12}$ E) $\dfrac{5}{16}$

13) **If** $a = \dfrac{4b+8}{3b+7}$, **express b in terms of a.**

A) $\dfrac{8+7a}{3a+4}$ B) $\dfrac{8-7a}{3a-4}$ C) $\dfrac{7-8a}{4-3a}$ D) $\dfrac{7-8a}{4a+3}$ E) $\dfrac{7-9a}{4a+3}$

14) \$3000 amount of money is deposited into a bank account with annual 20% of simple interest. How much money could be withdrawn after 4 years?

    A) 4400   B) 5500   C) 5400   D) 6000   E) 5000

15) $6 \cdot \left(\dfrac{1}{a} + \dfrac{1}{b} + \dfrac{1}{c} \right) - 6 \cdot \left(\dfrac{1}{c} + \dfrac{1}{b} - \dfrac{1}{a} \right)$?

    A) 0   B) $\dfrac{12}{a}$ C) $\dfrac{12}{c}$ D) $\dfrac{12}{b}$ E) 12c

16) If $\sqrt{3x+1} + 3 = 5,$ then x=?

    A) 1   B) 2   C) 3   D) 4   E) 5

17) If f(x)=4x+4 and f(a)=32, then a=?

    A) 2   B) 3   C) 4   D) 5   E) 7

18) If $\dfrac{x^2 + 10x + 25}{x + 5} + \dfrac{x^2 + 5x + 6}{x + 3} = ax + b,$ then $(b)^a$=?

    A) 42   B) 44   C) 45   D) 46   E) 49

19) If 2x+3y=21 and 3x+2y=19, then $(x+y)^2$=?

    A) 54   B) 56   C) 60   D) 62   E) 64

20) What is the ratio of the volume of the cylinder to the volume of the cone according to the figure,

$\dfrac{V_{cylinder}}{V_{cone}} = ?$

    A) 1   B) 2   C) 3
    D) 4   E) 5

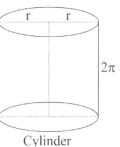

Cylinder   Cone

21) **144000 people visit a museum each year. How many people visit this museum in 4.5 months?**

   A) 52000   B) 54000   C) 51000   D) 62000   E) 53000

22) **Following are some information about the books in a library:**
   - **2% of the books get lost.**
   - **5% of the books wear off.**
   - **7% of the books need to be renewed.**

   If there are 6000 books in this library, how many books are lost or need to be renewed?

   A) 540   B) 560   C) 580   D) 600   E) 620

23) **Following table shows the number of passengers and their Nationalities in an airplane. What is the probability of the first passenger disembarking being a German or a male?**

	American	German	Italian
Female	30	40	25
Male	20	30	15
Total	50	70	40

   A) $\dfrac{19}{27}$ B) $\dfrac{17}{32}$ C) $\dfrac{21}{31}$ D) $\dfrac{21}{32}$ E) $\dfrac{21}{27}$

24) **Which of the following inequalities show the number of whose square is less than 3 more than 3 times the integer?**

   A) $x^2 \leq 2x+3$ B) $x^2 < 3x+3$ C) $x^2 \geq 2x+3$ D) $x^2 \geq 3x+3$ E) $x^2 \geq 4x+4$

25) $\dfrac{a}{b} = \dfrac{1}{11}$ if $\dfrac{2a+b}{a} = ?$

   A) 11   B) 12   C) 13   D) 14   E) 15

26) **Two workers named Adam and Matt are hired to paint a wall. Adam works twice as fast as Matt, and they finish the job in 24 hours. If Matt were hired alone for this job, how many hours would he need to complete?**

   A) 24   B) 37   C) 48   D) 72   E) 36

27) **If one of two numbers multiplied together is decreased by 20% and the other is increased by 60%, how would the result change?**

A) Decreases by 11%   B) Increases by 11%
C) Increases by 18%   D) Increases by 28%
E) Increased by 20%

28) **Given x<0, what is the smallest integer value of y that satisfies $6xy-30x<0$?**

A) 6   B) 8   C) 7   D) 6   E) 9

29) **If a=8, $4b(60-8a)^2$=?**

A) 32b   B) 18b   C) –32b   D) 64b   E) 16b

30) **Trucks need to pay $5 more than cars for a toll way. When 80 trucks and 20 cars use this road, $600 of fee is collected. Which of the following equations express the solution of this problem?**

A) 80(x–5)+20x=600   B) 80(x+5)+20x=600
C) 20(x+5)+80x=600   D) 20(x+5)+80x=600
E) 20(X+6)+60X=700

Please refer to the table below for questions 31–32.

Road	A	B	C
Road1	60	50	80
Road2	40	50	80
Road3	80	40	60

The table above shows the cruise speeds of three vehicles in three different roads, per hour.

31) **How far would vehicles A, B and C travel in 3 hours on Road 2 in total?**

A) 510   B) 530   C) 544   D) 560   E) 540

32) **What is the average speed of vehicles A, B and C on road 3?**

    A) 60   B) 65   C) 64   D) 68   E) 66

33) **The graph above shows the most popular sports activities and the number of students attending to these activities at a school. Which of the following information about the graph is correct?**

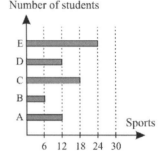

A → volleyball,
B → taekwondo,
C → tennis,
D → football,
E → basketball

A) The number of students attending tennis activities is twice the number of student attending football activities.

B) The number of students attending to volleyball activities and tennis activities are equal.

C) The number of students attending tennis and basketball activities are 44.

D) The number of students attending to volleyball activities is twice the number of student attending to taekwondo activities.

E) The number of students attending tennis and basketball activities are 66.

34) **A university has 40,000 students, while there are 80,000 books in its library, and 25,000 students use the library in a year. Which of the following is correct according to the information above ?**

A) 50% of the students use the library.

B) The number of books is less than the number of students.

C) 15,000 students do not use the library in a year.

D) The avarage number of books per student is 4.

E) The avarage number of books per student is 8

35) **Which of the following expressions indicate the difference of the sum of Grade 1 students and the sum of Grade 2 students?**

	Average age of 10 students	Average age of 15 students
Grade 1	X	
Grade 2		x+a

    A) 5x+15a   B) 6x+15a   C) 10x+15a   D) 5x+5a   E) 6x+7a

36) Solve the equation: 6(10-n)=4(n+8) for n.

    A) 2   B) 2.6   C) 2.8   D) 3   E) 3.8

Please refer to the table below for questions 37–38.

	Airline A	Airline B	Airline C	Airline D
Male	400	500	600	300
Female	300	400	700	400

The table above shows the number of daily passengers of four airlines.

37) What is the ratio of the number of females on their favorite airline to the entire number of female passengers?

    A) $\dfrac{6}{19}$ B) $\dfrac{7}{19}$ C) $\dfrac{7}{18}$ D) $\dfrac{8}{19}$ E) $\dfrac{7}{11}$

38) What is the ratio of the number of males on their least favorite airline to the total number of male passengers?

    A) $\dfrac{1}{3}$ B) $\dfrac{1}{4}$ C) $\dfrac{1}{5}$ D) $\dfrac{1}{6}$ E) $\dfrac{1}{8}$

Please refer to the graph below for questions 39–40.

The graph shows the number of passengers using an airport in a week.

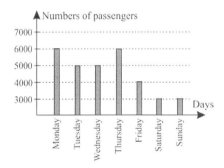

39) What is the ratio of average daily passengers in weekdays to the average daily passengers in weekends?

    A) $\dfrac{26}{15}$ B) $\dfrac{26}{17}$ C) $\dfrac{27}{16}$ D) $\dfrac{27}{17}$ E) $\dfrac{29}{17}$

40) Which of the below information about the graph is correct?

    A) The numbers of passengers using the airport on Monday and Tuesday are equal to each other.

    B) The avarage number of passengers on Monday and Tuesday is 5,000

    C) Total number of passengers on Tuesday and Friday is 9,000

    D) A total of 7,000 passengers have used the airport during the weekend.

    E) Total number of passengres on Tuesday is 6000

41) Which of the following are the roots of equation $y-3=4x^2+9x+2$?

A) $\left(1, \dfrac{4}{5}\right)$ 　　B) $\left(-1, \dfrac{5}{4}\right)$ 　　C) $\left(-1, -\dfrac{5}{4}\right)$ 　　D) $\left(2, \dfrac{4}{5}\right)$ 　　E) $\left(2, \dfrac{3}{7}\right)$

42) $d_1\|d_2\|d_3$, $x+y=$?

A) 70
B) 88
C) 90
D) 100
E) 80

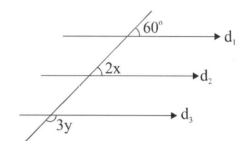

43) If $x^2=x+2$, then $x^2+x^3+x^4=$?

A) $10x+8$ 　　B) $8x+12$ 　　C) $9x+10$ 　　D) $10x+6$ 　　E) $8x+10$

44) If O is the center of the circle in the figure with a radius of 6cm, and $x=\angle AOB \rightarrow \angle ACB=30^\circ$, what is the ratio of shaded region to unshaded region?

A) $\dfrac{1}{11}$ 　　B) $\dfrac{2}{11}$ 　　C) $\dfrac{4}{11}$

D) $\dfrac{5}{11}$ 　　E) $\dfrac{3}{11}$

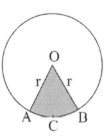

45) How many parabol are there in the graph?

A) 1 　　B) 2 　　C) 3
D) 4 　　E) 0

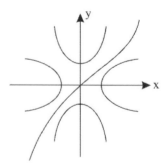

46) If x and y are integers, and $-7\leq x\leq 14$ and $5\leq y\leq 12$, what is the greatest value of $\dfrac{2x+6}{y+6}$?

A) $\dfrac{34}{13}$ 　　B) $\dfrac{34}{11}$ 　　C) $\dfrac{36}{11}$ 　　D) $\dfrac{36}{13}$ 　　E) 3

47) If $2x = \dfrac{3a}{3y+2}$, then $6xy+3+4x = ?$

A) 4a+5   B) 4a+3   C) 3a+3   D) 3a+2   E) 4a+4

48) Find the coordinates of the center of the circle with equation $x^2+y^2+6x+8y+10=0$?

A) (6, 8)   B) (−6, −8)   C) (−3, 4)   D) (−3, −4)   E) (4,8)

49) $\dfrac{x^2+4x+3}{(x+1)} + \dfrac{x^2+9x+14}{(x+2)} = ?$

A) x+10   B) 3x+10   C) 2x–10   D) 2x+10   E) 3x+12

50) Which of the following is the equation of the circle in the figure?

A) $x^2+y^2=5$
B) $x^2+y^2=5^2$
C) $x^2+y^2=\sqrt{5}$
D) $x^2+y^2=625$
E) $x^2+y^2=10$

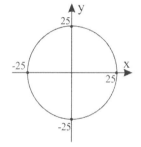

51) The number of male athletes in a group of 57 is one more than three times of the female athletes. How many female athletes are there in this group?

A) 14   B) 15   C) 16   D) 17   E) 18

52) What is the minimum integer value of x that satisfies $\dfrac{x}{3} - \dfrac{x}{7} > 4$?

A) 12   B) 16   C) 18   D) 20   E) 22

53) If 3x+3y=21, then 5x+5y=?

A) 31   B) 32   C) 33   D) 34   E) 35

54) If 300g of walnuts are sold for $4.2 how much does 800g of walnuts cost?

A) 9   B) 10   C) 11   D) 11.2   E) 12.2

55) Copy machine A can copy 40 pages in a minute, while copy machine B can copy 50 pages. How many pages can be copied in 6 minutes by using both machines?

A) 340   B) 370   C) 440   D) 450   E) 540

56) The perimeter of a square is 40cm. What will the new perimeter be, if the edge length is decreased by 10 % how many percent?

A) 23   B) 27   C) 30   D) 32   E) 36

57) What is the sum of x values that satisfy the conditions of y=3x+1 and y=−3(x+2)^2+1 equation system?

A) 1   B) 2   C) 3   D) -5   E) 5

58) A class consists of 6 female and 8 male students. If the average age of female students is 15 and the classroom average is 18, what is the average age of male students?

A) 12   B) 16   C) 18   D) 20   E) 20.25

59) If x-6=y, then evaluate the value of |4x-4y| + |6y-6x|.

A) 60   B) 55   C) 40   D) 30   E) 50

60) $\begin{cases} 2a + 3b = 12 \\ 3a + 2b = 13 \end{cases}$, a+b=?

A) 5   B) 5.5   C) 7   D) 4   E) 6

TEST – 2.7
- Questions -

1) Jack completes a task in 2x days, while it takes 2y days for Arthur to complete the same task. If they work together, they complete it in 7 days. Express y in terms of x .

A) $\dfrac{7x}{2x+7}$　　B) $\dfrac{7x}{2x-7}$　　C) $\dfrac{2x+7}{2x}$　　D) $\dfrac{2x-7}{2x}$　　E) 7x-6

2) If f(x)=x^2+4x and f(x+1)=ax^2+bx+c, a+b+c=?

A) 11　　　　B) 12　　　　C) 13　　　　D) 14　　　　E) 10

3) The Sum of the ages of a mother and daughter is equal to 50, while the ratio of their ages is to 4. Which of the following is the set of solution equations for this problem, if x is the mother age and y is the daughter's?

A) $\begin{cases} x+y=50 \\ x-y=0 \end{cases}$　　　　B) $\begin{cases} x+y=50 \\ x+2y=0 \end{cases}$　　　　C) $\begin{cases} x+y=50 \\ x-4y=0 \end{cases}$

D) $\begin{cases} x+y=50 \\ 2x+y=0 \end{cases}$　　　　　　E) $\begin{cases} x+y=50 \\ 2x+y=0 \end{cases}$

4) Which of the following expressions is true for the equation 6(x–3)=6(3–x)?

A) These exist no solution set
B) The solution set consists of two roots
C) One of the solutions of this equation is negative
D) The solution set of the equation is {3}
E) The soultion set of the equation is (4)

5) The table below shows the amount of fish caught in a city located at sea shore. In which year the amount of fish caught has increased the most by percentage?

Year	Fish caught (tons)
2010	20,000
2011	24,000
2012	30,000
2013	32,000
2014	38,000

A) 2010　　　B) 2011　　　C) 2012　　　D) 2013　　　E) 2014

6) The relationship between the purchasing price and sale price of a good is given in the above graphic. What is the profit margin of this good?

A) 30%   B) 40%   C) 45%
D) 50%   E) 55%

7) $\dfrac{2x^2 - 98}{x^2 - 14x + 49} = ?$

A) $\dfrac{x+7}{x-7}$ B) $\dfrac{2x+7}{x-7}$ C) $\dfrac{2x+14}{x-9}$ D) $\dfrac{2x+14}{x-7}$ E) $2x+7$

8) If $f(x)=x^2+4$ and $g(x)=1-x$, which of the following expressions is correct for $f(g(x))$?

A) This function is of third degree
B) The constant of the function is 4
C) The cooficient of x is -2
D) When the graph of this new function drawn, it would be concave dawnwards.
E) The constant of the function is 8

9) If $f(x)=x^2+3x$, then $f(2x)=?$

A) $4x^2+6x$ B) $6x^2+4x$ C) $4x^2+4x$ D) $6x^2+6x$ E) $4x+3$

10) If $f(6-x)=x^2+2x+3$, $f(8)=?$

A) 6   B) 5   C) 4   D) 3   E) 7

11) Each edge of the cube in the figure is 5cm. What is ratio of the total surface area to the volume of this cube?

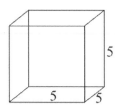

A) $\dfrac{5}{6}$ B) $\dfrac{6}{5}$ C) $\dfrac{4}{3}$

D) $\dfrac{3}{4}$ E) $\dfrac{5}{7}$

12) A bookstore profits $480 if it sells the SAT books for $20, and loses $180 if it sells for $16. Which of the following is the solution set of this problem?

A) 20x–480=16x–180

B) 20x+480=16x+480

C) 20x–480=16x+180

D) 16x–480=20x+180

E) 16x-380+20x+180

13) If ∠C=90°, and |AB|=6cm. What is the ratio of the perimeter to the area of the triangle in the figure?

A) $\dfrac{6+\sqrt{3}}{3\sqrt{3}}$

B) $\dfrac{6+2\sqrt{3}}{3\sqrt{3}}$

C) $\dfrac{4+2\sqrt{3}}{3\sqrt{3}}$

D) $\dfrac{5+2\sqrt{3}}{3\sqrt{3}}$

E) $\dfrac{5+7\sqrt{3}}{3\sqrt{3}}$

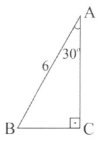

14) If lines y=mx+b and y=nx+c are perpendicular to each other, which of the following expressions is correct?

A) m=n   B) m+n=0   C) m·n=–1   D) $m = \dfrac{-1}{c}$ E) 2m+n=0

15) If points A(2, 4), B(3, 7) and C(6, y) are on the same line, find the value of y.

A) 11   B) 13   C) 14   D) 16   E) 12

16) Following are the prices of books at a bookstore:

– math: $4

– physics: $5

– chemistry: $6

How many math books could be bought with the amount of money paid for 12 physics books?

A) 15   B) 16   C) 17   D) 18   E) 19

17) If $\dfrac{a+b}{b} = 11$, $\dfrac{b}{a+b} = ?$

A) $\dfrac{1}{3}$ B) $\dfrac{1}{5}$ C) $\dfrac{1}{7}$ D) $\dfrac{1}{8}$ E) $\dfrac{1}{11}$

18) What is the value of m in the inequality $4(2m+3) - 3m > -13$?

    A) m>6   B) m<–5   C) m>7   D) m>–6   E) m>–5

19) If the equation of the line d_1 is $ax+by+c=0$, then $a+b+c=$?

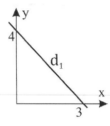

    A) 3   B) 4   C) 6

    D) –4   E) –5

20) If $f(2x–4)=x^2+3x+4$, then $f(6)=$?

    A) 22   B) 34   C) 41   D) 43   E) 44

21)

A	B	C	D

The total weight of four boxes A, B, C and D is 424kg. Boxes A and C have equal weights and B weights 44kg more than D. What is the total weight of two boxes A and D?

    A) 190   B) 198   C) 202   D) 205   E) 210

22) What is the volume of the cube whose total surface area is $24x^2$ cm^2 ?

    A) 8x   B) $8x^2$ C) $8x^3$ D) 9x   E) $16x^3$

23) What is the solution set of the inequality $\dfrac{x}{2} - \dfrac{x}{5} \geq 6$?

    A) x≥5   B) x≥10   C) x≥15   D) x≥20   E) x=12

24) Which of the following is correct for the equation $\dfrac{x^2 + 6x + 9}{(x+3)^2} = -3$?

    A) There exists no solution set for the equation

    B) There exists a solution set for the equation

    C) The equation has two roots

    D) One of the roots is positive and the other root is negative

    E) The questions has to three roots.

25) If $f(x)=4x^2-8x$ and $g(x)=f\left(\dfrac{x}{2}\right)$, then g(4)=?

   A) 1   B) 2   C) 3   D) 0   E) 5

Please refer to the following graph for questions 26–27.

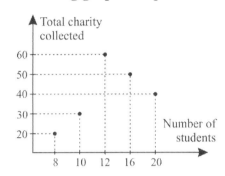

The graph above shows the number of students at five clubs in a school and the charities collected by these clubs.

26) What is the ratio of students of the two clubs which has collected the highest amount of charity?

   A) $\dfrac{3}{4}$ B) $\dfrac{3}{5}$ C) $\dfrac{2}{3}$ D) $\dfrac{4}{7}$ E) $\dfrac{8}{9}$

27) What is the approximate average charity per student?

   A) 5   B) 4   C) 3   D) 3.5   E) 7.5

28) 9/10 of a water tank is full. How many percent of this tank would be empty if 2/3 of the current water in the tank is used?

   A) 70%   B) 60%   C) 40%   D) 35%   E) 44%

29) The three squares in the figure have edge lengths of a, 2a and 3a respectively. What is the ratio of the total area of these three squares to the total perimeter?

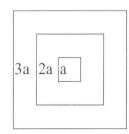

   A) $\dfrac{7a}{12}$ B) $\dfrac{7a^2}{12}$ C) $\dfrac{5a^2}{12}$

   D) $\dfrac{5a}{12}$ E) 4.4a

30) If |AB|=4x and |AC|=x in the right triangle in the figure, cosα=?

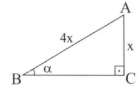

A) $\dfrac{4}{5}$ B) $\dfrac{\sqrt{15}}{4x}$ C) $\dfrac{\sqrt{15}}{4}$

D) 5   E) $\dfrac{7}{9}$

31) A teacher keeps duty at lunch at a boarding school every 5 days ,including weekends. If his first duty is on Thursday, what day will his 11th duty be?

A) Tuesday   B) Thursday   C) Friday   D) Wednesday   E) Sunday

32) A company conducts an exam to the candidates who apply for job. The table below shows the point intervals and the number of candidates who fall into the intervals. If the company plans to recruit 40 people, how many people from the interval of 78–68 points would not be recruited?

Points	Number of candidates
100–90	12
89–79	14
78–68	16
67–57	30

A) 2   B) 3   C) 4   D) 5   E) 6

Please refer to the tables below for questions 33–35.

Following table shows the price of watermelon per kilogram with respect to the months.

Months	May	June	July	August	September
Price	7	6	5	4	3

and the following table shows the percentage of the watermelons that a farmer has sold with respect to the months.

Months	May	June	July	August	September
%	10	20	20	40	10

This farmer has sold 3600kg of watermelon in 5 months.

33) How many kg of watermelon has this farmer sold in July?

A) 600   B) 700   C) 720   D) 800   E) 840

34) **How much money has this farmer earned in August?**

A) 4660   B) 4888   C) 5260   D) 5760   E) 4800

35) **Which month has this farmer earned the least amount of money?**

A) September   B) August   C) July   D) June   E) may

36) **Some students have donated $5 for a charity while others have donated $10 in a school. If $185 has been collected from 25 students, which of the following is the solution equation of this problem, if x is the number of students who donated $10?**

A) $5(25-x)+10x=185$
B) $5(x-25)+10x=185$
C) $10(25-x)+5x=185$
D) $10(x-25)+5x=185$
E) $12(x-10)+10x=195$

37) **What is the 6th term of the geometric sequence 6, 18, 54, … ?**

A) 1248   B) 1348   C) 1468   D) 1458   E) 1558

38) **If the parabola $y=x^2-10x+21$ intercepts x axis at points a and b, $|a-b|$=?**

A) 5   B) 4   C) 3   D) 2   E) 1

Please refer to the table below for questions 39–40.

The Following table shows the percentages of expenses of a private school.

Expenditure	Percentage of total expenses
Salary	40
Food	25
Stationery	15
Transportation	5
Rent	15

39) **If the information in the table were to be given as a pie chart, what would the central angle of the rent expense be in degrees?**

A) 50   B) 52   C) 54   D) 56   E) 55

40) **If the rent costs $120,000, how much does transportation cost?**

A) 60,000   B) 50,000   C) 44,000   D) 40,000   E) 48000

Following table shows the quotation of a bookstore for the library of a school.

Total number of same type books.	Unit price
300 or less	4
301–599	3
600 or more	2

41) How much does the school need to pay for 250 math, 350 English and 602 Science books?

A) 3354 B) 3254 C) 3154 D) 3056 E) 3288

Please refer to the figure below for questions 42–43.

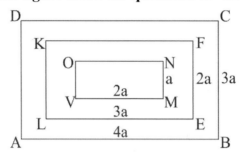

Three rectangles within each other are depicted in the figure.

42) What is the sum of perimeters of these three rectangles?

A) 36a B) 32a C) 30a D) 28a E) 30a

43) What is the sum of the areas of these three rectangles, calculated independently?

A) $26a^2$ B) $25a^2$ C) $24a^2$ D) $20a^2$ E) $24a$

44) $\angle A = \angle B = \angle C$, $|BC| = 12\text{cm}$, $4\angle D = \angle E = \angle F$, $|DE| = 18\text{cm}$. According to the figure $\dfrac{|BC|}{|FE|} = ?$

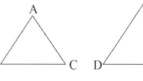

A) $\dfrac{3}{2}$ B) $\dfrac{3}{4}$ C) $\dfrac{3}{5}$

D) $\dfrac{2}{3}$ E) $\dfrac{5}{3}$

45) If $\sin 32^\circ = \cos x$, x=? ($0 < x < 90^\circ$)

    A) 32   B) 39   C) 48   D) 58   E) 38

Please refer to the figure below for questions 26–27.

Years	Physics	Chemistry	Biology
2011	140	100	90
2012	120	90	90
2013	100	80	80
2014	80	60	80
2015	60	60	70

The table above shows the number of books purchased for a high school library with respect to years.

46) About how many percent has purchase of physics books decreased in 2013 with respect to 2012?

    A) 17%   B) 18%   C) 19%   D) 20%   E) 16%

47) What is the average of all books purchased in 2011 and 2012?

    A) 100   B) 105   C) 110   D) 120   E) 130

48) Tables at a picnic area are for 6 and 8, while there are 18 tables in total. If the area can seat 128 people, how many 6–seater tables are there?

    A) 6   B) 7   C) 8   D) 10   E) 11

49) Which is the sum of the polynomials $(-4x^3+6x^2+7x+4)$ and $(4x^2-7x+8)$?

    A) $-4x^3+10x^2+2$ B) $4x^3+10x^2+2$ C) $-4x^3+10x^2-7$

    D) $10x^2+7x+12$ E) $-4x^3+10x^2+12$

50) If ABCD is a parallelogram, and $\angle A = 66^\circ$, $\angle y - \angle x$=?

    A) 48   B) 50   C) 52

    D) 54   E) 56

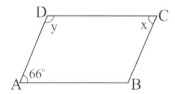

51) Half of a stick is divided into 7 pieces, while the other half is divided into 11 pieces. If the difference between the long and short pieces is 4cm, what is the original length of the stick?

   A) 134   B) 144   C) 148   D) 150   E) 154

52) What is the slope of the line 7x+3y+12=0 ?

   A) 7/8   B) 7/4   C) -7/3   D) 1/7   E) 5/9

53) If ABCDEF is a regular hexagon, ∠AFE=α and ∠FEA=x, then α−x=?

   A) 60   B) 70   C) 75
   D) 80   E) 90

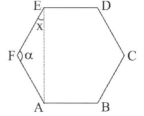

54) Some cards are numbered from 1 to 12 and put in a box. What is the probability of a card drawn having a prime number or a number smaller than 7 on it?

   A) 2/3   B) 2/7   C) 1/5   D) ¼   E) 5/9

55) The ratio of George age to Jack's ages is 4/5 today. What would it be in 10 years, if George is 4?

   A) 12/7   B) 13/7   C) 14/9   D) 14/13   E) 14/15

56) The price of a toy sold with a profit margin of 30% is increased for another 30%. What is the new profit margin of the toy?

   A) 18   B) 28   C) 39   D) 49   E) 69

57) The table below shows the number of aircrafts that belong to four airlines:

Airline	Number of aircrafts
A	40
B	50
C	30
D	60

If the table was to be shown by a pie chart, what would be central angle of airline C be?

A) 34 B) 44 C) 54 D) 55 E) 60

58) The graph above shows the inverse relationship between the distance travelled by a car and the fuel left in the tank. Find out x according to the graph.

A) 1 B) 2 C) 3
D) 4 E) 5

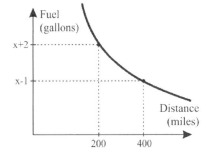

59) ABCD is a parallelogram.
$\angle A = 2x$, $\angle B = 110^0$, x=?

A) 30 B) 32 C) 34
D) 36 E) 35

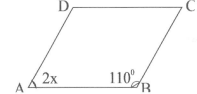

60) d_1: $2x+3y=12$ and d_2: $y=3x+4$. Sum the slopes of lines d_1 and d_2.

A) $\frac{7}{3}$ B) $\frac{6}{5}$ C) $\frac{11}{3}$ D) $\frac{7}{6}$ E) $\frac{11}{7}$

TEST – 2.8
- *Questions* -

1) The graph shows the distribution of the cars sold by three different manufacturers. Which of the following shows the ratio of A:B:C?

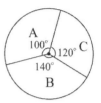

A) 6:5:7   B) 5:7:6   C) 7:5:6

D) 4:5:6   E)1:2:3

2) Which of the following is correct for the equation $7(x+7)+7=6(x+6)+6$?

A) The equation has two roots

B) The solution set of this equation is empty

C) The equation has a positive and a negative root

D) The solution set of the equation is {-14}

E) The questions has three roots

3) m_1 being the slope of the equation $y=3x+4$ and m_2 being the slope of the equation $y = \sqrt{2}x + 6$, $(m_2)^{m_1} = ?$

A) $\sqrt{2}$ B) $2\sqrt{2}$ C) $3\sqrt{2}$ D) 4   E) 2

4) What is the vertex of the function $f(x)=-6x^2+12x+36$?

A) (1, 12)   B) (1, 24)   C) (3, 43)   D) (4, 32)   E) (1, 42)

5) When half of the square of a number is summed with itself, the result is equal to 6 times of the number. Which of the following equation expresses this ?

A) $x^2+x=6$ B) $\dfrac{x^2}{2}+\dfrac{x}{2}=6x$ C) $\dfrac{x^2}{2}+x=6x$

D) $x^2+\dfrac{x}{2}=6x$)   E) $x^2+x=8$

6) If the ratio of A to B is 2:3 and the ratio of B to C is 5:7, which of the following information is correct if A, B and C are integers?

A) The minimum value of A+B is equal to 25

B) The minimum value of B+C is equal to 46

C) The greatest number is B

D) The smallest number is C

E) The smallest number is A

7) A classroom consists of some students who study Turkish, some who study German and some who study neither of them. If
   - 30% of the students study Turkish
   - 40% of the students study German
   - 30% of students study none of them,

   and if the number of students who study both languages is 12, how many students are there in this classroom?

   A) 120   B) 115   C) 100   D) 90   E) 110

8) Find the area between the line 4x+3y-24=0 and, x and y axes.

   A) 12   B) 19   C) 18   D) 24   E) 16

9) The edges of the rectangular prism in the figure are x, 2x and 3x cm. What is the ratio of the surface area to the volume of this rectangular prism?

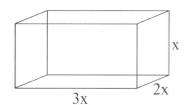

   A) $\dfrac{22}{7x}$ B) $\dfrac{11}{3x}$ C) $\dfrac{3x}{11}$

   D) $\dfrac{13x}{11}$ E) $\dfrac{4x}{11}$

10) How much would the area of a square increase if the edge length is increased for 20%.

   A) 11%   B) 22%   C) 39%   D) 44%   E) 33%

11) The parabola $y=ax^2+bx+c$ intercepts the x axis at points 3 and 4, while it intercepts y axis at 12. Find a+b+c=?

   A) 6   B) 7   C) 8   D) 15   E) 10

12) If |DE|=8, |EB|=4 and |AE|=|EC|, then |AE|=?

   A) $3\sqrt{2}$ B) $4\sqrt{2}$ C) $3\sqrt{5}$

   D) $5\sqrt{3}$ E) $7\sqrt{3}$

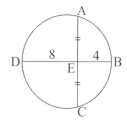

13) If there are 2x+10 female students in a classroom and 40% of the students in this classroom are female, how many male students are there in this classroom?

A) 3x+10   B) 3x+11   C) 3x+15   D) 2x+15   E) 3x+12

Please answer questions 14-15 according to the information below.

Name	Score of Exam 1	Score of Exam 2
Jack	500	620
George	320	380
Michael	120	160
Jessica	820	1060
John	100	124

Following table shows the exam results of five students, while the maximum point for each exam is 1200.

14) Which student has increased his/her score the most by percentage of their first exam?

A) Michael   B) Jessica   C) John   D) Jack   E) George

15) Which student has increased his/her score the least by percentage of their first exam?

A) Jack   B) George   C) Jessica   D) John   E) Michael

16) $3^{\frac{2}{3}} \cdot 3^{\frac{3}{2}} = ?$

A) 1   B) 2   C) $3^{\frac{13}{6}}$ D) $3^{\frac{13}{7}}$ E) 3

17) If $\angle B = 90^{\circ}$, $|AB|=1$ and $|BC|=2$, tanC+cotC=?

A) $\dfrac{3}{5}$ B) $\dfrac{5}{3}$ C) $\dfrac{5}{2}$

D) $\dfrac{2}{5}$ E) $\dfrac{2}{7}$

18) $\dfrac{(x+3)^2 + (x-3)^2}{x^2+9} = ?$

A) x^2+9 B) x^2-9 C) $2x^2+18$ D) 2   E) $\dfrac{x^2-9}{x^2+9}$

19) If $\dfrac{1}{x}+\dfrac{1}{y}=\dfrac{1}{2}$ and $\dfrac{1}{x}-\dfrac{1}{y}=\dfrac{1}{3}$, 5x=?

    A) 11   B) 12   C) 14   D) 15   E) 13

20) If parabola $y=ax^2+10x+25a$ is tangent to x axis and concave upwards, 3a=?

    A) 1   B) 2   C) 3   D) 4   E) 5

21) Jack completes a task alone in 6 days, while Jack and Jessica complete the same task together in 4 days. How many days does it take for Jessica to complete this task alone?

    A) 9   B) 11   C) 12   D) 18   E) 10

22) Which of the following information is correct for the equation $\sqrt{2x+10}=4$?

A) The root of equation is 6

B) There exists no solution set for the equation

C) The only root of the equation is +3.

D) The two roots of the equation are ±3

E) The only root of the equation is 4

23) If the line y intercepts x axis at -6 and y axis at 4, (m+n)=?

    A) $\dfrac{14}{3}$ B) $\dfrac{14}{5}$ C) $\dfrac{13}{3}$

    D) $\dfrac{-13}{3}$ E) $\dfrac{13}{8}$

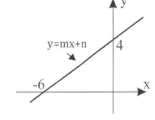

24) Some classrooms in a high school have 12 students, while others have 13 students. If there are 148 students and 12 classrooms in this school, which of the following expressions is the equation system that gives the solution of the problem?

A) $\begin{cases} x+y=25 \\ 13x+12y=148 \end{cases}$ B) $\begin{cases} x+y=12 \\ 13x+12y=148 \end{cases}$ C) $\begin{cases} x+y=12 \\ 13x+12y=169 \end{cases}$

D) $\begin{cases} x+y=25 \\ 13x-12y=148 \end{cases}$ E) $\begin{cases} x+y=26 \\ 13x-12y=148 \end{cases}$

25) Jack designs a book cover in 3 hours 20 minutes and earns $150. About how many minutes does he need to work to earn $1240?

A) 1353   B) 1453   C) 1473   D) 1653   E) 1243

26) The graph above shows the number of female and male spectators who go to watch a team's basketball match with respect to weeks. What is the percentile decrease of female spectators in week III with respect to week I?

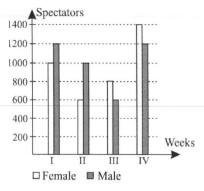

A) 10%   B) 15%   C) 22%

D) 25%   E) 20%

Questions 27-28 are based on the following information:

Some students in a classroom donate $10 for a charity while others donate $20 a classroom. If $360 has been collected from 30 students.

27) Which of the following is the solution equation of this problem?
A) 5(30-x)+10x=360
B) 10(30-x)+20x=360
C) 10(30+x)+20x=360
D) 5(30+x)-20x=360
E) 5(30+2x)+10x=360

28) How many students have donated $20?

A) 3   B) 4   C) 5   D) 6   E) 7

29) If $f(x)=3x^3-3$ and $f(a)=78$, which of the following a values satisfies this condition?

A) 3   B) 2   C) 1   D) 0   E) 4

30) Two vehicles start to move towards each other from cities A and B with constant velocities of V and 2V, and they meet after a time of t. If the distance between these two cities is 90 miles, v·t=?

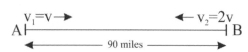

A) 40   B) 33   C) 25   D) 20   E) 30

31) If f(x)=3x^3-x^3+4x^2+2, f(i)=?

    A) -2i-2   B) -4i+2   C) -2i-4i   D) -2i+4i   E) -4i-2

32) Marbles numbered from 1 to 12 are put in a bag. If marbles are not put back into the bag after being drawn, what is the probability of drawing two   prime numbers in a row?

    A) $\frac{5}{21}$ B) $\frac{5}{17}$ C) $\frac{4}{33}$ D) $\frac{5}{33}$ E) $\frac{5}{19}$

Questions 33-34 based on the following information:

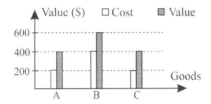

33) What is the profit ratio of the goods A and C?

    A) 55%   B) 75%   C) 150%   D) 200%   E) 50%

34) What is the ratio of average price to average cost?

    A) 7/4   B) 7/5   C) 4/9   D) 7/11   E) 4/11

35) According to the graph, how many kg of olives is necessary to produce 28l of olive oil?

    A) 64   B) 75   C) 78

    D) 84   E) 74

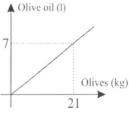

36) What is the equation of of a circle centered at (3, 4) and has a diameter of 10cm?

    A) (x-3)^2+(y-4)^2=100   B) (x-3)^2+(y-4)^2=10

    C) (x-3)^2+(y-4)^2=25   D) (x+3)^2+(y+4)^2=25

    E) (x+6)^2+(y+3)^2=25

37) 30% of the students in a high school are female. If there are 1200 students in this high school, what is the difference between the number of male and female students?

    A) 420   B) 469   C) 480   D) 580   E) 460

38) If |BC|=4cm, and |CD|=16cm, and A(ABC)=7cm^2, A(ABD)=?cm^2

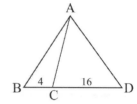

    A) 35   B) 36   C) 40

    D) 44   E) 42

39) The pie chart in the figure shows the ratio of tourists visiting four states. The amount of tourists visiting Oklahoma, Kansas, Arkansas and Texas is proportional with 2, 4, 6 and 8, respectively. What is the central angle of the pie that shows the amount of tourists visiting Oklahoma?

    A) 111   B) 72   C) 54   D) 36   E) 108

40) 6 pencils, 3 erasers and 9 notebooks cost $27. How much would 3 notebooks, an eraser and 2 pencils cost?

    A) 18   B) 13   C) 12   D) 9   E) 15

Questions 41-42 are based on the following information:

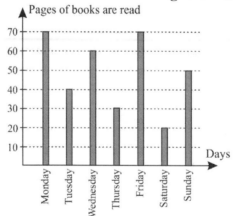

41) The graph above shows the number of pages of books that a student has read within a week. Which of the following expressions is right?

    A) The student has read 80 pages during the weekend

    B) The student has read equal number of pages on Tuesday and Sunday

    C) The student has read the greatest number of pages on Monday and Friday

    D) The student has read the least number of pages on Thursday

    E) The student has read the least number of pages on Sunday

42) **What is the ratio of average number of pages in the weekdays to the average number of pages in the weekend?**

   A) $\dfrac{54}{35}$ B) $\dfrac{59}{35}$ C) $\dfrac{44}{35}$ D) $\dfrac{35}{44}$ E) $\dfrac{39}{26}$

43) **What is the total surface area of the cube with a volume of $27x^3y^3 cm^3$?**

   A) $64x^2y^2$ B) $32x^2y^2$ C) $32xy$ D) $81x^2y^2$ E) $54x^2y^2$

44) **If $\angle B=90^o$, $\angle C=30^o$, $|AB|=x$ and**
   $\angle F=\angle D$, $\angle E=90^o$, $|DE|=y$, $\dfrac{y}{x}=?$

   A) $\sqrt{2}$ B) $\sqrt{3}$
   C) $\sqrt{5}$ D) $2\sqrt{5}$
   E) 5

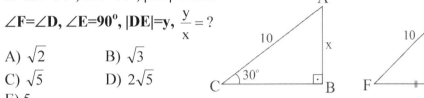

45) $A=\begin{bmatrix} 4 & 3 \\ 2 & 1 \end{bmatrix}$, $B=\begin{bmatrix} 7 & 8 \\ 9 & 7 \end{bmatrix}$ if $A+B=?$

   A) $\begin{bmatrix} 11 & 11 \\ 11 & 8 \end{bmatrix}$ B) $\begin{bmatrix} 11 & 11 \\ 12 & 8 \end{bmatrix}$ C) $\begin{bmatrix} 12 & 12 \\ 12 & 8 \end{bmatrix}$ D) $\begin{bmatrix} 9 & 6 \\ 7 & 3 \end{bmatrix}$ E) $\begin{bmatrix} 6 & 4 \\ 4 & 4 \end{bmatrix}$

46) **The price of 5 math books in a bookstore is equal to 7 physics books. What is the ratio of the price of a math book to a physics book?**

   A) 3   B) 2   C) 1.4   D) 1.8   E) 2.4

47) **Either a rectangle or a triangle is drawn on cards and these cards are put in a box. If the number of rectangles on the cards is twice the number of triangles, and there are totally 55 edges drawn on the cards, how many cards are there with rectangles?**

   A) 12   B) 9   C) 8   D) 4   E) 10

Questions 48-50 are based on the following information:

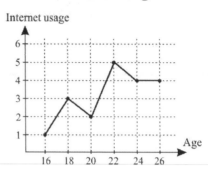

48) **Which two age groups have equal amount of internet usage?**

    A) 16-18   B) 18-20   C) 20-22   D) 24-26   E) 12-24

49) **About h ow many hours of Internet would the 23-year age group use?**

    A) 4.5   B)5   C)5.2   D) 5.6   E) 6

50) **What is the approximate average daily Internet usage of all 16 age groups?**

    A) 3.16   B) 3.25   C) 3.40   D) 3.50   E) 4

51) **If $3<x\leq6$ and $2\leq y<5$, $\max(x^2-y^2)=$?**

    A) 30   B)32   C) 33   D) 334   E) 35

Questions 52-53 are based on the following information:

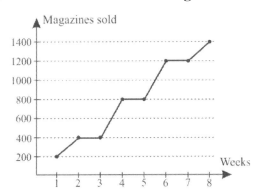

52) **The graph above shows the number of copies sold by a new magazine for 8 weeks. How many weeks has this magazine had constant sales?**

A) 2   B) 3   C) 4   D) 5   E) 6

53) **What two-week interval represent the average sales of magazines over the 8 weeks?**

A) 800   B) 700   C) 600   D) 500   E) 400

54) **According to the four given graphs in the figure, a+b+c+d=?**

A) 3   B) 4   C) 5

D) 6   E) 7

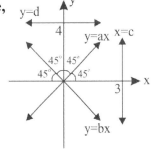

55) **If the parabola $y=x^2-bx+c$ intercepts x axis at 4 and 3, c-b=?**

A) 3   B) 4   C) 5   D) 6   E) 7

56) If the volume of the rectangular prism in the figure is 72cm^3, x=?

A) 1   B) 2   C) 3

D) 4   E) 5

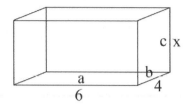

57) What is the total surface area of the prism in the above figure?

A) 102   B) 108   C) 110   D) 120   E) 126

58) If $(\pi-3)^2+(3-\pi)^2=a\pi^2-b\pi+c$, a+b+c=?

A) 5   B) 5   C) 7   D) 8   E) 9

59) If $\dfrac{6n+3}{4}=\dfrac{2n-5}{5}$, then 22n=?

A) 35   B) -35   C) 36   D) -36   E) 34

60) A tin contains 84 lb. of olive oil and another tin contains 105 lb. of flare oil. Both oils will be mixed and filled into bottles of equal volume such that there will be no remaining oil. What is the least number of bottles that are needed?

A) 4   B) 5   C) 6   D) 8   E) 9

TEST – 2.9
- Questions -

1) Which of the following is true for the lines 4x+3y-12=0 and 3x+4y-16=0?

   A) Multiplication of the slopes of these two lines is equal to -1.
   B) Sum of the slopes of these two lines is equal to -25/12.
   C) These two lines are parallel to each other.
   D) These two lines are perpendicular to each other.
   E) First line slope is 4/3

2) Two edges of a right triangle are x and y, while its hypotenuse is z, its area is A and its perimeter is B. Which of the following information about this triangle is true?

   A) x+y=2A and x·y·z=B
   B) x·y=2A and x+y+z=B.
   C) x·z=2A and x+y+z=A.
   D) x·y=2B and x+y+z=A.
   E) x+y=3A, and x.y.z=2B

3) How many elements are there in the solution set of equation $x^2 - 2\sqrt{3}\,x = -3$?

   A) 0   B) 1   C) 2   D) 3   E) 4

4) The perimeter of an equilateral triangle is 30cm. If the edges are decreased for 10%, what would the new perimeter be?

   A) 30   B) 26   C) 85   D) 24   E) 27

5) If the equation of the line d_1 is 2x+3y=12, 2a+3b=?

   A) 12   B) 18   C) 22
   D) 24   E) 20

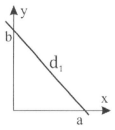

6) **Which of the following information about the graph above is wrong?**

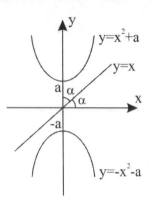

A) The parabolas are symmetrical
B) The angle α is equal to 45°
C) a and –a are the peak points of the parabolas
D) The peak points of the parabolas are (-a, a) and (0, -a)
E) The angel is α is equal to 60

7) **If $(x+2)(x+3)+x+2=(x+a)(x+b)$, then $(a+b)^{(a+b)}$=?**

A) 3^3 B) 4^4 C) 5^5 D) 62 E) 6^6

8) **Which of the following are the roots of equation $x^2+3x=16$?**

A) $-3+\sqrt{73}$ and $-3-\sqrt{73}$ B) $+3+\sqrt{73}$ and $-3-\sqrt{73}$

C) $\dfrac{-3-\sqrt{73}}{2}$ and $\dfrac{-3+\sqrt{73}}{2}$ D) $-3+2\sqrt{73}$ and $+3+2\sqrt{73}$

E) $-4+2\sqrt{73}$ and $+4+2\sqrt{73}$

9) **If $|AC|=h$, $|BC|=6$, $|DC|=8$ and $\angle ACD=90^o$,**

$$\dfrac{A(ABD)}{A(ACD)} = ?$$

A) $\dfrac{7}{4}$ B) $\dfrac{4}{7}$ C) $\dfrac{8}{9}$

D) $\dfrac{9}{8}$ E) $\dfrac{7}{8}$

10) $A = \begin{bmatrix} 12 & 11 \\ 7 & 4 \end{bmatrix}$, $B = \begin{bmatrix} 7 & 1 \\ 8 & 3 \end{bmatrix}$ if $A - B = ?$

A) $\begin{bmatrix} 5 & 10 \\ 1 & 2 \end{bmatrix}$ B) $\begin{bmatrix} 6 & 4 \\ 1 & 2 \end{bmatrix}$ C) $\begin{bmatrix} 6 & 4 \\ 3 & 2 \end{bmatrix}$ D) $\begin{bmatrix} 9 & 3 \\ 7 & 2 \end{bmatrix}$ E) $\begin{bmatrix} 5 & 10 \\ -1 & 1 \end{bmatrix}$

11) What is the area of the circle which has a diameter of 4π cm?

A) 4π B) $4\pi^2$ C) $4\pi^3$ D) $4\pi^4$ E) $8\pi^2$

12) Six of a dozen of eggs are broken. What is the probability of all four randomly selected eggs out of this dozen being broken?

A) $\dfrac{1}{22}$ B) $\dfrac{1}{55}$ C) $\dfrac{1}{66}$ D) $\dfrac{1}{33}$ E) $\dfrac{1}{44}$

13) If $f(x)=x^2+10x+26$ and $g(x)=(x+5)^2$, which of the following show the relationship between $f(x)$ and $g(x)$?

A) $f(x)+g(x)=1$ B) $f(x)-g(x)=1$ C) $f(x)-g(x)^2=1$

D) $f(x)+2g(x)=1$ E) $f(x)=g(x)^2$

14) $f(4)+f(-2)+f(3)=?$

A) -2
B) 12
C) 13
D) 14
E) 11

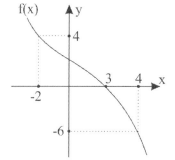

15) $|BD|=|DC|=r$, $|AD|=h$ and $|FE|=|EK|=r$, $|KL|=2h$. According to the information above, find the ratio of volumes, $\dfrac{V_{cone}}{V_{cylinder}}=?$

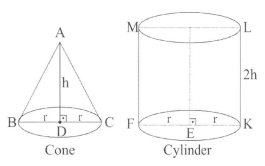

Cone   Cylinder

A) $\dfrac{1}{6}$ B) $\dfrac{1}{3}$

C) 6   D) 3

E) 9

16) ABC is right angle. x=?

A) 20   B) 30   C) 36

D) 40   E) 45

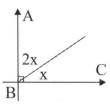

17) What is the Minimum integer value of x that satisfies $4x-16\geq0$ condition?

A) 4   B) 3   C) 6   D) 7   E) 5

18) $A = \begin{bmatrix} 12 & 24 \\ 9 & 15 \end{bmatrix}$, $B = \begin{bmatrix} 2x & 3y \\ 9 & 15 \end{bmatrix}$ if $x + y = ?$

A) 10   B) 11   C) 12   D) 13   E) 14

19) If the radius of the circle is 4cm and $\angle AOB=60°$, What is the perimeter of triangle AOB?

A) 11   B) 12   C) 13

D) 14   E) 15

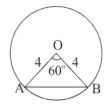

20) ABCD and LEKF in the figure are squares. If |AB|=3a and |FE|=a, what is the ratio of the area of ABCD to LEFK?

A) 6   B) 7   C) 8

D) 9   E) 10

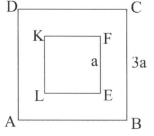

21) Following are the prices of three books in a bookstore:

Math: $2.22

Physics: $6.66

Chemistry: $5.55

If $26.64 has been paid for 6 books, which of the following shows the books bought?

A) 2 math and 2 physics   B) 2 math and 2 chemistry
C) 3 math and 3 physics   D) 3 math and 3 chemistry
E) 4 math and 1 physics

22) A bookstore sells SAT books in 2015 for $15, where the same store has sold these books for $12 in 2014. This bookstore has sold 30 books within 2 years and has earned $420. How many books have been sold for $12?

A) 10   B) 11   C) 14   D) 16   E) 12

23) The graph above shows the number of students according to the distance between their homes and school. How many students live between 4-6 miles to school?

A) 100   B) 110
C) 115   D) 120
E) 130

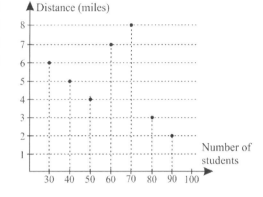

24) If $\angle A = 2\alpha$, $\angle D = 124^\circ$, $\angle B = 2x$ and ABCD is a rhomboid, $x + \alpha = ?$

A) 97   B) 88   C) 86
D) 80   E) 90

25) The graph above shows the price of some nuts with respect to amount. How much does 900g of nuts cost?

A) $5.6   B) $6   C) $6.3
D) $6.9   E) $7.7

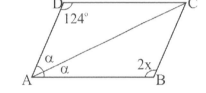

Please answer questions 26-27 according to the information below.

Books read	Female Students
4	5
6	6
8	7
10	8

Books read	Male Students
5	4
7	6
9	8
11	10

The graphs above show the number of students in a classroom and the number of books they have read in 4 weeks.

26) What is the ratio of books read to students, assuming no same book was read twice.?

A) $\dfrac{10}{9}$ B) $\dfrac{10}{7}$ C) $\dfrac{11}{9}$ D) $\dfrac{11}{12}$ E) $\dfrac{11}{8}$

27) What is the ratio of the books read in a week by female students to all the books read?

A) $\dfrac{7}{60}$ B) $\dfrac{8}{70}$ C) $\dfrac{7}{50}$ D) $\dfrac{6}{50}$ E) $\dfrac{7}{66}$

28) Which of the following is the equation of the line above?

A) 2y+x=4   B) 2x-y=4   C) 2x+y=4
D) 3x+2y=6   E) 3x+4y=12

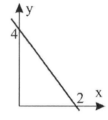

29) The graph above shows the distance covered by a car with respect to time. How far does this car go in 6 hours?

A) 240 miles   B) 250 miles
C) 260 miles   D) 280 miles
E) 260 miles

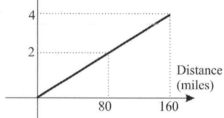

30) What is the ratio of geometrical mean to arithmetical mean of the prime numbers between 5 and 13, not including 5 and 13?

A) $\dfrac{\sqrt{66}}{7}$ B) $\dfrac{\sqrt{77}}{9}$ C) $\dfrac{\sqrt{55}}{7}$ D) $\dfrac{\sqrt{88}}{9}$ E) 11

31) The number of male athletes is four more than three times the number of female athletes in a group of 84 athletes. How many female athletes are these in this group?

A) 20   B) 24   C) 22   D) 23   E) 21

32) **If ABCD is a rectangle and**
$\dfrac{|AB|}{|BC|} = \dfrac{1}{2}$, $\sin\alpha + \cos\alpha = ?$

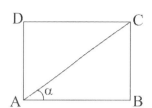

A) $\dfrac{2}{\sqrt{5}}$ B) $\dfrac{3}{\sqrt{5}}$ C) $\dfrac{4}{\sqrt{5}}$

D) $\dfrac{5}{\sqrt{5}}$ E) 3

Please answer questions 33-35 according to the information below. Following table shows the costs and profit margins of the computer brands A, B, C and D.

Brand	Cost ($)	Profit Margin (%)
A	400	20
B	500	25
C	600	30
D	800	10

33) **How many C computers should be sold for $3,900 of sales?**
A) 3   B) 4   C) 5   D) 6   E) 7

34) **How much total profit is made when 2 brand A, 2 brand B, and 2 brand C computers are sold?**
A) 715   B) 780   C) 790   D) 800   E) 770

35) **What is half of the price of the least profit- making brand?**
A) 880   B) 444   C) 430   D) 440   E) 410

36) **What is the ratio of the volume of the rectangular prism to the cube in the figure?**

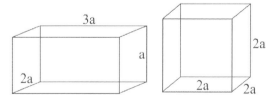

A) $\dfrac{3}{4}$ B) $\dfrac{4}{3}$

C) $\dfrac{2}{3}$ D) $\dfrac{9}{4}$

E) $\dfrac{5}{6}$

37) The table below shows the amount sold and income of four books. Which of these four books is the cheapest?

Books	Amount sold	Income
A	20	1000
B	30	1200
C	40	1600
D	25	6250

A) A   B) C   C) D   D) B and C   E) B

38) What is the average fuel consumption in 100 miles of the car that spends 36 gallons of fuel in 720 miles?

A) 6   B) 5.5   C) 4.4   D) 4   E) 5

39) How many games are played in a basketball league which consists of 8 teams, if teams play with each other for only once?

A) 30   B) 28   C) 25   D) 24   E) 26

40) Jack drives his car with a constant speed of 60 miles per hour. How far would he go in 280 minutes?

A) 320 miles   B) 333 miles   C) 280 miles   D) 260 miles   E) 300 miles

41) What is 40% of the number whose 30% is 6?

A) 14   B) 12   C) 10   D) 8   E) 6

42) $A = \begin{bmatrix} 4 & 3 \\ 2 & 1 \end{bmatrix}$, $B = \begin{bmatrix} 1 & 2 \\ 3 & 4 \end{bmatrix}$ if $2A + 3B = ?$

A) $\begin{bmatrix} 11 & 12 \\ 13 & 14 \end{bmatrix}$ B) $\begin{bmatrix} 12 & 13 \\ 14 & 15 \end{bmatrix}$ C) $\begin{bmatrix} 9 & 10 \\ 11 & 12 \end{bmatrix}$ D) $\begin{bmatrix} 7 & 10 \\ 11 & 12 \end{bmatrix}$ E) $\begin{bmatrix} 13 & 14 \\ 15 & 16 \end{bmatrix}$

43) If lines 2x+3y=12 and ax+7y=16 are perpendicular to each other, what is the value of a?

A) $\dfrac{21}{2}$ B) $\dfrac{-21}{2}$ C) $\dfrac{-23}{2}$ D) $\dfrac{25}{2}$ E) $\dfrac{22}{7}$

44) **70% of the students of a university's civil engineering department consist of international students, while 30% of these international students are Asian. What is the percentage of non-Asian international students in this department?**

Λ) 49%   B) 48%   C) 45%   D) 44%   E) 46%

45) **What is the radius of the sphere whose volume is $160\pi cm^3$?**

A) $2\sqrt{15}$ B) $2\sqrt[3]{15}$ C) $3\sqrt{15}$ D) $3\sqrt[3]{15}$ E) 30

46) **According to the graphs below, m+n=?**

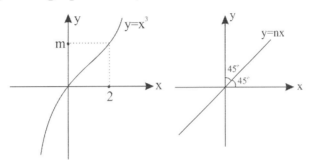

A) 9   B) 10   C) 11   D) 13   E) 12

47) **Water in a 26-liter container in filled into 0.8l bottles. How much water, in liters is there in the last bottle which is partially filled?**

A) 0.4   B) 0.6   C) 0.8   D) 0.9   E) 0.09

Please answer questions 48-50 according to the information below.

School	Number of Students	Charity collected ($)
A	30	$900
B	40	$800
C	44	$880
D	60	$2400

The table above shows the number of students at certain schools and the amount of charity collected in these schools.

48) **What is the approximate percentage of the charity collected in school D in the entire charity collected?**

A) 48%   B) 52%   C) 55%   D) 60%   E) 70%

49) Which school has the highest average charity per student?

    A) A   B) B   C) C   D) D   E) A and B

50) What is the average charity per school?

    A) 4300   B) 1245   C) 4400   D) 4460   E) 4560

51) An athlete runs some certain distance in the first day, and runs 100m less than three times of the distance he has run in the previous day in the following days. If he runs 7300m in three days, how much did he run on the first day?

    A) 700   B) 680   C) 640   D) 600   E) 590

52) Algebra books in a bookstore are sold for \$6, while geometry books are sold for \$4. If a person who buys 8 books from this store pays \$44, how many of these books are algebra books?

    A) 3   B) 4   C) 5   D) 5.5   E) 6

53) If the equation of the line in the figure is $2x+3y=12$, $\tan\alpha=?$

    A) 1.2   B) 1.6   C) 2

    D) 2/5   E) 2/3

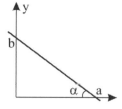

54) What is the sum of prime numbers between 20 and 30?

    A) 44   B) 48   C) 50   D) 51   E) 52

55) The table above shows the best seller models in a car dealer within a month. If this graph were drawn as a pie chart, what would be the approximate approcentral angle of the least selling model?

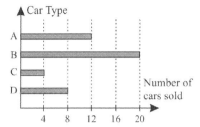

A) 33%   B) 34%   C) 36%
D) 40%   E) 44%

56) The table above shows the number of students in classrooms of a school. What is the ratio of female students to male students at this school?

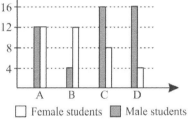

A) 3.16   B) 3.25   C) 3.40
D) 3.50   E) 0.75

57) If the difference between 30% and 20% of number A is 10, what is the half of number A?

A) 44   B) 46   C) 47   D) 48   E) 50

58) A box full of notebooks weight 56kg. If the weight of the notebooks in this box is 13 times of the box, what is the weight of the empty box?

A) 3   B) 3.25   C) 4   D) 4.2   E) 4.4

59) The perimeter of a rectangle is 80cm, and the proportion of sides is 3:7. Calculate the length of the shorter side.

A) 12   B) 11   C) 10   D) 9   E) 8

60) ABCD is square. Find the perimeter KBFE if AB=16cm.

A) 24   B) 26   C) 28
D) 32   E) 40

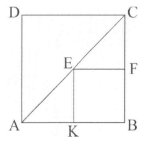

TEST – 2.10
- Questions -

1) A tin contains 84 lb. of olive oil and another tin contains 105 lb. of flare oil. Both oils will be mixed and filled into bottles of equal volume such that there will be no remaining oil. What is the least number of bottles that are needed?

   A) 9   B) 8   C) 7   D) 6   E) 5

2) The perimeter of a rectangle is 80cm, and the proportion of sides is 3:7. Calculate the length of the longer side.

   A) 28   B) 26   C) 24   D) 22   E) 20

3) ABCD is square. Find the perimeter KBFE if AB=24cm.

   A) 40   B) 48   C) 49

   D) 50   E) 52

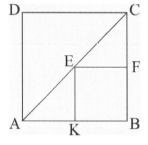

4) Jack can complete a task in 12 days. George can complete the same task in 16 days. If they work together, what fraction of the task can they complete at the end of 1 day?

   A) $\dfrac{7}{48}$ B) $\dfrac{7}{43}$ C) $\dfrac{48}{7}$ D) $\dfrac{6}{43}$ E) 8

5) If 2a+b+c=14, a+2b+c=16, a+b+2c=18, then a+b+c=?

   A) 10   B) 9   C) 12   D) 13   E) 11

6) One sack of feed will last a canary, pigeon, or chicken 100, 60, and 40 days ,respectively. With one sack of feed, for about how many days can all 3 birds eat?

   A) 25 B) 22 C) 21 D) 19 E) 26

7) Which of the following is a rational number?

   A) $\dfrac{\sqrt{3}}{\sqrt{2}}$ B) $\sqrt{5}$ C) $\sqrt{7}$ D) $\dfrac{\sqrt{100}}{\sqrt{289}}$ E) 1.5

8) $d_1 \| d_2 \| d_3$, x=FD=?

   A) 3 B) 4 C) 5
   D) 6 E)7

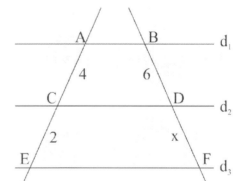

9) 2x+3y-8=0, find the slope and y-intercept.

   A) $\dfrac{2}{3}, -8$ B) $-\dfrac{2}{3}, 8$ C) $\dfrac{2}{3}, 8$ D) $8, -\dfrac{2}{3}$ E) $-\dfrac{2}{3}, \dfrac{8}{3}$

10) The expression 6a+6b-6c+12d is equivalent to which of the following?

   A) 6(a+b+c+d) B) 6(a+2b-c+d) C) 6(2a+b+c-d)
   D) 6(a+b-c+2d) E) 4a+6b+3c+2d

11) What is the slope of the line of the equation 7x-6y=15?

A) $\dfrac{6}{7}$　　　B) $\dfrac{-6}{7}$　　　C) $\dfrac{7}{6}$　　　D) $\dfrac{-7}{6}$　　　E) $\dfrac{7}{9}$

12) If a bookstore sells every book for $5 each, the store will make a $120 profit, and if the bookstore sells every book for $4 each, the store will be at $100 loss. With the information given, how many books does the bookstore have?

A) 100　　　B) 110　　　C) 180　　　D) 220　　　E) 230

13) There are 64 men and 16 women in a room. How many married couples should join the room to make the number of men 3 times greater than the number of women?

A) 6　　　B) 8　　　C) 10　　　D) 12　　　E) 13

14) If y=-4, what is the value of $\dfrac{y^2-9}{y-3} = ?$

A) -1　　　B) -2　　　C) -3　　　D) -4　　　E) 5

15) There are 4 yellow, 7 red, 5 green and 4 blue murbles in one box. What is the probability of a randomly choosen marble to be green?

A) $\dfrac{1}{2}$　　　B) $\dfrac{1}{3}$　　　C) $\dfrac{1}{4}$　　　D) $\dfrac{1}{6}$　　　E) $\dfrac{1}{7}$

TEST – 2.1
- Solutions -

1) **The correct answer is (C)**

If $\dfrac{2x-4}{3} = 4m$ then 2x–4=3·4m, 2x–4=12m, 2x=12m+4,

$\dfrac{2x}{2} = \dfrac{12m+4}{2}$, x=6m+2, 3x=3(6m+2) $\Rightarrow$ 3x=18m+6

2) **The correct answer is (A)**

$\log_2 8 = \log_2 2^3 = 3\log_2 2 = 3$, $\log_3 81 = \log_3 3^4 = 4\log_3 3 = 4$, $\log_5 25 = \log_5 5^2 = 2\log_5 5 = 2$

3) **The correct answer is (A)**

Let each person has x pencils at the beginning, which means the number of pencils is 15x. Since each person would have 10 pencils less when distributed to 20 people, the number of pencils would be 20(x–10), and as the number of pencils would be equal to each other in both situations, 15x=20(x–10)

4) **The correct answer is (D)**

If he has earned $150 on Saturday, then
    m=30+10n=150, 30+10n=150, 10n=150–30=120, 10n=120, n=12
therefore he has worked for 12 hours on Saturday. Similarly for Sunday,
    m=40+9n=130, 40+9n=130, 9n=130–40=90, 9n=90, n=10
therefore he has worked for 10 hours on Sunday.
Total number of hours he has worked is, 12+10=22 hours.

5) **The correct answer is (B)**
Expanding the parentheses,
$x(x+y)+y(x+y)+(x+y)^2 = x^2+xy+y^2+yx+x^2+2xy+y^2 =$
$= 2x^2+4xy+2y^2 = 2(x^2+2xy+y^2) = 2(x+y)^2$

6) **The correct answer is (C)**
Pricing formula is P=6a+4b, where a=60cm and b=40cm.
    Therefore P=6a+4b
    P=6·60+4·40=360+160=520

7) **The correct answer is (B)**

$h = V_0 \cdot t - \dfrac{1}{2}gt^2$ where $V_0 = 2V$ and $t = 4s$

Therefore $h = V_0 \cdot t - \dfrac{1}{2}gt^2$ and $h = 2V \cdot 4 - \dfrac{1}{2}g4^2$ and $h = 8V - 8g$

8) **The correct answer is (A)**

If $\dfrac{a-2}{b-2} = \dfrac{1}{3}$, then $3(a-2) = 1(b-2)$

Therefore $3a - 6 = b - 2$ and $b = 3a - 4$. Replacing b in equation

$$\frac{3a}{2b+8} = \frac{3a}{2(3a-4)+8} = \frac{3a}{6a-8+8} = \frac{3a}{6a} = \frac{1}{2}$$

9) **The correct answer is (A)**

$2x + 3y = 21$

$3y - x = 12$

Let us multiply the second equation by 2 and sum them up

$2x + 3y = 21$

$\underline{6y - 2x = 24}$

$6y + 3y = 21 + 24$, so $9y = 45$, $y = 5$

Replacing y with 5 in any of the equations, say, the first one,

$2x + 3y = 21$, $2x + 3 \cdot 5 = 21$, $2x + 15 = 21$,

$2x = 21 - 15 = 6$, $2x = 6$, $x = 3$, then $(x, y) = (5, 3)$

10) **The correct answer is (C)**

$f(x) = ax^2 + 4$ so $f(2) = a2^2 + 4 = 4a + 4$

$f(1) = a1^2 + 4 = a + 4$ since $\dfrac{f(2)}{f(1)} = \dfrac{1}{3} = \dfrac{4a+4}{a+4}$,

$1(a+4) = 3(4a+4)$, $a + 4 = 12a + 12$, $11a = -8$ and therefore $a = -8/11$,

11) **The correct answer is (C)**

We need to build a ratio here. Since the trees are parallel, ratios of their height to the length of their shadows must be equal to each other.

   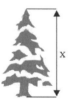

First three   Shade   Second three   Shade

Therefore x being the shadow length of the second tree,

$\dfrac{m}{m+4} = \dfrac{n}{x}$, and $x = \dfrac{n(m+4)}{n}$.

12) **The correct answer is (A)**

Expanding the denominators,

$$\frac{\frac{1}{3^x}-\frac{1}{2^x}}{\frac{1}{3^x}+\frac{1}{2^x}}=\frac{\frac{2^x}{6^x}-\frac{3^x}{6^x}}{\frac{2^x}{6^x}+\frac{3^x}{6^x}}=\frac{\frac{2^x-3^x}{6^x}}{\frac{2^x+3^x}{6^x}}=\frac{2^x-3^x}{2^x+3^x}$$

13) **The correct answer is (B)**

$$\frac{3^x+3^{x+1}+3^{x+2}}{3^{x+1}+3^{x+2}+3^{x+3}}=\frac{3^x(1+3^1+3^2)}{3^x(3^1+3^2+3^3)}=\frac{3^x\cdot13}{3^x\cdot39}=1/3$$

14) **The correct answer is (D)**

Equation of a line passing through two known

point is found by $\frac{y-y_1}{y_1-y_2}=\frac{x-x_1}{x_1-x_2}$

The line passes through origin A(0, 0) and B(3, 9),

therefore $\frac{y-9}{9-0}=\frac{x-3}{3-0}$ and $\frac{y-9}{9}=\frac{x-3}{3}$,

3(y–9)=9(x–3), and y–9=3x–9, and y=3x

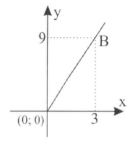

15) **The correct answer is (C)**

(x+4)(x+5)=x²+5x+4x+4.5=x²+9x+20

(x+4)(x+5)= x²+3ax+5b, therefore 3a=9 and a=3 , 5b=20 and b=4

Replacing a and b in the equation

$\frac{a+b}{b-a}=\frac{3+4}{4-3}=7$

16) **The correct answer is (A)**

If a>0 and 3a²–9a=0, then 3a(a–3)=0 therefore either 3a=0 or (a–3)=0

Since a>0, first situation is rejected, leaving us with (a–3)=0, and a=3

17) **The correct answer is (E)**

ΔAED and ΔACB are similar triangles.

Therefore $\frac{3}{6}=\frac{4}{x+4}$, 3(x+4)=6.4, 3x+12=24, 3x=12, x=4

simplifying the terms, $\frac{1}{2}=\frac{4}{x+4}$, resulting x+4=8, and x=4

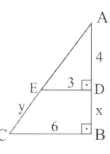

18) **The correct answer is (E)**

Summing up these two equations,

　　2a+3b=18

　　6b+7a=27

　　9a+9b=45, therefore 9(a+b)=45, and a+b=5

19) **The correct answer is (E)**

For two angles complementing each other to 90°, sin of one is equal to the cos of the other. Therefore sin14=cos(90–14)=cos76, and x=76

Meaning x+y=90, sin(x)=cos(90-x)

Sin(14)=cos(90-14)=cos76, and x=76

20) **The correct answer is (A)**

$$\sqrt{(a+b)+2\sqrt{ab}} = \sqrt{a} + \sqrt{b}$$

$$\sqrt{5+2\sqrt{6}} = \sqrt{(3+2)+2\sqrt{3\cdot2}} = \sqrt{3} + \sqrt{2}$$

$$\frac{\sqrt{5+2\sqrt{6}}}{\sqrt{3}+\sqrt{2}} = \frac{\sqrt{3}+\sqrt{2}}{\sqrt{3}+\sqrt{2}} = 1$$

21) **The correct answer is (C)**

According to the table, number of physics and biology books sold is 700, while 300 history and chemistry books have been sold. Therefore the answer is 700–300=400

22) **The correct answer is (A)**

Let us name the money each sibling receives as A, B, C and D. Total money distributed to the siblings is $2400, so A+B+C+D=2400 and this amount of money is distributed proportional to 2, 4, 6, and 8. Therefore "k" being a constant to be calculated, $\frac{A}{2} = \frac{B}{4} = \frac{C}{6} = \frac{D}{8}$ =k, and replacing k with A, B, C, and D, A+B+C+D=2k+4k+6k+8k=2400, yielding to 20k=2400 and k=120. The sibling who had taken the largest sum of money has taken 8k, therefore 8k=8·120=960

23) **The correct answer is (D)**

y=144, x=36, y–x=144–36=108.

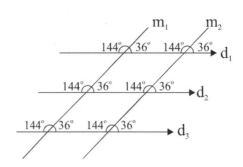

24) **The correct answer is (D)**

Finding the difference means subtraction. Therefore
(8a+6b–3c)–(6a+8b–3c)=8a+6b–3c–6a–8b+3c=2a–2b

25) **The correct answer is (A)**

$$\log 1000 = \log 10^3 = 3, \quad \log \frac{1}{100} = \log 10^{-2} = -2 \log 10 = -2$$

$$\log 1000 + \log \frac{1}{100} = 3 - 2 = 1$$

26) **The correct answer is (D)**

Put the numbers in order -6, -4, 2, 11, 20.
The one in the middle, 2 is the median.

27) **The correct answer is (A)**

Total charity collected=1600+1500+1800+600=5500
Ratio of charity collected at school B to the total charity collected=
=1500/5500 =15/55=3/11

28) **The correct answer is (A)**

$|\pi-4|+|\pi-3|+|\pi-2|=?$

Remember that $\pi = 3.14$ and $(\pi-4)<0$, while $(\pi-3)>0$ and $(\pi-2)>0$,
therefore $\pi-4|+|\pi-3|+|\pi-2|=-(\pi-4)+(\pi-3)+(\pi-2)=-\pi+4+\pi-3+\pi-2=\pi-1$

29) **The correct answer is (B)**

$Ep = k \cdot \dfrac{q_1 \cdot q_2}{d}$, therefore Ep·d=k· q_1. q_2, and k= $\dfrac{E_p \cdot d}{q_1 \cdot q_2}$

30) **The correct answer is (D)**

Reducing the distance by 50% means dividing the distance by two, therefore the ratio of the new distance to the original distance would be $d_2 = d_1/2$. The ratio of the energies in two situations would be

$$\frac{Ep_2}{Ep_1} = \frac{k \cdot \frac{q_1 \cdot q_2}{d_2}}{k \cdot \frac{q_1 \cdot q_2}{d_1}}, \text{ replacing } d_1 \text{ with } d_2, \quad \frac{Ep_2}{Ep_1} = \frac{k \cdot \frac{q_1 \cdot q_2}{d_1/2}}{k \cdot \frac{q_1 \cdot q_2}{d_1}} = \frac{2 \cdot k \cdot \frac{q_1 \cdot q_2}{d_1}}{k \cdot \frac{q_1 \cdot q_2}{d_1}}, \text{ simplifying}$$

the terms, with each other, $\dfrac{Ep_2}{Ep_1} = 2 = 200\%$

31) **The correct answer is (B)**

Minimalizing $|3x-12|$ means keeping the term at zero, that is $|3x-12|=0$
Therefore $3x-12=0$, $3x=12$, and $x=4$

32) The correct answer is (D)

Number of students at school D for 2014 has been given as 325, which has increased for 75, reaching 400 for 2015. By using direct proportion,
If 325 increases for 75 then 100 increases for x,
325/75=100/x, 325x=75·100, x=7500/325=23

33) The correct answer is (C)

Salary expenses at school A has increased for 32–24=for 8 points
Salary expenses at school B has increased for 39–31=for 8 points
Salary expenses at school C has increased for 33–30–for 3 points
Salary expenses at school D has increased for 26–20=for 6 points
Salary expenses at school E has increased for 32–25=for 7 points,

34) The correct answer is (A)

The table provides information about the salary expenses only. Therefore average budget of the schools cannot be found.

35) The correct answer is (B)

We need to find tanα to find the water consumption after week 3

$\tan\alpha=\dfrac{20}{5}=\dfrac{x}{3}$, therefore 5x=20·3, 5x=60 and x=$\dfrac{60}{5}$, x=12

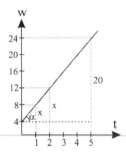

36) The correct answer is (B)

To find out the relationship between the time (t) and consumed water (w), we need to establish a function between time and water as w=f(t)=at+b, a and be being constants. Now we need to find out a and b. The figure "a" is the slope of the line, therefore a=tanα=$\dfrac{20}{5}$ =4, and at t=0, w=4, therefore 4=4·0+b, and b=4 too. The function is found as w=f(t)=4t+4

37) The correct answer is (A)

Following the graph, f(–6)=6, f(4)=4 and f(6)=4,
f(–6)+f(4)+f(6)=6+4+4=14

38) The correct answer is (A)

Since –8<a<4, (a–4) would be negative for all possible a values, therefore
|a–4|=–(a–4)
Similarly, (a+8) would be positive for all possible a values, therefore
|a+8|=a+8
|a–4|+|a+8|=–(a–4)+(a+8)= –a+4+a+8=12

39) **The correct answer is (C)**

Let the number of 5–room houses be x and 4–room houses be y. Since the number of houses on the street is 30, x+y=30, and having 132 rooms in these houses means 5x+4y=132. Solving these two equations with two unknowns, let us multiply the first equation by four first;

x+y=30 $\Rightarrow$ 4x+4y=120 and subtract from each other

$$5x+4y=132$$
$$- \quad (4x+4y=120)$$
$$5x+4y-4x-4y=132-120, \text{ therefore } x=12.$$

40) **The correct answer is (E)**

Let the original price of the TV set be x. Since the price increases for 40%, the new price would be determined by x+40%x=308,

$$x+\frac{4x}{10}=308, \text{ and } \frac{10x+4x}{10}=308,$$

therefore 14x=3080 and $x=\dfrac{3080}{14}=220$

41) **The correct answer is (D)**

The increase in the number of students attending basketball=410–300=110
The increase in the number of students attending football=370–300=70
The increase in the number of students attending tennis=290-200=90
The increase in the number of students attending swimming=500–320=180
The increase in the number of students attending volleyball=160–130=30

42) **The correct answer is (A)**

Volleyball is the sport that had the least number of increase.
Total number of students who attended to any sport in
2015=410+370+290+500+160=1730.

The ratio of volleyball attenders to the entire students= $\dfrac{160}{1730}=\dfrac{16}{173}$

43) **The correct answer is (C)**

|AB| defines the radius of the circle.
A(4, 8), B(5, 9)

$$|AB|=\sqrt{(x_2-x_1)^2+(y_2-y_1)^2}=$$
$$=\sqrt{(9-8)^2+(5-4)^2}=\sqrt{1+1}=\sqrt{2}$$

$(x-x_1)^2+(y-y_1)^2=r^2$, (equation of a circle)
$(x-4)^2+(y-8)^2=\left(\sqrt{2}\right)^2$
$(x-4)^2+(y-8)^2=2$

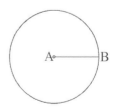

44) The correct answer is (E)

$V=V_0-gt$, and $V_0=50$m/s, $g=10$m/s^2, t=2s, replacing these values in the equation, $V=V_0-gt=50-2\cdot10=30$m/s

45) The correct answer is (D)

Let the number of students selected for the basketball team be b and the number of students selected for the football team be f. Since each student is to be selected for either football or basketball team, classroom size=f+b=f+24, because we know that 24 students have been selected for the basketball team (b=24), therefore $\dfrac{3}{7}=\dfrac{f}{f+24}$, 7f=3f+72, 4f=72, and f=18

46) The correct answer is (A)

Since this is a pie chart, the sum of angles (A+B+C+D)=360 and the total number of guests in the hotel is 18+12+16+6=52. Each guest must be represented by an angle of 360/52=6,9 degrees. Since there are 12 engineers, the angle of their pie must be 12x6,9=83.1 degrees.

47) The correct answer is (A)

The slope of a line is m where y=mx+b. Therefore the slope of the line $y=3x+\sqrt{2}$ is 3, and the slope of the line $y=\sqrt{2}x+3$ is $\sqrt{2}$. Their sum is $3+\sqrt{2}$.

48) The correct answer is (C)

Dividing P(x) by Q(x),

$$
\begin{array}{rl|l}
& x^3+4x^2+4x-8 & \underline{\;x^2+2x\;} \\
- & \underline{x^3+2x^2} & x+2 \\
& 2x^2+4x-8 & \\
- & \underline{2x^2+4x} & \\
& 0+0-8 &
\end{array}
$$

$P(x)=(x^2+2x)\cdot(x+2)-8$

49) The correct answer is (D)

Let the equation of the parabola be $y=a(x-r)^2+k$. The peak point of the parabola would be (3, –3)=(r, k).

For (0, 9), $9=a\cdot(-3)^2-3$ and 12=9a, therefore, $a=\dfrac{4}{3}$

Thus the equation is 2nd $y=f(x)=\dfrac{4}{3}(x-3)^2-3$

$f(4)=\dfrac{4}{3}(4-3)^2-3=\dfrac{4}{3}-3=\dfrac{-5}{3}$

50) **The correct answer is (A)**

There are $\dfrac{80-2}{2}+1=40$ even numbers between 2 and 80, while there are 5 odd numerals {1, 3, 5, 7 and 9}. When we add them up, the result is 40+5=45. The probability of having an even number or an odd number under 10 numeral is $\dfrac{45}{80}=\dfrac{9}{16}$

51) **The correct answer is (E)**

There are 16 teams in the league and the first game takes 2 teams to play. Therefore we need to calculate

$C(16; 2)=\binom{16}{2}=\dfrac{16!}{(16-2)!2!}=\dfrac{16.15.14!}{14!2!}=\dfrac{16.15}{2}=120$

52) **The correct answer is (E)**

Let the minimum number of chocolates be x. Since one chocolate is left when packed by 4, 6 and 9, x=4a+1=6b+1=9c+1, and x–1=4a=6b=9c. Therefore we need to find the least common multiplier of these three numbers, LCM(4,6,9)=36. As there is one chocolate left in each situation, the minimum number of chocolates, x=36+1=37

53) **The correct answer is (E)**

The number of visiting students from 440 to 490, therefore 50 increase from 400 means x increase from 100, and x=$\dfrac{100 \cdot 50}{440}$=11.4%

54) **The correct answer is (A)**

Let A be the set of even numbers between 1 and 11, B be the set of odd numbers between 2 and 12 and C be the set of prime numbers between 4 and 14.
A= {2,4,6,8,10}, B={3,5,7,9,11} and C={5,7,11,13}.
Therefore $\dfrac{A+B}{A+B+C}=\dfrac{30+35}{30+35+36}=\dfrac{65}{101}$

55) **The correct answer is (C)**

The volume of a cylinder is calculated by V=□r²h,
therefore V=π|AB|²|BD|=π·2²·3=12π=36

56) **The correct answer is (A)**

$f(x)=\dfrac{x^3+8}{x^2-9x}$ is undefined when $x^2-9x=0$, therefore x=0 and x=9 makes the function undefined.

57) **The correct answer is (E)**

Since 1kg=1000g, if 1000g costs \$16 then 1800g costs x and
1000/16=1800/x

$x=\dfrac{16 \cdot 1800}{1000}=28.8, \quad \$28.8$

58) **The correct answer is (A)**

Since the units digit in 663 (3) is less than 5, it must be rounded to 660, and since the units digit in 986 (6) is greater than 5, it must be rounded to 990. Therefore 660+990=1650.

59) **The correct answer is (C)**

$x^2+8x+7=0$
$(x+7)\cdot(x+1)=0$
$x+7=0, x=-7$
$x+1=0, x=-1 \qquad \{-7; -1\}$

60) **The correct answer is (C)**

$|-2\pi|+|2\pi-1|=$
$|-2\pi|=2\pi, |2\pi-1|=2\pi-1,$
$2\pi+2\pi-1=4\pi-1$
$*|2\pi-1|=2\pi-1$ because $2\pi-1>0, 2\pi-1\approx5.3$

TEST – 2.2
- *Solutions* -

1) **The correct answer is (D)**

   If 6x+6=16, then 6x=16–6=10, and 3x=5 and x=5/3
   Replacing 3x with 5 in the equation
   $9x^2+3x+4=9(5/3)^2+3\cdot(5/3)+4=25+5+4=34$

2) **The correct answer is (D)**

   In the given equation system, let us multiply the first equation by –2, and sum them up
   $\begin{cases} x+y=5 \\ 2x+4y=18 \end{cases}$ + $\begin{cases} -2x-2y=-10 \\ 2x+4y=18 \end{cases}$ yielding to –2x–2y+2x+4y=18–10
   therefore 2y=8, and y=4. Replacing this y value in any equation, say the first one, we obtain the x value x+y=5 and x+4=5, therefore x=1

3) **The correct answer is (A)**

   Let us name the number of second hand sets that can be bought as y. Buying 20 new TV sets, we need to pay 20x amount of money and this amount of money must be equal to the amount that we would buy second hand sets. Therefore 20x=y(x–m), and since we are looking for y value, y=20x/(x–m)

4) **The correct answer is (B)**

   Summing up the terms in the equation,
   $8x^2+12xy+9y^2-4x^2=4x^2+12xy+9y^2=(2x+3y)^2$

5) **The correct answer is (B)**

   If $\sqrt{2x^2+2m-12}-\sqrt{2x^2}=0$, then If $\sqrt{2x^2+2m-12}=\sqrt{2x^2}$, and taking square of both sides, $2x^2+2m-12=2x^2$, where $2x^2$ would cancel each other. Therefore 2m–12=0, 2m=12 and m=6.
   Substituting m with 6, 6m+6=6·6+6=42

6) **The correct answer is (B)**

   The equation of a line is found by the formula $\frac{y-y_1}{y_1-y_2}=\frac{x-x_1}{x_1-x_2}$. Line d_1 in the figure passes through (0, 3) and (2, 0) points. Therefore, $\frac{y-3}{3-0}=\frac{x-0}{0-2}$ and, $\frac{y-3}{3}=\frac{x}{-2}$, leading to $\frac{x}{2}+\frac{y}{3}=1$. Similarly for line d_2, which passes through (–3,0) and (0,–3), $\frac{y-0}{0-(-3)}=\frac{x-(-3)}{-3-0}$, and $\frac{y}{3}=\frac{x+3}{-3}$, yielding to x+y=–3

7) **The correct answer is (D)**

If $m=7^2+7$, then $7^3+7^2=7(7^2+7)=7m$

8) **The correct answer is (A)**

$180(n-2)=n \cdot m$. Replacing m with 140 in the formula, $180(n-2)=140n$, $9(n-2)=7n$, and $9n-18=7n$, therefore $2n=18$ and $n=9$

9) **The correct answer is (B)**

Since the equation of a line is found by the formula $\dfrac{y-y_1}{y_1-y_2}=\dfrac{x-x_1}{x_1-x_2}$, and the line passes through points $(0, \sqrt{2})$ and $(\sqrt{3}, 0)$, the equation of this line turns out to be $\dfrac{x}{\sqrt{3}}+\dfrac{y}{\sqrt{2}}=1$. Expanding both sides of the equation by $\sqrt{6}$ yields to $x\sqrt{2}+y\sqrt{3}=\sqrt{6}$, and $y\sqrt{3}=\sqrt{6}-x\sqrt{2}$ therefore $y=-x\dfrac{\sqrt{2}}{\sqrt{3}}+\dfrac{\sqrt{6}}{\sqrt{3}}=ax+b$, therefore $a=-\sqrt{\dfrac{2}{3}}$ and $b=\sqrt{2}=\dfrac{\sqrt{6}}{\sqrt{3}}$ and

$a+b=-\dfrac{-\sqrt{2}}{\sqrt{3}}+\dfrac{\sqrt{6}}{\sqrt{3}}=\dfrac{\sqrt{6}-\sqrt{2}}{\sqrt{3}}$.

10) **The correct answer is (C)**

The equation of line d_1 is $y=x$, since the slope is positive, while the equation of line d_2 is $y=-x$, since the slope is negative, and the equation of line d_3 is $x=3$.

11) **The correct answer is (B)**

The questions has three 19s but no more than two of any other numbers. Correct answer 19.

12) **The correct answer is (B)**

If $4a^2=m^2+n^2$, then $a^2=\dfrac{m^2+n^2}{4}$ and $a=\sqrt{\dfrac{m^2+n^2}{4}}=\dfrac{\sqrt{m^2+n^2}}{2}$. Since the perimeter of rhombus is equal to 4a, $4a=4 \cdot \dfrac{\sqrt{m^2+n^2}}{2}=2\sqrt{m^2+n^2}$

13) **The correct answer is (C)**

For any given quadratic equation $ax^2+bx+c=0$, sum of the roots $(x_1+x_2)=-\dfrac{b}{a}$ and multiplication of the roots $x_1 \cdot x_2=\dfrac{c}{a}$. In the given equation of $n^2-9n+20=0$, $a=1$, $b=-9$ and $c=20$. Therefore sum of the roots, $-\dfrac{b}{a}=\dfrac{-(-9)}{1}=9$, and the multiplication of the roots, $\dfrac{c}{a}=\dfrac{20}{1}=20$. Therefore the ratio to be found is $\dfrac{9}{20}$.

14. **The correct answer is (C)**

Find the range, substract the smallest from the largest number.
28-(-6)=28+6=34

15) **The correct answer is (A)**

$$\frac{(2+\pi)^2}{2+\pi}+\frac{(3-\pi)^2}{3-\pi}+\frac{\pi(\pi+2)}{\pi+2}=2+\pi+3-\pi+\pi=5+\pi$$

16) **The correct answer is (A)**

Let the toll fee for cars be x, which means toll fee for trucks is (x+5). Since we know 80 trucks and 20 cars have used the tollway, the total toll fee could be written as 80(x+5)+20x=600, therefore 80x+400+20x=600, 100x=200, and x=2. As trucks need to pay $5 more (x+5), they need to pay 2+5=7

17) **The correct answer is (B)**

$(\pi+k)^2+(\pi^2+3k\pi+k^2)=\pi^2+2k\pi+k^2+\pi^2+3k\pi+k^2=2\pi^2+5k\pi+2k^2=$
$=a\pi^2+bk\pi+ck^2$ a=2, b=5, c=2, a+b+c=2+5+2=9

18) **The correct answer is (E)**

Since each shape has 2 diagonals, total number of diagonals=2x3=6

19) **The correct answer is (E)**

Applying Pythagorean theorem, $|AB|^2+|BC|^2=|AC|^2$, therefore $2^2+|BC|^2=4^2$, and $|BC|^2=16-4$, resulting $|BC|=2\sqrt{3}$, which means that ABC is a special triangle. The edge across the 30 degree angle is the half of hypotenuse, and the edge across the 60 degree angle is $\frac{\sqrt{3}}{2}$ times the hypotenuse.

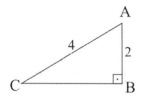

Therefore $\frac{\angle A}{\angle C}=\frac{60}{30}=2$.

20) **The correct answer is (E)**

For $\begin{cases} 4x+6y=10 \\ mx+12y=16 \end{cases}$ equation system to have empty set as solution set, ratio of coefficient of x and y must be equal, that is $\frac{4}{m}=\frac{6}{12}$, therefore 6m=48 and m=8

21) **The correct answer is (A)**

Let the number of tickets sold to the children be x and the number of tickets sold to the adults be y, which means x+y=80. The total fee collected 440=3x+7y, and solving these two equations together, $\begin{cases} x+y=80 \\ 3x+7y=440 \end{cases}$

22) **The correct answer is (B)**

Let the classroom size be 100x, which means 40x of the students would be males and 60x students would be females. Then the number of blonde students would be $\frac{60x \cdot 20}{100}=12x$, which means (60x–12x)=48x students are non–blondes. $\frac{48x}{100x}=48\%$.

23) **The correct answer is (D)**

In the equation m=1.25+0.25n, n is the number of liters since m=$9.25 has been paid, 9.25=1.25+0.25n, 0.25n=9.25–1.25=8, and n=8/0.25=32.

24) **The correct answer is (C)**

Dividing 1446 by 24, the remainder is 6, which means we have to go forward for 6 hours. 8:30a.m+6hrs=2.30p.m

25) **The correct answer is (D)**

First we have to find out how much fuel has been sold in 3 days. If 84 tons have been sold in 4 days then x tons have been sold in 3 days. 84/x=4/3, and x=84·3/4=63 tons of fuel has been sold in 3 days. Since the initial stock is 120 tons, the remaining fuel is 120–63–57 tons.

26) **The correct answer is (B)**

The greatest odd number that could be written is 96543, while the smallest even number that could be written is 34596, so the difference is 96543–34596=61947

27) **The correct answer is (A)**

The general equation for parabola is $y=a(x–x_1)(x_1–x_2)$, where x_1 and x_2 are the points that the parabola cuts x axis, and a is a coefficient. Therefore, $y=a(x–2)(x–4)$, which means $y=a(x^2–6x+8)$. Since the parabola cuts y axis at (0, 4), we may evaluate this point as $4=a(0^2–6·0+8)=8a$, therefore $a=\dfrac{4}{8}=\dfrac{1}{2}$. Therefore the equation is $y=\dfrac{x^2}{2}–3x+4$, meaning $a=\dfrac{1}{2}$, b=–3 and c=4, resulting $a+b+c=\dfrac{1}{2}–3+4=\dfrac{3}{2}$.

28) **The correct answer is (C)**

Ahmet is 2n and Mehmet is 3m years old. Ahmet's current age is three times of Mehmet's current age. Therefore 2n=3x3·m=9m. two years later, both of their ages would increase by 2.The sum of this change would be 2+2=4.the total sum would be 9m+4

29) **The correct answer is (A)**

Let this market sell the apricot for $x per kilogram, Since selling price=buying price+profit, and the market would earn 14x if the apricot is sold for $14 and 10x, if it is sold for $10, 14x=A+110 and 10x=A–40.

30) **The correct answer is (B)**

$f(0)=2·3^0=2·1=2$, $f(1)=2·3^1=2·3=6$, $f(2)=2·3^2=2·9=18$, $f(3)=2·3^3=2·27=54$, therefore $f(x)=2·3^x=2·9=18$

31) **The correct answer is (D)**

1 math book=$15, 3 physics books=3·20=$60. 60% discount means only 40% of the original price should be paid, one should pay 60·40%=$24 for the physics books. 6 chemistry books=6·30=$180. Applying the discount , one needs to pay 180·40%=$72. Therefore total amount to be paid is 15+24+72=111 dollars.

32) The correct answer is (D)

Let 100x of the eggs be collected from farm A and 100y of them be collected from farm y. therefore 100x+100y=4000. Since 3% of the broken eggs will come from farm A and 4% from farm B, the equation will be 3x+4y=120.

33) The correct answer is (C)

Pages 4, 14, 24, 34, 40, 41, 42, 43 use 4 once, while 44 uses it twice, totaling 10 times.

34) The correct answer is (E)

2000 passengers have landed in the first hour, while 5000 others landing in the second hour. Since we are asked for 90 minutes, we need to take only half of the second hour, 5000/2=2500, and when we sum up with the first hour, 2000+2500=4500.

35) The correct answer is (A)

Mass center of a homogeneous wire is the middle of it. Therefore when we cut a portion of it, its mass center would shift for half of the length cut off. Therefore we can formulate it as *Cut portion=(original length–new length)=2(shift in center of mass)*. Let the original length of the wire be x, therefore 3x/11=2x9, and x=66cm.

36) The correct answer is (D)

Let us count and calculate the rectangles and their perimeter one by one

ABCD	2(4+2)	12
ANFK	2(1+2)	6
NBEF	2(1+2)	6
KECD	2(4+1)	10
KFRD	2(1+2)	6
FECR	2(1+2)	6
ABEK	2(4+1)	10
Total		**56cm**

37) The correct answer is (C)

Let us calculate the tax first. Tax=9x%90 =90x9/100=0.81 dollars, therefore the price including tax would be 90+8.1=98.1 dollars.

38) The correct answer is (A)

Let us count the triangles: ABC, AED, AMF, MEK, BNE, DLF and DOC, totaling 7.

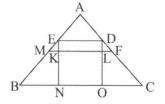

39) **The correct answer is (C)**

According to the figure, Algebra I covers 80 degrees, whereas Algebra II covers 120 and Algebra III covers 160 degrees, therefore the ratio is 80:120:160, simplifying to 2:3:4.

40) **The correct answer is (A)**

Since the distance is equal to the velocity multiplied by time ($x=V{\cdot}t$), velocity of vehicle K could be calculated from $x_K=V_K{\cdot}t_K$, and $270=V_k{\cdot}3$, $V_K=90$km/h. Similarly, $x_L=V_L{\cdot}t_L$, and $300=V_L{\cdot}3$, $V_L=100$km/h. Since these two vehicles move at opposite directions, total velocity could be summed up, which means the vehicles get close to each other at a velocity summed up of each other ($x=(V_K+V_L){\cdot}t$). Since the distance to be traveled by both vehicles is 900 km, $900=(V_K+V_L){\cdot}t=(100+90){\cdot}t$, therefore $t=900/190=90/19$ hours.

41) **The correct answer is (A)**

Let us name the number of students as x, then the price of the present would be 45x–65 when each student pays 45 dollars, and 30x+60 when each student pays 30 dollars. Since the price of the present is constant, these two must be equal to each other, and 45x–65=30x+60.

42) **The correct answer is (C)**

$$\log_7 \sqrt{7} = \log_7 7^{\frac{1}{2}} = \frac{1}{2}\log_7 7 = \frac{1}{2} = a. \quad a = \frac{1}{2}, \quad (a)^2 = \left(\frac{1}{2}\right)^2 = \frac{1}{4}$$

43) **The correct answer is (E)**

$E_p = \dfrac{kx^2}{2}$, and replacing x with 20 and k with 10,

$$E_p = \frac{10 \cdot 20^2}{2} = \frac{10 \cdot 400}{2} = \frac{4000}{2} = 2000$$

44) **The correct answer is (B)**

Since the circle passes from the origin, BOA=90, therefore |BA| is both the hypotenuse of BOA triangle, and the diameter of the circle. Naming the midpoint of |BA| as m, it could be calculated as m($\frac{6+0}{2}$, $\frac{0+8}{2}$)= (3,4), and since |AO|=6 and |BO|=8, the radius of this triangle could be calculated by using Pythagoras's theorem as |BA|=2r=10cm, r=5cm, Therefore $(x–3)^2+(y–4)^2=25$

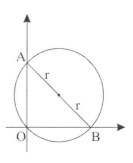

45) The correct answer is (C)

Slope of a line is calculated by $m = \dfrac{y}{x}$, therefore, $m_1=2$, $m_2=-2$ and $m_3=\sqrt{3}$, and the sum of them is $2-2+\sqrt{3}=\sqrt{3}$

46) The correct answer is (B)

In the given graph, $f(x+3)=0$ at 3 points, that are -4, 3, and 5. Therefore, for the first point, $x+3=-4$, and $x=-7$, for the second point $x+3=3$, and $x=0$, and finally for the last point, $x+3=5$, and $x=2$.
Sum of these x values is : $-7+0+2=-5$

47) The correct answer is (D)

The table only informs about the employees who have been late to work, but it does not provide any information about the number of employees in the company. Therefore the correct answer: D

48) The correct answer is (A)

The equation of a line passing through two known point is found by $\dfrac{y-y_1}{y_1-y_2}$ $=\dfrac{x-x_1}{x_1-x_2}$, therefore the equation of line d_1 is $\dfrac{x}{3}+\dfrac{y}{-4}=1$, and $-4x+3y=-12$, and similarly for line d_2 it is $\dfrac{x}{3}+\dfrac{y}{-2}=1$, and $-2x+3y=-6$.

49) The correct answer is (B)

$f(x)$ cuts the x axis where $x=0$, therefore $f(0)=0^2+25=25$, so it cuts y axis at 25 $(0,25)$. Solving it for $y=0$, $0=-x^2+25$, $x^2=25$, $x=\pm5$, so it cuts x axis at -5 and $5\cdot(5, 0)$, $(-5, 0)$.

50) The correct answer is (D)

Shaded region is $A(ABCD)-A(KLEF)=a^2-b^2$, since both of them are squares. Since $a^2-b^2=x$ and $a^2+b^2=y$, summing these two equations up, $2a^2=x+y$ and $a^2=(x+y)/2$.

51) The correct answer is (E)

Let the number of female athletes be x in this group, which means that the number of male athletes is $2x+5$. Since the sum of these two must be equal to 44, $x+2x+5=44$, therefore $3x+5=44$, $3x=39$ and $x=13$.

52) The correct answer is (A)

Since they buy the same products and the least amount is asked, we need to find out the GCD(120,140, 80, 60)=20. This means they have bought 6, 7, 4 and 3 pieces respectively. Summing them up, $6+7+4+3=20$

53) **The correct answer is (C)**

If $f(x)=ax^2+bx+2$, $f(1)=7$ and $f(2)=16$, then $f(1)=7=a \cdot 1^2+b \cdot 1+c=a+b+2=7$ and $a+b=5$, $f(2)=a \cdot 2^2+b \cdot 2+2=4a+2b+2=16$ and $4a+2b=14$ and $2a+b=7$. Solving these two equations together, $a+b=5$, if we multiply both sides with -1, $-a-b=-5$ and summing up $2a+b=7$, $-a-b=-1$, $a=2$ and $b=3$, $a/b=2/3$

54) **The correct answer is (C)**

let notebook be n and pencils be p $8n+6p=60$ and $6n+8p=80$ when we sum them up $14n+14p=140$ then $n+p=10$

55) **The correct answer is (D)**

Scoring formula for the exam is $S=0.25A+25$. Since the first student has answered all 100 questions correctly, his/her point is $S_1=100 \cdot 0,25+25=50$. The other one cannot answer 60 questions, which means he/she has answered 40 questions, so his/her point is $S_2=40 \cdot 0.25+25=35$. Therefore the sum of their points is $50+35=85$

56) **The correct answer is (D)**

$|AB|^2=BC \cdot BD$, $6^2=4 \cdot (4+2r)$, $36=4 \cdot (4+2r)$, $9=4+2r$, $2r=5$, $r=2,5$

57) **The correct answer is (C)**

$$a = \frac{V^2}{r} = \frac{20^2}{2} = \frac{400}{2} = 200$$

58) **The correct answer is (E)**

$$a = \frac{V^2}{r} \Rightarrow V^2 = ar = 18 \cdot 2, \ V^2 = 36, \ v = 6$$

59) **The correct answer is (B)**

The actual increase = 24000-20000=4000
The percentage increase is
$$\left(\frac{4000}{20000} \right) \cdot x100\% = 20\%$$

60) **The correct answer is (D)**

$(x+3)^2+(x-3)^2=2A$,
$x^2+6x+9+x^2-6x+9=2A$
$2x^2+18=2A$, $x^2+9=A$

TEST – 2.3
- Solutions -

1) **The correct answer is (B)**

   Since machine A can fill up 360 bottles in an hour, it can fill 360/60=6 bottles in a minute. This means 150x6=900 bottles in 150 minutes. Similarly, since machine B can fill 220 bottles in an hour, it can fill 220/60=11/3 bottles in a minute. This means 150x11/3=550 bottles in 150 minutes, totaling 900+550=1450 bottles.

2) **The correct answer is (B)**

   Taking into parenthesis of $\sqrt{3}$, $\dfrac{\sqrt{3}}{a}+\dfrac{\sqrt{3}}{b}+\dfrac{\sqrt{3}}{c}=\sqrt{3}\left(\dfrac{1}{a}+\dfrac{1}{b}+\dfrac{1}{c}\right)$.

   Replacing $\left(\dfrac{1}{a}+\dfrac{1}{b}+\dfrac{1}{c}\right)$ with $\sqrt{3}$, $\Rightarrow \sqrt{3}\cdot\sqrt{3}=3$

3) **The correct answer is (A)**

   $\dfrac{1}{3}+\dfrac{1}{2}-\left(-\dfrac{1}{2}+\dfrac{1}{3}\right)=\dfrac{1}{3}+\dfrac{1}{2}+\dfrac{1}{2}-\dfrac{1}{3}=\dfrac{1}{2}+\dfrac{1}{2}=1$, $a^1=a$

4) **The correct answer is (D)**

   Let the number of classrooms for 10 students be x and the number of classrooms for 13 students be y, which means **x+y=20**. This means there are 10x students studying in the small classrooms and 13y students studying in larger classrooms. Since the total number of students is 224, 10x+13y=224.

5) **The correct answer is (B)**

   If $\dfrac{6}{\pi}=\dfrac{14}{\pi+x}$ then 14π=6(π+x), 7π=3(π+x)

   therefore 7π=3π+3x, 3x=4π and $x=\dfrac{4\pi}{3}$.

6) **The correct answer is (E)**

   Summing up these equations, $+\begin{cases}3x-4y=6\pi\\6x-5y=12\pi\end{cases}$,

   therefore 9x-9y=18π and 9(x-y)=18π, $x-y=\dfrac{18\pi}{9}=2\pi$.

7) **The correct answer is (A)**

Since for x=0 f(0)=1, this condition is only satisfied by choices A and D. and since for x=-1 f(-1)=-1, this condition is only satisfied by choice A.

8) **The correct answer is (C)**

The equation of the line d_1 is n·y=mx+n, therefore the slope is $\frac{m}{n}$. The equation of the line d_2 is m·y=nx+m, therefore the slope is $\frac{n}{m}$. Therefore the ratio of the slopes is $\dfrac{\dfrac{m}{n}}{\dfrac{n}{m}} = \dfrac{m^2}{n^2}$.

9) **The correct answer is (A)**

In order to have an empty set as solution set, the ratio of coefficients of x and y must be equal to each other, which means $\dfrac{9}{m} = \dfrac{-6}{12}$, $m = \dfrac{9 \cdot 2}{-6} = -18$

10) **The correct answer is (A)**

For $y=x^2+4$, x=0 at A, therefore $y=0^2+4=4$, and
For $y=-x^2-3$, x=0 at B, therefore $y=0^2-3=-3$
Therefore the distance between A and B is 4–(–3)=7

11) **The correct answer is (D)**

Since ABC is an equilateral triangle, its interior angles are equal to each other and mA=mB=mC=x=60. As DEFG is a square and |DF| is a diagonal. The diagonals divide the angles equally in squares, therefore y=90/2=45.
Then $\dfrac{x + y}{x - y} = \dfrac{60 + 45}{60 - 45} = \dfrac{105}{15} = 7$.

12) **The correct answer is (D)**

Let the roots of equation $y=x^2-8x+7$ be x_1 and x_2.

Since $x_1 + x_2 = \dfrac{-b}{a} = \dfrac{-(-8)}{1} = 8$ and $x_1 \cdot x_2 = \dfrac{c}{a} = \dfrac{7}{1} = 7$, $\dfrac{(x_1 + x_2)}{(x_1 \cdot x_2)} = \dfrac{8}{7}$

13) The correct answer is (B)

$$\dfrac{\dfrac{3}{a}+\dfrac{3}{b}}{\dfrac{a}{3}+\dfrac{b}{3}}=\dfrac{\dfrac{3b}{ab}+\dfrac{3a}{ba}}{\dfrac{a+b}{3}}=\dfrac{\dfrac{3b+3a}{ab}}{\dfrac{a+b}{3}}=\dfrac{\dfrac{3(a+b)}{ab}}{\dfrac{(a+b)}{3}}=\dfrac{\dfrac{3}{ab}}{\dfrac{1}{3}}=\dfrac{3}{ab}\cdot 3=\dfrac{9}{ab}$$

14) The correct answer is (C)

The roots of a quadratic equation are found by ($\Delta=b^2-4ac$)

$x_{1,2}=\dfrac{-b\pm\sqrt{\Delta}}{2a}$, Since $\Delta=(-2)^2-4\cdot 1\cdot(-12)=52$, and

$\sqrt{\Delta}=\sqrt{52}=2\sqrt{13}$

$x_1=\dfrac{2+2\sqrt{13}}{2\cdot 1}=\sqrt{13}+1$, and $x_2=\dfrac{2-2\sqrt{13}}{2\cdot 1}=1-\sqrt{13}$

15) The correct answer is (C)

I.   When we double the velocity of the object, the acceleration would increase for 4 times.

II. When we half the radius, the acceleration would double.

III. When we half the velocity, the acceleration would decrease for 4 times

Therefore the correct answer is II and III.

16) The correct answer is (A)

$x(x^4-25)=600x$, therefore $x^4-25=600$ and $x^4=625=5^4$. Therefore $x=\pm 5$

17) The correct answer is (A)

$\dfrac{1}{3x_{(4)}}-\dfrac{1}{4x_{(3)}}=\dfrac{1}{3_{(4)}}+\dfrac{1}{4_{(3)}}$ and $\dfrac{4-3}{12x}=\dfrac{4+3}{12}$, $\dfrac{1}{12x}=\dfrac{7}{12}$ and $x=\dfrac{1}{7}$

18) The correct answer is (A)

An exterior angle of a triangle is equal to the sum of non-adjacent interior angles. Therefore x=60+40=100

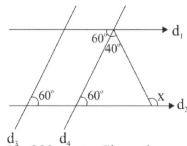

19) The correct answer is (C)

The amount to be paid for the copies is 24x12=288 cents. Since the cost would have been 4 cents in machine A, the number of pages would have been x=288/4=72 pages.

20) The correct answer is (C)

$|BD|^2+|AD|^2=|AB|^2$, therefore $3^2+|AD|^2=5^2$, and $|AD|=4$

$\sin x = \dfrac{AD}{AB} = \dfrac{4}{5}$, $\tan y = \dfrac{AD}{DC} = \dfrac{4}{6} = \dfrac{2}{3}$,

$\sin x + \tan y = \dfrac{4}{5} + \dfrac{2}{3} = \dfrac{12+10}{15} = \dfrac{22}{15}$

21) The correct answer is (D)

The number of female students=16+8+10+4=38 and the number of male students=16+10+4+4=34 Therefore total number of students=38+34=72 The ratio of female students to male students is 38/34=19/17 There are 12 male and 12 female students in class A, therefore the ratio is 1. But the classroom with the highest percentage of female students is 10/14=71%

22) The correct answer is (A)

There are (12+18+8)=38 passengers in the plane. The probability of firs passenger disembarking being an American is 12/38. Since there would be one passenger and one American less after disembarking, there will be 11 Americans and 37 passengers left, so the probability of second passenger being an American would be 11/37, and the probability of both passengers being Americans would be 12x11/38x37=66/703

23) The correct answer is (A)

Since a physics book costs $90 and the profit margin is 30%=30x90/100=$27, the book would be sold for 90+27=$117. Therefore the number of books sold is 702/117=6

24) The correct answer is (B)

Replacing n with 0, choices A, C and D cannot satisfy the f(n) condition in the table, and replacing n with 1, only choice B can satisfy the f(n) condition in the given table. Therefore the correct answer is B.

25) The correct answer is (D)

Let the sum of all attending students be 100x, and the number of students attending both activities be y, therefore 30x+y+50x=100x, and y=20x. Since we know that 60 students have attended both activities, y=60=20x, and x=3. As the number of students who have attended football is 30x, 30x=30·3=**90** students have attended football activities.

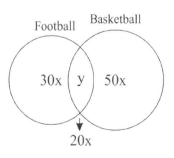

26) **The correct answer is (A)**

The sum of the polynomials would be
$4x^3+2x^2+3x+4+4x^2-3x-4=4x^3+2x^2+4x^2+3x-3x+4-4=4x^3+6x^2$

27) **The correct answer is (A)**

Since $\dfrac{2\pi+x}{3}=\dfrac{7}{2}$, then $2(2\pi+x)=21$,

$4\pi+2x=21$ and $2x=21-4\pi$, $x=\dfrac{21-4\pi}{2}$

28) **The correct answer is (D)**

Naming notebooks as n and pencils as p, let us sum both equations

$\begin{array}{r} 10n+5p=9 \\ +\quad 5n+10p=6 \\ \hline 15n+15p=15 \end{array}$, therefore $15(n+p)=15$, $n+p=1$

29) **The correct answer is (C)**

Since there is inverse proportion between the work completed and the number of workers, (the more workers, the less time to complete),

27 workers complete in 86 hours
14 workers complete in x hours
$27 \cdot 86 = 14x$ and $x = 27 \cdot 86/14 = 165.8 = 166$ hours

30) **The correct answer is (D)**

According to the formula, $\upsilon^2=g \cdot R \cdot \tan\alpha=10 \cdot 10 \cdot \tan45$, since $\tan45=1$,
$\upsilon^2=100$, and $\upsilon=10m/s$.

31) **The correct answer is (B)**

Dividing 1840 minutes into 60 results 30 hours and 40 minutes, which means 1 day, 6 hours and 40 minutes. 8:00am+6:40=2:40pm

32) **The correct answer is (B)**

By definition, a **function** is a relation where a value from the set the first components of the ordered pairs is associated with exactly one value from the set of second components of the ordered pair. Therefore a given x value of a function could be related to only one y value. This is true for all but $y=\sqrt{x}$, since a value of x corresponds to two y values. Therefore there are 3 functions in the given figure.

33) **The correct answer is (B)**

$\log_3 3^7 = 7$, $\log_4 4^8 = 8$, $7\log_7 4 = 4$, $7+8+4=19$

34) **The correct answer is (A)**

Since the car would be parked for h hours, payment must be calculated by m=0.25xh

35) **The correct answer is (C)**

$\log 18 = \log(2 \cdot 9) = \log 2 + \log 9 = \log + \log_3 2 = \log 2 + 2\log 3 = a + 2b$.

36) **The correct answer is (B)**

According to the graph, m is one of the roots of the equation $x^2 + bx - 18 = 0$. Remember that for quadratic equations $ax^2 + bx + c = 0$, the sum of the roots ($x_1 + x_2 = -b/a$) and multiplication of the roots ($x_1 \cdot x_2 = c/a$). Therefore $x_1 + x_2 = 6-3 = -b/1$ and b=−3, since a=1 for this equation. Similarly, $x_1 \cdot x_2 = c/a$ and $6 \cdot m = -18/1$ and m=−3, and b+m=−3−3=−6.

37) **The correct answer is (D)**

Let us count the number that numeral 7 is used: 7, 17, 27, 37, 47, 57, 67, 70, 71, 72, 73, 74, 75, 76, 77, 78, 79, 87, 97. Numeral 7 has been used for 20 times in these numbers. To make it 21, it must be used once more, and the closest number is 107. Therefore the minimum number of pages must be 107.

38) **The correct answer is (C)**

Let us name this number as x. then 3x/7=6m, 3x=42 and x=14m. Since we are calculating 5/14th of this number, $5x/14 = 5 \cdot 14m/14 = 5m$

39) **The correct answer is (C)**

Having the minimum number of square plots means having the maximum edge for a square. Therefore we are looking for HCF (110, 160)=10. Dividing the total land area into the plot area, $110 \cdot 160/10 \cdot 10 = 176$
HCF=highest common factor

40) **The correct answer is (C)**

According to the given graph, there have been 2400, 1200 and 2400 visitors in January, March and May respectively. Therefore the average of these three months would be (2400+1200+2400)/3=2000.

41) The correct answer is (D)

According to the graph, most popular models are E and C.

42) The correct answer is (C)

Third edge of a triangle can neither be smaller nor greater than the sum of other two edges. Therefore x being the length of the third edge, 20–14<x<20+14 and 6<x<34, which means the maximum value of x could be 33. Therefore the maximum peripheral of the garden is 20+14+33=67.

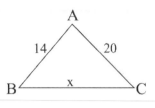

43) The correct answer is (A)

The sum of exterior angles of a triangle is 360.
Therefore 110+134+x=360 and x=116

44) The correct answer is (B)

x=v·t, where x is the distance, v is the velocity and t is the time. Since both vehicle would cover 140m together to meet, x=140, and since they move towards each other. We need to sum up their velocities. Therefore 140=(4v+3v)·t, and t=140/7v=20/v.

45) The correct answer is (B)

The volume of a cylinder is calculated by V=Πr²h, where r is the radius and h is the height of the cylinder. Therefore V=Π(2Π)²·3Π=12Π⁴cm³.

46) The correct answer is (D)

Let us find the points where the line 2x+3y=18 cuts the axes first. For x=0, 3y=18 and y=6, and for y=0, 2x=18 and x=9. Therefore the area of the triangle between the x and y axes and this line is, A=6·9/2=27

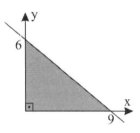

47) The correct answer is (E)

The original area of the rectangle is A=30·20=600cm². When the edges are decreased by 10%. The new edge lengths would be a'=a·0.9=20·0.9=18cm and b'=b·0.9=30·0.9=27cm. Therefore the area of the new rectangle would be A''=18·27=486cm², and the difference would be 600–486=114.

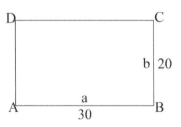

48) The correct answer is (B)

If x workers finish in b days, then (x+y) workers finish in k days. Since there is an inverse proportion, x·b=(x+y)·k, and $k = \dfrac{x \cdot b}{x + y}$

49) The correct answer is (C)

The total angles occupied by four professions in the graph must be 360, therefore A+B+C+D=360. Since there are 8 doctors, 4 teachers, 20 engineers and 16 faculty members, naming the angle occupied by one person as "x", 8x+4x+20x+16x=360 and x=7.5. Therefore the angles representing each profession should be A=8·7.5=60, B=4·7.5=30, C=20·7.5=150 and D=16·7.5=120.

50) The correct answer is (E)

Summing both equations up, $\dfrac{1}{x} + \dfrac{3}{y} = 4$ and $\dfrac{4}{x} - \dfrac{3}{y} = 3$,

$\dfrac{1}{x} + \dfrac{4}{x} + \dfrac{3}{y} - \dfrac{3}{y} = 4 + 3$, $\dfrac{5}{x} = 7$, and $x = \dfrac{5}{7}$.

51) The correct answer is (E)

The number of even numbers in an interval is calculated by:
The number of terms=(last term–first term)/2+1=(124–10)/2+1=58.

52) The correct answer is (E)

The least paper consuming schools are A (20 packs), B (10 packs) and E (30 packs). Therefore their average consumption is (20+10+30)/3=20 packs.

53) The correct answer is (E)

An inscribed angle that covers the same portion of intercepted arc with a central angle is half of that central angle.
Therefore $\angle ACB = \angle AOB/2 = 64/2 = 32$

54) The correct answer is (E)

Since there are 5 high school students, they need to pay 5·3=$15, while 6 university students need to pay 6·5=$30, and senior citizens need to pay 10·4=$40. The total amount would be 15+30+40=$85.

55) The correct answer is (E)

Summing up the polynomials,
$2x^3+3x^2+6x+4-(4x^3-x^2+2x-6)=ax^3+bx^2+cx+d$,
$2x^3+3x^2+6x+4-4x^3+x^2-2x+6=-2x^3+4x^2+4x+10$,
therefore a=-2, b=4, c=4 and d=10, (a+b+c+d)=-2+4+4+10=16

56) The correct answer is (C)

Since $\begin{cases} y \le -4 \cdot 5^x + 625 \\ y \le 5^x \end{cases}$ then $5^x \le -4 \cdot 5^x + 625$ and $5^x + 4 \cdot 5^x \le 625$,

$(4+1)5^x=625$, $5 \cdot 5^x=625$, and $5^{x+1}=625=5^4$, therefore x+1=4, x=3

57) The correct answer is (A)

n(n–3)=2D, therefore D=n(n–3)/2.
Replacing n with 7, D=7·(7–3)/2=7·4/2=14.

58) The correct answer is (C)

Let us find the number of edges first. 2D=n(n–3), 2.35=n(n–3) and therefore $n^2-3n=70$ or $n^2-3n-70=0$, which means (n–10)(n+7)=70. Therefore n=10 or n=–7. Since a polygon with –7 edges is impossible, we have to get n=10. Therefore the perimeter is 10·2=20cm.

59) The correct answer is (B)

AC=12 if $BA = \dfrac{AC}{2} = \dfrac{12}{2} = 6$, $BC = \dfrac{AC}{2}\sqrt{3} = \dfrac{12}{2}\sqrt{3} = 6\sqrt{3}$
Perimeter (ABC)=AB+AC+BC=12+6+$6\sqrt{3} = 18 + 6\sqrt{3}$

60) The correct answer is (B)

P=2(a+b)=44,   A=a·b
  a+b=22   120= a·b
$AC^2=a^2+b^2=(a+b)^2-2a\cdot b=(22)^2-2\cdot120$
  |AC|= $\sqrt{244} = 2\sqrt{61}$

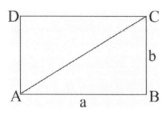

TEST – 2.4
- *Solutions* -

1) **The correct answer is (A)**

   Since ABC is a straight angle, $\angle ABD + \angle DBC = 180^o$. Given $\angle ABD - \angle DBC = 58^o$ too, when we sum up both equations, $2 \cdot \angle ABD = 238^o$ and $\angle ABD = 119^o$

2) **The correct answer is (C)**

   $$\left(\sqrt{3x} + \sqrt{2x}\right)^2 = \left(\sqrt{3x}\right)^2 + 2\sqrt{3x} \cdot \sqrt{2x} + \left(\sqrt{2x}\right)^2 =$$
   $$= 3x + 2\sqrt{3x \cdot 2x} + 2x = 5x + 2x\sqrt{6}$$

3) **The correct answer is (D)**

   Since $f(x)=x^2+2x$ and $g(x)=x-2$, $f(g(x))=(g(x))^2+2g(x)=(x-2)^2+2(x-2)$.
   Replacing x with 2a, $f(g(2a))=(2a-2)^2+2(2a-2)=4a^2-8a+4+4a-4=4a^2-4a$.

4) **The correct answer is (B)**

   $(x+y)^2-(y-x)^2+(2xy)^2=x^2+2xy+y^2-(y^2-2xy+x^2)+4x^2y^2=$
   $=x^2+2xy+y^2-y^2+2xy-x^2+4x^2y^2=4xy+4x^2y^2=4xy(1+xy)$

5) **The correct answer is (C)**

   Simplifying the expressions, $\dfrac{(x+y)^2}{x+y} + \dfrac{(x-y)^2}{x-y} = x+y+x-y = 2x$

6) **The correct answer is (A)**

   Let us expand the parentheses first,
   $(4+4i) \cdot (3-3i) = 4 \cdot 3 - 4 \cdot 3 \cdot i + 3 \cdot 4 \cdot i - 3 \cdot 3 \cdot i^2 = 12-12i+12i-(-12)=12+12=24$

7) **The correct answer is (C)**

   Let us expand both sides of the equation first,
   $(x+2y)^2+(y-2x)^2=A(x^2+y^2)$,
   $x^2+4xy+4y^2+y^2-4xy+4y^2=A(x^2+y^2)$,
   $x^2+4y^2+y^2+4y^2=A(x^2+y^2)$,
   $5x^2+5y^2=5(x^2+y^2)=A(x^2+y^2)$, therefore A=5

8) **The correct answer is (C)**

Since color book cover and color publishing would increase the cost, I and III should be avoided.

9) **The correct answer is (C)**

$y=0$ for A and B, means A and B are the roots of given equation. Therefore $f(x)=x^2-8x+12=0$ for $x=A$ and $x=B$. solving accordingly, $(x-6)(x-2)=0$ and $A=6$ and $B=2$. Therefore solution$=6^2+2^6=36+64=100$

10) **The correct answer is (B)**

Let us name the number of tickets sold to the children as x and the number of tickets sold to the adults as y. Since the total number of tickets sold is 160, $x+y=160$, and since the total revenue is 880, the revenue from children would be ax and the revenue from adults would be $(a+3)y$, then $ax+(a+3)y=880$

11) **The correct answer is (D)**

$\log_3 21=\log_3(7\cdot 3)=\log_3 3+\log_3 7=1+\log_3 7$

12) **The correct answer is (A)**

Since $\dfrac{1}{a}+\dfrac{1}{b}=\dfrac{1}{2}$ and $\dfrac{1}{a}-\dfrac{1}{b}=\dfrac{1}{4}$, summing them up

$\dfrac{1}{a}+\dfrac{1}{b}+\dfrac{1}{a}-\dfrac{1}{b}=\dfrac{1}{2}+\dfrac{1}{4}$, and $\dfrac{2}{a}=\dfrac{2}{4}+\dfrac{1}{4}=\dfrac{3}{4}$,

therefore $\dfrac{4}{a}=2\cdot\left(\dfrac{2}{a}\right)=2\cdot\dfrac{3}{4}=\dfrac{3}{2}$.

13) **The correct answer is (D)**

Parallel lines have equal slopes, and the slope of the line $y=x\sqrt{3}+3$ is $\dfrac{y}{x}=\sqrt{3}$. Therefore the slope of the new line is $=\sqrt{3}$ too. Since a point and the slope of the line is known, $y-y_1=m(x-x_1)$, and A(3, 4), therefore $y-4=\sqrt{3}(x-3)$, $y-4=x\sqrt{3}-3\sqrt{3}$, and $y=x\sqrt{3}-3\sqrt{3}+4$

14) **The correct answer is (C)**

Since this is a linear function and we know two points on this line, A(4, 200) and B(6, 300), Let us find the slope of this line first.

$$m = \frac{y_2 - y_1}{x_2 - x_1} = \frac{300 - 200}{6 - 4} = \frac{100}{2} = 50$$

As y=mx+n, for any point 200=50·4+n, n=0, therefore the is y=50x

15) **The correct answer is (D)**

Solving the equation, 4(x+4)=3(x–3)+3(3–x),

4x+16=3x–9+9–3x=0, 4x=–16 and $x = \frac{-16}{4} = -4$

16) **The correct answer is (A)**

$\left(\frac{\pi}{2} + \frac{\pi}{3} + \frac{\pi}{4} \right) = \pi \left(\frac{1}{2} + \frac{1}{3} + \frac{1}{4} \right) = \pi \left(\frac{6+4+3}{12} \right) = \frac{13\pi}{12}$, Since π=180 ,

$$\frac{13\pi}{12} = \frac{13 \cdot 180}{12} = 195^\circ$$

17) **The correct answer is (A)**

$\frac{5}{x} - \frac{5}{9} = \frac{2}{x}$, therefore $\frac{5}{x} - \frac{2}{x} = \frac{5}{9}$ and $\frac{3}{x} = \frac{5}{9}$, $x = \frac{3 \cdot 9}{5} = \frac{27}{5}$

18) **The correct answer is (C)**

x^2–2x+2=3x–4, therefore x^2–5x+6=0 and (x–3)(x+2)=0, resulting x_1=3 and x_2= -2

19) **The correct answer is (A)**

x=0 at y intercept. Therefore y–6=6(x–2) and y–6=6(0–2), y–6=–12, and y=–6

20) **The correct answer is (E)**

Let us take the square of both sides of the equation.

$\sqrt{3x + 2} = \sqrt{2x + 3} \Rightarrow \left(\sqrt{3x + 2} \right)^2 = \left(\sqrt{2x + 3} \right)^2$ and $3x + 2 = 2x + 3$

3x–2x=3–2 and x=1. Therefore $4x^2+4x=4 \cdot 1^2+4 \cdot 1=4+4=8$

21) **The correct answer is (A)**

Let us start with converting the given time into minutes, and then find the LCF of the resulting minutes and finish with converting the resulting minutes into hour. $\frac{1}{3}h = 20\,min$, $\frac{1}{4}h = 15\,min$ and $\frac{1}{6}h = 10\,min$.

LCF(10, 15, 20)=60, and 1h=60

22) **The correct answer is (C)**

$log_5 125 = log_5 5^3 = 3log_5 5 = 3$
$log_3 27 = log_3 3^3 = 3log_3 3 = 3$
$log_4 64 = log_4 4^3 = 3log_4 4 = 3$

23) **The correct answer is (D)**

The numbers on red balls would be (5, 6, 7, 8, 9, 10, 11, 12, 13, 14, 15), while the green balls would be numbered as (7, 8, 9, 10, 11, 12, 13, 14, 15, 16, 17). Even green balls would be (8, 10, 12, 14, 16), totaling 5, and even red balls would be (6, 8, 10, 12, 14) totaling another 5. Therefore P(even)= $\frac{10}{22} = \frac{5}{11}$.

24) **The correct answer is (E)**

0, 4, 8, 12, 16, 20, 24, 28, 32, 36, 40, 44, 48, 52, 56, 60, …

25) **The correct answer is (D)**

This sort of problem is solved by using the formula $f(x) = a \cdot (1-r)^x$, therefore $f(m) = 2400 \cdot (1-0.06)^m = 2400 \cdot (0.94)^m$

26) **The correct answer is (A)**

Since f(x)=0,84x+0,6 and f(x)=5,64, 5.64=0.84x+0.6 and 0.84x=5.04,

$x = \frac{5,04}{0,84} = 6\,years$

27) **The correct answer is (B)**

The interior angle of an equilateral triangle is 60, and the exterior angle is 120, therefore the ratio is $\frac{60}{120} = \frac{1}{2}$

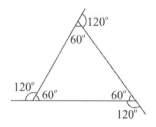

28) The correct answer is (C)

Summing up these two equations, $2 \cdot 3^x + 3 \cdot 3^y + 3 \cdot 3^x + 2 \cdot 3^y = 33 + 27$,

Therefore $5 \cdot 3^x + 5 \cdot 3^y = 60$, $5(3^x + 3^y) = 60$, and $3^x + 3^y = \dfrac{60}{5} = 12$

29) The correct answer is (D)

The number of weekday shoppers is $1000+400+600+200+800=3000$, and the number of weekend shoppers is $600+400=1000$, therefore the ratio is $\dfrac{1000}{3000} = \dfrac{1}{3}$.

30) The correct answer is (C)

A truck occupies and area of $3 \cdot 8 = 24m^2$, and since 20 trucks can part at this lot, the area of this lot is $20 \cdot 24 = 480m^2$. A car occupies $3 \cdot 2 = 6m^2$, so the number of cars that can park in this lot is $\dfrac{480}{6} = 80$.

31) The correct answer is (C)

Let Ahmet have read x pages of book in the first day, then the following would be the number of pages he has read in the consecutive days would be $(x+20)$, $(x+40)$, … $(x+100)$. Since he has read $1/8^{th}$ of the book in the first day, the book is 8x pages long, therefore
$x+(x+20)+(x+40)+(x+60)+(x+80)+(x+100)= 8x=6x+300$,
therefore $2x=300$ and $x=150$, $8x=1200$

32) The correct answer is (B)

Since $|AB|^2=|BC| \cdot |BD|$, $|AB|^2=6 \cdot (6+4)=60$ and
$|AB|=\sqrt{60} = \sqrt{4 \cdot 15} = \sqrt{4} \cdot \sqrt{15} = 2\sqrt{15}$

33) The correct answer is (D)

The number of printed books is $900+1200+1500=3600$, while the number of faulty books printed in February is 20. Therefore the answer is $\dfrac{20}{3600} = \dfrac{1}{180}$.

34) The correct answer is (B)

Let the number of male students be x and the number of female students be y. therefore x·20%=y·30% and 2x=3y, or x=$\frac{3y}{2}$. Since there are 300 students at this school, x+y=300 and replacing x, $\frac{3y}{2}$+y=300, therefore the number of female students=y=120. As 70% of them do not play basketball, $\frac{120 \cdot 70}{100} = 84$.

35) The correct answer is (C)

If parabolas y=x²–6x+13 and y=a(x–b)²+c are identical, then x²–6x+13= =a(x–b)²+c. Therefore x²–6x+13=a(x²–2bx+b²)+c=ax²–2abx+ab²+c. Since x²=ax², a=1, –2ab=–6 and ab²+c=13. Replacing a with 1, in the second expression, –2ab=–2b=–6, b=3. Replacing a and b in the last expression, ab²+c=1·3²+c=9+c=13, therefore c=4 and a+b+c=1+3+4=8

36) The correct answer is (D)

A) The total number of graduates is =400+500+600+700=2200, and the average is $\frac{2200}{4} = 550$

B) The ratio of greatest number of graduates to least number of graduates= $\frac{700}{400} = \frac{7}{4}$ (not $\frac{4}{7}$)

C) The average of graduates is 550 and the closest number is 500 and 600

D) The least number of graduates come from B University.

37) The correct answer is (D)

There is no information about the price of transportation forms in the graph, therefore D is the correct answer.

38) The correct answer is (B)

Daily number of passengers is 4800+3600+2400+1200=12000, multiplying by 7, weekly number of passengers is 84000.

39) The correct answer is (B)

The average number of passengers for 3 days is $\frac{3 \cdot 120000}{4} = 90000$.

40) The correct answer is (D)

Since there is an inverse ration in this question,
If x workers complete in 2^m days
(x+a) workers complete in y days.

Therefore $x \cdot 2^m = y(x+a)$ and $y = \dfrac{x \cdot 2^m}{(x+a)}$

41) The correct answer is (A)

40% more of 80 is $\dfrac{80 \cdot (100+40)}{100} = 112$, and 40% less of 80 is $\dfrac{80 \cdot (100-40)}{100} = 48$, therefore $\dfrac{A}{B} = \dfrac{112}{48} = \dfrac{7}{3}$.

42) The correct answer is (A)

According to the graph, the average pages would be
$\dfrac{(400+300+500+100+300)}{5} = 320$

43) The correct answer is (C)

The graph shows that 24 tons of water has emptied in 36 minutes and the pool can hold 124 tons of water. Therefore if 24 tons empties in 36 minutes, Then 124 tons empties in t minutes. Therefore 24·t=124·36, and t=186 minutes =3 hours and 6 minutes.

44) The correct answer is (D)

If $x^2-5x+6=0$, then (x–3)(x–2)=0, therefore the roots of this equation are x=2 and x=3. $|x_1-\pi|+|x_2-\pi|=|2-\pi|+|3-\pi|$. Since 2<$\pi$ and 3<π, $|2-\pi|=-2+\pi$ and $|3-\pi|=-3+\pi$, Therefore $|x_1-\pi|+|x_2-\pi|=-2-\pi-3+\pi=2\pi-5$.

45) The correct answer is (A)

Let us call pencils as p and notebooks as n, then 10p+6n=57 and 4n=9p,
Therefore $\dfrac{n}{p} = \dfrac{9}{4} = \dfrac{9x}{4x}$. 10n+6p=57, 10·9x+6·4x=57, 90x+24x=57, 114x=57, $x=\dfrac{1}{2}$. Notebook is =9x=9·$\dfrac{1}{2}$ =4.5. \$4.5

46) The correct answer is (D)

Correct answer is D, since values change in all other graphs.

47) The correct answer is (B)

For the given line $4x+5y+20=0$, $5y=-4x-20$ and $y=-\dfrac{4x}{5}-4$, therefore $m_1=-\dfrac{4}{5}$. Multiplying the slopes of two perpendicular lines result in $m_1 \cdot m_2=-1$. Therefore $m_2 \cdot \left(-\dfrac{4}{5}\right)=-1$, $m_2=\dfrac{5}{4}$.

48) The correct answer is (C)

Finding out where x and y axes are.C.,Using (0.0) as a point, $3(0)+2(0)>12$ is false .thus the shade is on the other side of the line intercepted results in (0, 6) and (4, 0). Therefore $3x+2y\geq12$.is graph C.

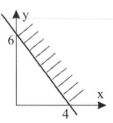

49) The correct answer is (C)

As seen from the graph, $f(-6)=-3$, $f(-4)=0$, $f(7)=6$, and $f^{-1}(6)=7$, therefore $\dfrac{f(-6)+f(-4)}{f^{-1}(6)}=\dfrac{-3+0}{7}=-\dfrac{3}{7}$.

50) The correct answer is (D)

Since the edges are located at A(–8, 4) and B(8, 4) the diameter is equal to

$2r=\sqrt{(8-(-8)^2+(4-4)^2}=16$, and $r=8$.

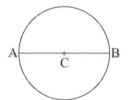

The center would be located at

$\left(\dfrac{x_1+x_2}{2},\dfrac{y_1+y_2}{2}\right)=(0,\ 4)$.

A circle's general equation is $(x-a)^2+(y-b)^2=r^2$, Therefore $(x-0)^2+(y-4)^2=64$

51) The correct answer is (A)

The sum of parents' ages would be (28+6+32+6)=72 in 6 years, while the sum of the children's ages would be (6+6+8+6+4+6)=36, therefore the ratio would be $\dfrac{72}{36}=2$.

52) The correct answer is (D)

Since x+144=180, x=180–144=36 and 4y=144, y=36,

therefore $\dfrac{x}{2}+2y=\dfrac{36}{2}+36\cdot2=90$.

53) The correct answer is (E)

First four positive even number are 2, 4, 6 and 8, therefore their sum is 2+4+6+8=20. First four prime numbers are 2, 3, 5, and 7, and their sum is 2+3+5+7=17. Therefore the ratio is $\dfrac{20}{17}$.

54) The correct answer is (E)

The mode used is $P(b)=m \cdot n^b$, since $P(b)=50000$ and $m=48000$,

and b=1 year, $n^b = \dfrac{50000}{48000} = 1.04$ therefore n=1.04.

55) The correct answer is (E)

First day: 200 pages,

Second day: 200·(1+10%)=220 pages,
Third day: 220·(1+10%)=242 pages and
Fourth day: 242·(1+10%)=266 pages.
Therefore he would read 200+220+242+266=928 pages.

56) The correct answer is (E)

This means we need to find out the solution of the equation.

$2x \cdot (2x+6) - 2 = (2x-6) \cdot 2x + 2$, therefore expanding the parantheses,

$4x^2 + 12x - 2 = 4x^2 - 12x + 2$, and 12x+12x=4, 24x=4 and $x = \dfrac{4}{24} = \dfrac{1}{6}$.

57) The correct answer is (D)

If 4x–3y=14 and 2x–y=10, then we obtain 2x=y+10 from the second equation. When we replace this in the first equation, 2(y+10)–3y=14 and 2y+20–3y=14, therefore y=6. Replacing y with 6 in any of the two equations, (say, second one), 2x–y=10 and 2x–6=10, therefore 2x=16 and x=8. Finally, x–y=8–6=2.

58) The correct answer is (A)

Since $f(x)=(x+2)^2$ and $g(x)=4x^2+16x+16$, $f(x)=x^2+4x+4$, therefore

$$\frac{g(x)}{f(x)} = \frac{(4x^2+16x+16)}{(x^2+4x+4)} = \frac{4(x^2+4x+4)}{(x^2+4x+4)} = 4$$

59) **The correct answer is (C)**

$$x^2+y^2+Ax+By+C=0 \quad M\left(-\frac{A}{2}, -\frac{B}{2}\right)=M(-a, b)$$

$$x^2+y^2+12x+10y+20=0 \quad A=12, B=10$$

$$M\left(-\frac{A}{2}, -\frac{B}{2}\right)=M\left(-\frac{12}{2}, -\frac{10}{2}\right)=(-6; -5)$$

60) **The correct answer is (B)**

$$\frac{x+y}{x-y}=\frac{3}{2} \quad \Rightarrow \quad 3(x-y)=2(x+y)$$

$$\frac{x}{y}=\frac{5y}{y}=5 \qquad 3x-3y=2x+2y \Rightarrow 3x-2x=2y+3y, \ x=5y$$

TEST – 2.5
- Solutions -

1) **The correct answer is (B)**

Let us expand the parentheses and simplify then, $(6a^2+6a+6)-(4a^2-4a-4)=$
$6a^2+6a+6-4a^2+4a+4=6a^2-4a^2+6a+4a+6+4=2a^2+10a+10=2(a^2+5a+5)$

2) **The correct answer is (C)**

Multiplication of the numbers with the same bases but different powers is

done by summing their powers. $x^{\frac{2}{3}} \cdot x^{\frac{3}{2}} \cdot x^{\frac{-14}{6}}$. Therefore,

$$\frac{2}{3}+\frac{3}{2}-\frac{14}{6} \Rightarrow \frac{2}{3_{(2)}}+\frac{3}{2_{(3)}}-\frac{14}{6_{(1)}}=\frac{4+9-14}{6}=-\frac{1}{6}, \; x^{\frac{2}{3}} \cdot x^{\frac{3}{2}} \cdot x^{\frac{-14}{6}}=x^{-\frac{1}{6}}=\frac{1}{x^{1/6}}$$

3) **The correct answer is (C)**

$$\frac{3}{2}\left(\frac{1}{a}+\frac{1}{b}+\frac{1}{c}\right)-\frac{6}{4}\left(-\frac{1}{a}+\frac{1}{b}+\frac{1}{c}\right)=\frac{3}{2}\cdot\frac{1}{a}+\frac{3}{2}\cdot\frac{1}{b}+\frac{3}{2}\cdot\frac{1}{c}+\frac{3}{2}\cdot\frac{1}{a}-\frac{3}{2}\cdot\frac{1}{b}-\frac{3}{2}\cdot\frac{1}{c}=$$

$$=\frac{3}{2a}+\frac{3}{2a}=\frac{6}{2a}=\frac{3}{a}$$

4) **The correct answer is (D)**

The points where a parabola intercept x axis are the roots of that parabola
equation, as y=0 at where x axis is intercepted. Therefore,

$y=x^2-6x+5$
$x^2-6x+5=0$ $(x-5)\cdot(x-1)=0$
x   -5   x=5   x=1
x   -1 x_1=5 x_2=1

$$\frac{\sqrt{x_1}+\sqrt{x_2}}{\sqrt{5}-1}=\frac{\sqrt{5}+\sqrt{1}}{\sqrt{5}-1}=\frac{\sqrt{5}+1}{\sqrt{5}-1}=\frac{(\sqrt{5}+1)(\sqrt{5}+1)}{(\sqrt{5}-1)(\sqrt{5}+1)}=\frac{(\sqrt{5}+1)^2}{5-1}=$$

$$=\frac{5+2\sqrt{5}+1}{4}=\frac{6+2\sqrt{5}}{4}=\frac{3+\sqrt{5}}{2}$$

5) **The correct answer is (A)**

Let us divide both sides of the equation into two,

$$\frac{6a+4b+8c}{2}=\frac{24}{2}, \quad 3a+2b+4c=12, \; 15a+10b+20c=5(3a+2b+4c)=5\cdot12=60$$

6) **The correct answer is (B)**

Let us extract α from equation. $A = \dfrac{\pi r^2 \alpha}{360} \Rightarrow A \cdot 360 = \pi r^2 \alpha, \ \alpha = \dfrac{A \cdot 360}{\pi r^2}$

7) **The correct answer is (E)**
Square roots of negative numbers are imaginary

.

8) **The correct answer is (A)**

f(x)=ax+b,
f(2) → f(2)=2a+b=8
f(3) → f(3)=3a+b=4
f(2)+f(3)=2a+3a+b+b=12, 5a+2b=12

9) **The correct answer is (D)**

d_1=2x+3y=12,   for x=0, 2·0+3y=12, y=4 (0, 4)

for y=0, 2x+3·0=12, x=6 (6, 0)

Therefore the area of the triangle is $\dfrac{6 \cdot 4}{2} = 12$.

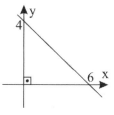

10) **The correct answer is (A)**

Let us sum up both equations first.

6N+4P+2E=20
+ 3N+5P+7E=16
9N+9P+9E=36, therefore 9(N+P+E)=36, N+P+E=4

11) **The correct answer is (C)**

$DE = \dfrac{BC}{2} = \dfrac{6x+4}{2} = (3x + 2)$ BC-DE=(6x+4)-(3x+2)=6x-3x+4-2=3x+2

12) **The correct answer is (B)**

In an arithmetic series, d denotes the differences between terms (e.g. a_4-a_3).

13) **The correct answer is (C)**

Since the power is an odd number, we can take 7+h root of both sides,
3a-4=a+10, 3a-a=4+10, 2a=14, a=7

14) **The correct answer is (D)**

Since the points B and C are tangent, |AB|=|AC|=r=5, and the center of the circle is O(5, -5). Since the equation of the circle is $(x-a)^2+(y-b)^2=r^2$, therefore $(x-5)^2+(y+5)^2=25$.

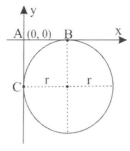

15) **The correct answer is (B)**

If two lines are perpendicular to each other, multiplication of their slopes is equal to -1. Slope of $d_1 = \sqrt{3}$, slope of $d_2=a$ and $a\sqrt{3} = -1$, $a = -\dfrac{1}{\sqrt{3}}$.

16) **The correct answer is (E)**

Since this number is divisible by both 5 and 13, we need to find out LCF(5, 13)=65. The only number divisible by 65 between 230 and 270 is 260 $\rightarrow$ (65x4=260).

17) **The correct answer is (E)**

When we connect the diagonals, the hexagon gets divided into six identical triangles with edges of 5 cm. therefore the peripheral of the hexagon is 6x5=30cm.

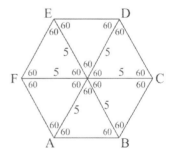

18) **The correct answer is (E)**

$$\dfrac{3+\dfrac{1}{x}}{3-\dfrac{1}{x}} = 3 \quad \Rightarrow \quad \dfrac{\dfrac{3x+1}{x}}{\dfrac{3x-1}{x}} = 3, \quad \dfrac{3x+1}{3x-1} = \dfrac{3}{1} \quad \Rightarrow$$

3x+1=9x-3, 1+3=9x-3x, 4=6x, $x = \dfrac{4}{6}$, $x = \dfrac{2}{3}$

19) **The correct answer is (C)**

3x-6y=0, 3x=6y, x=2y, $\dfrac{3}{x}+\dfrac{3}{y} = 6$, $\dfrac{3+6}{2y} = 6$, 9 = 12y, 3 = 4y, $y = \dfrac{3}{4}$

x=2y $\Rightarrow$ $x = 2 \cdot \dfrac{3}{4} = \dfrac{3}{2}$

20) **The correct answer is (D)**

$3x+4y=12$

$6x+ay=24$

$\dfrac{3}{6}=\dfrac{4}{a}=\dfrac{12}{24} \Rightarrow \dfrac{4}{a}=\dfrac{1}{2}$, $a=8$

21) **The correct answer is (A)**

Let there be x people in this group. The sum of ages of this group would increase for 10x in 10 years. Therefore $150+10x=250$, $10x=100$ and $x=10i$ therefore this group consists of 10 friends.

22) **The correct answer is (D)**

$4(x-\pi)+3(\pi-x)=2(\pi+x) \Rightarrow 4x-4\pi+3\pi-3x=2\pi+2x \Rightarrow 4x-3x+3\pi-4\pi=2\pi+2x$,

$x-\pi=2\pi+2x$, $x-2x=2\pi+\pi$, $-x=3\pi$, $x=-3\pi$

23) **The correct answer is (E)**

Composite number is not prime number.

24) **The correct answer is (E)**

$3x^2y^5 \rightarrow$ degree is $(2+5)=7$.

25) **The correct answer is (D)**

Let us call $\dfrac{6}{10}+\dfrac{7}{12}$ as y. Then $\dfrac{6}{10}+\dfrac{7}{12}=x$

$+\dfrac{\dfrac{4}{10}+\dfrac{5}{12}=y}{1+1=x+y}$, $y=2-x$

26) **The correct answer is (C)**

Summing up the ratios, $40+20+10+10=80$, therefore the ratio of the students who do not want to go to college is $100-80=20\%$, which is equal to the students who want to study medicine. Therefore the correct answer is C.

27) **The correct answer is (A)**

The number of students aged between 20-24 is: $28+26=54$ for computer engineering, $30+24=54$ for economy, $22+20=42$ for medicine and $22+18=40$ for civil engineering. Therefore the correct answer is A.

28) The correct answer is (D)

This actually means the number of students aged 24-26.
Therefore computer engineering is the correct answer.

29) The correct answer is (D)

The graph shows that the student has solved the maximum number of questions on Wednesday (360) and the minimum number of questions on Thursday (60) therefore the sum is 360+60=420.

30) The correct answer is (D)

Let us name the initial kinetic energy as E_{k1} and final kinetic energy as E_{k2}, and initial velocity as v_1 and final velocity as v_2, then

$$E_{k1} = \frac{1}{2}mv^2 \text{ and } E_{k2} = \frac{1}{2}m(2v)^2 = \frac{1}{2}m \cdot 4v^2. \quad \frac{E_{k2}}{E_{k1}} = \frac{\frac{1}{2}m \cdot 4v^2}{\frac{1}{2}m \cdot v^2} = 4.$$

Therefore the increase is 400%.

31) The correct answer is (C)

This expression would be a-b<x<a+b.

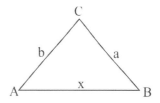

32) The correct answer is (C)

$\angle ABD + \angle DBC = 90^\circ$, $\dfrac{\angle ABD}{\angle DBC} = \dfrac{2x}{3x}$

$2x+3x=90^\circ$, $5x=90^\circ$, $x=18^\circ$. $z=3x=3 \cdot 18^\circ=54^\circ$.

33) The correct answer is (A)

There is an inverse proportion here. Therefore
If x workers finish in → b days
Then (x+y) workers finish in → m days

$x \cdot b=(x+y) \cdot m$ and $m = \dfrac{x \cdot b}{x+y}$.

34) The correct answer is (A)

$$\frac{1}{3}_{(4)} + \frac{1}{4}_{(3)} + \frac{1}{12}_{(1)} + \frac{1}{x} = \frac{1}{6}_{(2)}$$

$$\frac{4+3+1}{12} + \frac{1}{x} = \frac{2}{12}, \quad \frac{8}{12} + \frac{1}{x} = \frac{2}{12} \Rightarrow \frac{1}{x} = \frac{2}{12} - \frac{8}{12}, \quad \frac{1}{x} = \frac{-6}{12}, \quad x = -2$$

35) **The correct answer is (D)**

In this formula, P shows the total sales, x shows the number of mobile phones sold, and n shows the number of covers sold.

36) **The correct answer is (E)**

Let us multiply the second inequality by -1 and then sum them up.

$$6 < x \leq 12$$
$$+ \ -7 < -y \leq -4$$
$$\overline{-1 < x-y \leq 8}.$$

Therefore the largest value of x-y is 8.

37) **The correct answer is (C)**

If pipe I fills the pool within a hours, it fills 1/a of the pool within 1 hour. Similarly, pipe II fills 1/b and pipe III empties 1/c of it. If the pool is filled within t hours when all of them are open, then 1/t of the pool is filled within 1 hour. Therefore $\dfrac{1}{t} = \dfrac{1}{a} + \dfrac{1}{b} - \dfrac{1}{c}$ and $t = \dfrac{abc}{bc + ac - ab}$.

38) **The correct answer is (A)**

$2\sqrt{2x+3} + 4 = 13$ and $2\sqrt{2x+3} = 9$, taking square of both sides

$(2\sqrt{2x+3})^2 = 9^2$, $4 \cdot (2x+3) = 81$, $2x+3 = \dfrac{81}{4}$,

therefore $2x = \dfrac{81}{4} - 3 = \dfrac{81}{4} - \dfrac{12}{4} = \dfrac{69}{4}$, $x = \dfrac{69}{8}$.

39) **The correct answer is (E)**

40) **The correct answer is (E)**

Following table shows the unit price and the quantity of the products purchased, as well as total expenditure

Quantity	Unit price	Expenditure (=unit price x quantity)
2	60	120
4	40	160
6	X	6x
8	80	640
10	20	200
	TOTAL	1120+6x

Since the total expenditure is 1600, 1600=1120+6x, therefore 6x=480 and x=80.

41) **The correct answer is (E)**

The graph shows that the company has published 20,000 books in 2000 and 100,000 books in 2008, which means (100,000-20,000)=80,000 of increase in 8 years. Building a direct proportion,

80,000 of increase in 8 years means

60,000 of increase in x years. Therefore x=8· $\dfrac{60000}{80000}$ = 6 years.

42) **The correct answer is (E)**

$144x^4-225y^2=(12x^2)^2-(15y)^2=(12x^2-15y)\cdot(12x^2+15y)$

43) **The correct answer is (C)**

f(-2)=5,   f(3)=0,   f(5)=-4, $\dfrac{f(-2)+f(3)}{f(5)}=\dfrac{5+0}{-4}=-\dfrac{5}{4}$

44) **The correct answer is (C)**

$y\geq x^2-4x-12$, $y=x^2-4x-12$, for y=0, $x^2-4x-12=0$ and (x-6)(x+2)=0, therefore x=6 and x=-2, (6, 0), (-2, 0). For x=0, y=-12, therefore (0, -12).

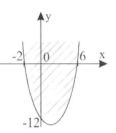

45) **The correct answer is (A)**

Let us take the initial edge as 10 units, which means the area is A=a·a=10x10=100 units. When the edge length is decreased for 10%, the new edge length would be 10x90%=9 units. Therefore the new area would be 9·9=81 units. This means (100-81)=19 units of decrease in 100 units, which is 19%.

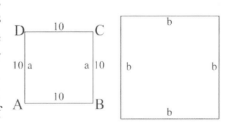

46) **The correct answer is (C)**

A parabola being concave upwards means a positive "a" value in the general equation of $y=ax^2+bx+c$. Therefore parabolas I, II and III are concave upwards, which means there are 3 of them.

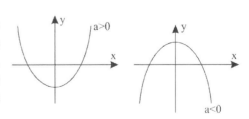

47) **The correct answer is (D)**

The total number of students is 30+30+32+28=120, while the number of male students is 10+18+16+10=54. Therefore the probability of getting a male student is 54/120. Besides, there are 12 female students who want to study computer engineering, which brings another 12/120. Please note that the male students who want to study computer engineering is already included in male students. Therefore the probability is 54/120+12/120=66/120=11/20.

48) **The correct answer is (A)**

Similarly, the number of female students is 66, and the number of male students wh want to be a teacher is 10, therefore the probability is (66+10)/120=76/120=19/30

49) **The correct answer is (D)**

Tollways A and B would be used by (200+600)=800 cars in an hour, which makes 2x800=1600 in two hours, not 2000. Therefore D is the correct answer choice.

50) **The correct answer is (C)**

For known two points, slope is calculated by $\dfrac{y_2 - y_1}{x_2 - x_1} = \dfrac{8-4}{2-6} = \dfrac{4}{-4} = -1$.

51) **The correct answer is (B)**

The ratio of children is 100-(70+20)=10. The number of female spectators is 20%·6000=1200 and the number of child spectators is 10%·6000=600. Therefore the ratio is 1200/600=2.

52) **The correct answer is (E)**

There are 3 triangles in the figure. Their perimeters are as: ABC=6+6+8=20, ABD=6+3+4=13, ADC=6+3+4=13, Totaling 20+13+13=46.

53) **The correct answer is (E)**

Game once in two weeks means 52/2=26 games in a year. Since a game lasts 90 minutes=1.5 hours, total time would be 26·1.5=39 hours.

54) **The correct answer is (E)**

$ax^2+bx+c=(2x+4)^2=4x^2+16x+16$,
a=4, b=16, c=16, $\Rightarrow$ a+b+c=36

55) The correct answer is (E)

Let their edges be a and b, therefore $\frac{a}{b} = \frac{3}{2}$. The volume of a cube is a^3.

Therefore the ratio would be $\frac{a^3}{b^3} = \frac{3^3}{2^3} = \frac{27}{8}$.

56) The correct answer is (B)

$f(g(x)) = 4x + 3 = 4(2x+4) + 3 = 8x + 16 + 3 = 8x + 19 \Rightarrow f(g(2)) = 8x + 19 = 8 \cdot 2 + 19 = 35$,

$g(f(x)) = 2x + 4 = 2(4x+3) + 4 = 8x + 10$, $g(f(3)) = 8 \cdot 3 + 10 = 34$

$\frac{f(g(2))}{g(f(3))} = \frac{35}{34}$

57) The correct answer is (E)

$y = 3x + 2$, $y = (x-1)^2 + 5$, $y = x^2 - 2x + 1 + 5$, $y = x^2 - 2x + 6$,

$3x + 2 = x^2 - 2x + 6$

$x^2 - 5x + 4 = 0$

$x \quad\quad -1$

$x \quad\quad -4$

$(x-1) \cdot (x-4) = 0$

$x_1 = 1$, $x_2 = 4$, and $x_1 + x_2 = 1 + 4 = 5$.

58) The correct answer is (E)

Let us call this number as x. Therefore $x \cdot 30\% - x \cdot 24\% = 12 = x \cdot 6\%$. Therefore $6x/100 = 12$, and $x = 200$. Half of 200 is 100.

59) The correct answer is (D)

$f(x) = 3x + 3$, $g(x) = 2x + 2$, $f(g(2)) = ?$

$f(g(x)) = 3g(x) + 3 = 3 \cdot (2x+2) + 3 = 6x + 9$

$f(g(2)) = 6(2) + 9 = 6 \cdot 2 + 9 = 21$

60) The correct answer is (B)

$\pi r^2 = 5$, $r^2 = \frac{5}{\pi}$, $r = \sqrt{\frac{5}{\pi}}$

TEST – 2.6
- Solutions -

1) **The correct answer is (B)**

   There is an inverse proportion between the number of workers and completion time. Therefore, if 8 workers complete in 24 hours, then 6 workers complete in t hours. 8·24=6·t, therefore $t = \dfrac{8 \cdot 24}{6} = 32$.

2) **The correct answer is (A)**

   f(x)=2x+3 g(x)=4x+3
   f(2)=2·2+3=7   g(3)=4·3+3=15
   2f(2)=2·7=14   3g(3)=3·15=45
   2f(2)+3g(3)=14+45=59

3) **The correct answer is (D)**

   h=maximum height, V_o=initial velocity, S=horizontal distance, g=gravity. Therefore g is constant.

4) **The correct answer is (A)**

   The shortest distance is a line. Therefore ABC is a right triangle and we can use Pythagoras theorem. $|AB|^2+|BC|^2=|AC|^2$, $100+576=|AC|^2$.
   Therefore, $|AC|^2=676$, and AC=26km.

5) **The correct answer is (C)**

   Expanding the parentheses,
   $y=3(x+4)^2-3=3(x^2+8x+16)-3=3x^2+24x+48-3=3x^2+24x+45$
   $y=3(x^2+8x+15_{(5,3)})$
   $y=3(x+5)(x+3)$

6) **The correct answer is (D)**

   4x+3y=24, for x=0, 3y=24 and y=8, for y=0, 4x=24, and x=6. Therefore this line passes through (0, 8) and (6, 0).

   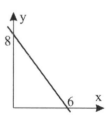

7) **The correct answer is (A)**

   The equation of a line with known slope and a known point is
   $y-y_o=m(x-x_o)$, therefore, since m=–2 and A(4, 7),
   y–7=–2(x–4), y–7=–2x+8, y=–2x+15

8)   **The correct answer is (B)**

$$\frac{4}{7}(x-1)(x+1)(x^2+1) = \frac{4}{7}(x^2-1)(x^2+1) = \frac{4}{7}(x^4-1)$$

9)   **The correct answer is (D)**

$$\frac{a^{\frac{5}{4}}}{a^{\frac{4}{5}}} = a^{\frac{5}{4}} \cdot a^{-\frac{4}{5}} = a^{\frac{5}{4}-\frac{4}{5}}, \quad a^{\frac{25-16}{20}} = a^{\frac{9}{20}} = a^{\frac{x}{mn}}$$

x=9, mn=20, therefore x+m+n=9+2+0=11.

10) **The correct answer is (D)**

The general formula for parabola is y=ax^2+bx+c.
Since a=−1 in our parabola, it is concave downward,
while its peak point would be (0, 10) as y=−x^2+10.
For x=0, y=10 and For y=0, x^2=10 and x=∓$\sqrt{10}$
Therefore the parabola intercepts y–axis at (0, 10)
and x–axis at $\left(-\sqrt{10}, 0\right)$ and $\left(\sqrt{10}, 0\right)$

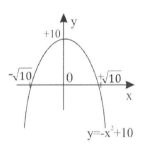

11) **The correct answer is (C)**

$(4x^3)^3 = 4^3(x^3)^3 = 64x^9$. Degree is 9.

12) **The correct answer is (E)**

$$\frac{2a+1}{5_{(3)}} + \frac{2a-1}{3_{(5)}} = \frac{3}{15}, \quad \frac{6a+3+10a-5}{15} = \frac{3}{15} \Rightarrow 16a-2=3, \ 16a=5, \ a = \frac{5}{16}$$

13) **The correct answer is (B)**

If $a = \frac{4b+8}{3b+7}$, then a(3b+7)=4b+8, 3ab+7a=4b+8, 3ab−4b=8−7a,

b(3a−4)=8−7a, $\Rightarrow$ $b = \frac{8-7a}{3a-4}$

14) **The correct answer is (C)**

Since c=$3000, n=20% and t=4 years, $I = \frac{c \cdot n \cdot t}{100} = \frac{3000 \cdot 4 \cdot 20}{100} = \$2400$.

Therefore $2400 of interest due to pay. Summing up with the capital, total
amount to be paid is 2400+3000=$5400.

15) **The correct answer is (B)**

$$6 \cdot \left(\frac{1}{a} + \frac{1}{b} + \frac{1}{c} \right) = 6 \cdot \left(\frac{1}{c} + \frac{1}{b} - \frac{1}{a} \right) \Rightarrow \frac{6}{a} + \frac{6}{b} + \frac{6}{c} = \frac{6}{c} + \frac{6}{b} - \frac{6}{a} \Rightarrow \frac{6}{a} + \frac{6}{a} = \frac{12}{a}$$

16) **The correct answer is (A)**

$\sqrt{3x+1} + 3 = 5$ and $\sqrt{3x+1} = 5 - 3 = 2$

$\left(\sqrt{3x+1} \right)^2 = 2^2$, and $3x+1=4$, $3x=4-1=3$, and $x=3/3=1$.

17) **The correct answer is (E)**

If f(x)=4x+4 and f(a)=32, replacing x with a, 4a+4=32, 4a=32–4=28, therefore, a=28/4=7.

18) **The correct answer is (E)**

$$\frac{x^2 + 10x + 25}{x + 5} + \frac{x^2 + 5x + 1}{x + 3}$$ could be simplified,

$$\frac{(x+5)(x+5)}{(x+5)} + \frac{(x+3)(x+2)}{(x+3)} = x + 5 + x + 2 = 2x + 7,$$

Therefore, $b^a = 7^2 = 49$.

19) **The correct answer is (E)**

Summing both equations, 2x+3y+3x+2y=21+19, 5x+5y=40, 5(x+y)=40 and x+y=8, therefore $(x+y)^2 = 8^2 = 64$.

20) **The correct answer is (B)**

Volume of the cylinder is calculated by $V_{cy} = \pi r^2 h$ and since h=2π in the figure, $V_{cy} = \pi \cdot r^2 \cdot (2\pi) = 2\pi^2 r^2$.

Volume of a cone calculated by $V_{cone} = \frac{1}{3} \pi r^2 h$, and since h=3π in the figure,

$V_{cone} = \frac{1}{3} \pi r^2 3\pi = \pi^2 r^2$. The ratio of two volumes is $\frac{V_{cylinder}}{V_{cone}} = \frac{2\pi^2 r^2}{\pi^2 r^2} = 2$.

21) **The correct answer is (B)**

144,000 annual visitors means $\frac{144,000}{12} = 12,000$ monthly visitors.

Therefore total visitors in 4.5 months would be 4.5x12,000=54,000.

22) **The correct answer is (A)**

The number of lost books is 6,000x2%=120, and the number of books that need to be renewed is 6,000x7%=420. Therefore the answer is 120+420=540.

23) **The correct answer is (D)**

The number of male passengers is 20+30+15=65, and the number of female passengers is 30+40+25=95, therefore the total number of passengers is 65+95=160. Therefore the probability of first passenger disembarking being a male is 65/160.

The number of German passengers is 40+30=70, but we are interested in female German passengers only, because male German passengers have already been calculated. Therefore the probability of first passenger disembarking being a female German is 40/160, and the total is $\frac{65}{160}+\frac{40}{160}=\frac{105}{160}=\frac{21}{32}$.

24) **The correct answer is (B)**

Let us call this number as x. Therefore $x^2 < 3 \cdot x + 3$.

25) **The correct answer is (C)**

26) **The correct answer is (D)**

Since Adam works twice fast as Matt , A=2M. Besides, the work completed is constant. Therefore $(A+M)\cdot24=M\cdot x$, replacing A with 2M, $24\cdot3M=M\cdot x$, and x=72 hours.

27) **The correct answer is (D)**

Lets us take 10 as base. 20% decrease means decrease to 8, and 60% increase means, increase to 16. The original multiplication would be 10x10=100, while the final multiplication would be 8x16=128. Therefore increase from 100 to 128 is 28%.

28) **The correct answer is (D)**

6xy–30x<0, 6xy<30x. Since x<0, dividing both sides by x changes the direction of inequality, therefore 6xy<30x and 6y>30, y>5 which means that the smallest possible y value is 6.

29) **The correct answer is (D)**

Replacing a with 8, $4b(60-8a)^2 = 4b(60-8\cdot8)^2 = 4b(60-64)^2 = 4b(-4)^2 = 64b$.

30) **The correct answer is (B)**

Let cars pay $x, then trucks need to pay x+5. Therefore the revenue would be 80(x+5)+20x=600.

31) **The correct answer is (A)**

Since x=vt, the distance covered by three vehicles could be calculated by summing up the velocities and multiplying by the time. Hence, $x=(v_1+v_2+v_3)t=(40+50+80)\cdot3=170\cdot3=510$

32) **The correct answer is (A)**

The average velocity would be $v_{av} = \dfrac{v_A + v_B + v_C}{3} = \dfrac{80+40+60}{3} = \dfrac{180}{3} = 60$.

33) **The correct answer is (D)**

The number of students attending to volleyball is 12, and the number od students attending to taekwondo is 6. Therefore the ratio is 12/6=2.

34) **The correct answer is (C)**

Total number of students is 40,000, and the number of students who use the library is 25,000. Therefore the number of students who don't use library is 40,000–25,000=15,000.

35) **The correct answer is (A)**

Let the total age of first graders be m, and the total age of second graders be n, then m=10x, and n=15(x+a)=15x+15a. Therefore the difference would be n–m=15x+15a–10x=5x+15a.

36) **The correct answer is (C)**

6(10-n)=4(n+8), 60-6n=4n+32, 60-32=6n+4n, 28=10n, n=2.8.

37) **The correct answer is (C)**

The number of female passengers is (300+400+700+400)=1800, and the favorite airline has 700 passengers. Therefore the ratio is 700/1800=7/18.

38) **The correct answer is (D)**

The number of male passengers is (400+500+600+300)=1800, and the least preferred airline has 300 passengers. Therefore the ratio is 300/1800=1/6.

39) **The correct answer is (A)**

Average weekday passengers is $\dfrac{6000 + 5000 + 5000 + 6000 + 4000}{5} = 5200$.

And average weekend passengers is $\dfrac{3000 + 3000}{2} = 3000$.

Therefore the ratio is $\dfrac{5200}{3000} = \dfrac{26}{15}$.

40) The correct answer is (C)

Total number of passengers on Friday and Tuesday is (5000+4000)=9000.

41) The correct answer is (C)

$y-3=4x^2+9x+2$, $\quad y=4x^2+9x+5$

$y=ax^2-bx+c \Rightarrow a=4$, $b=9$, $c=5$, and $D = \sqrt{b^2 - 4ac} = \sqrt{9^2 - 4\cdot4\cdot5}$, D=1

$x_1 = \dfrac{-b + \sqrt{D}}{2a} = \dfrac{-9 + \sqrt{1}}{2a} = \dfrac{-9 + 1}{8} = -1$,

$x_2 = \dfrac{-b - \sqrt{D}}{2a} = \dfrac{-9 - \sqrt{1}}{2a} = \dfrac{-9 - 1}{8} = \dfrac{-10}{8} = -\dfrac{5}{4}$

42) The correct answer is (A)

Since $d_1 \| d_2$, 2x=60 and x=30°, and
Since $d_1 \| d_3$, 3y+60=180, 3y=180−60=120, and y=120/3=40°.
Therefore x+y=30°+40°=70°.

43) The correct answer is (C)

If $x^2=x+2$, then
$x^2=x+2$,
$x^3=x\cdot x^2=x(x+2)=x^2+2x=x+2+2x=3x+2$
$x^4=(x^2)^2=(x+2)^2=x^2+4x+4=x+2+4x+4=5x+6$
$x^2+x^3+x^4=(x+2)+(3x+2)+(5x+6)=9x+10$.

44) The correct answer is (A)

haded region$=\dfrac{\pi r^2 \alpha}{360} = \dfrac{\pi r^2 \cdot 30}{360}$

Unshaded region$=\dfrac{\pi r^2(360-\alpha)}{360} = \dfrac{\pi r^2 \cdot (360-30)}{360} = \dfrac{\pi r^2 \cdot 330}{360}$

Therefore the ratio is $\dfrac{\dfrac{\pi r^2 \cdot 30}{360}}{\dfrac{\pi r^2 \cdot 330)}{360}} = \dfrac{30}{330} = \dfrac{1}{11}$

45) The correct answer is (B)

Only f(x) and g(x) are parabolas.

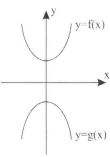

46) The correct answer is (B)

In order to maximize the ratio, we need to minimize the denominator and maximize the numerators. The minimum y value is $5 \leq y \leq 12$ inequality is 5. Similarly, the maximum x value in $7 \leq x \leq 14$ inequality is 14. Therefore

$$\frac{2x+6}{y+6} = \frac{2 \cdot 14 + 6}{5+6} = \frac{34}{11}.$$

47) The correct answer is (C)

$$2x = \frac{3a}{3y+2} \Rightarrow 2x(3y+2) = 3a,$$

$6xy + 4x = 3a$, $6xy = 3a - 4x$, $6xy + 4x + 3 = 3a - 4x + 4x + 3 = 3a + 3$

48) The correct answer is (D)

Center of a circle with equation of $x^2 + y^2 + Ax + By + C = 0$ is found by $M\left(\frac{-A}{2}, \frac{-B}{2}\right)$, therefore $\left(\frac{-6}{2}, \frac{-8}{2}\right)$ and $(-3, -4)$.

49) The correct answer is (D)

$$\frac{x^2+4x+3}{(x+1)} = \frac{(x+3)(x+1)}{(x+1)} = x+3, \quad \frac{x^2+9x+14}{(x+2)} = \frac{(x+2)(x+7)}{(x+2)} = x+7$$

$$\frac{x^2+4x+3}{(x+1)} + \frac{x^2+9x+14}{(x+2)} = x+3+x+7 = 2x+10$$

50) The correct answer is (B)

The centre of the circle is the origin, and the radius is $25=5^2$, Therefore $x^2+y^2=5^2$.

51) The correct answer is (A)

Let the number of female athletes be x, which means the number of male athletes is (3x+1). The total number of athletes is equal to the sum, and x+3x+1=57, 4x+1=57, 4x=56, and x=56/4=14.

52) The correct answer is (E)

$$\frac{x}{3} - \frac{x}{7} > 4 \text{ and } \frac{7x-3x}{21} > 4, \quad \frac{4x}{21} > 4 \text{ and } x > 21,$$

therefore minimum x value is 22.

53) The correct answer is (E)

x+3y=21, 3(x+y)=21, x+y=7
5x+5y=5(x+y)=5·7=35

54) **The correct answer is (D)**

Using direct proportion,
If 300g is $4.2
800g is x,
$$x = \frac{4.2 \cdot 800}{300} = \$11.2.$$

55) **The correct answer is (E)**

When they work together, they can copy (50+40)=90 pages. Multiplying by 6 minutes, 90x6=540pages.

56) **The correct answer is (E)**

Since the perimeter of a square is 4a=40cm, a=10cm, the edge of square is 10cm. Reducing by 10% means having only 90% of the original length. Therefore the new edge length would be 10x90%=9cm, and the perimeter would be 9x4=36cm.

57) **The correct answer is (D)**

$y=3x+1$, $y=-3(x+2)^2+1$
$3x+1=-3(x+2)^2+1$, $3x+1=-3(x^2+4x+4)+1$, $3x+1=-3x^2-12x-12+1$,
$3x^2+12x+12+3x=0 \Rightarrow 3x^2+15x+12=0$
$x^2+5x+4=0$
x   1
x   4
$(x+1)(x+4)=0$,
$x_1=-1$, $x_2=-4$,
$x_1+x_2=-1-4=-5$

58) **The correct answer is (E)**

Total age of the females is 6·15=90. Total age of the class is 18·(6+8)=252. Therefore the total age of the male students is 252-90=162. Since there are 8 male students, the average age would be 162/8=20.25

59) **The correct answer is (A)**

$x-6=y \Rightarrow x-y=6$
$|4x-4y|=4\cdot|x-y|$, $|6y-6x|=|6x-6y|=6\cdot|x-y|$,
$4\cdot|x-y|+6\cdot|x-y|=10\cdot|x-y|=10\cdot6=60$

60) **The correct answer is (A)**

$2a+3b=12$
$3a+2b=13$
+ _____
$5a+5b=25$, $\Rightarrow a+b=5$

TEST – 2.7
- Solutions -

1) **The correct answer is (B)**

Since there is an inverse ratio, let us calculate the job completed by both in a day first: $\dfrac{1}{2x}+\dfrac{1}{2y}=\dfrac{1}{7}$, and $\dfrac{1}{2y}=\dfrac{1}{7}-\dfrac{1}{2x}$, and $\dfrac{1}{2y}=\dfrac{2x-7}{14x}$,

therefore $2y=\dfrac{14x}{2x-7}$ and $y=\dfrac{7x}{2x-7}$.

2) **The correct answer is (B)**

$f(x)=x^2+4x$ and $f(x+1)=ax^2+bx+c$. Replacing x with x+1,
$f(x+1)=(x+1)^2+4(x+1)=x^2+2x+1+4x+4=x^2+6x+5$, therefore
a=1, b=6 and c=5, a+b+c=1+6+5=12.

3) **The correct answer is (C)**

Let us call the mother's age as x and the daughter's age as y. Then x+y=50 and x/y=4. Therefore x=4y and x–4y=0.

4) **The correct answer is (D)**

6(x–3)=6(3–x) therefore x–3=3–x, 2x=6 and x=3. The solution set is {3}.

5) **The correct answer is (C)**

Let us calculate the increases

For .2010: $\dfrac{24{,}000-20{,}000}{20{,}000}=\dfrac{4{,}000}{20{,}000}=20\%$

For .2011: $\dfrac{30{,}000-24{,}000}{24{,}000}=\dfrac{6{,}000}{24{,}000}=25\%$

For .2012: $\dfrac{32{,}000-30{,}000}{30{,}000}=\dfrac{2{,}000}{30{,}000}\approx 6{,}7\%$

For. 2013: $\dfrac{38{,}000-32{,}000}{32{,}000}=\dfrac{6{,}000}{32{,}000}\approx 19\%$

6) **The correct answer is (D)**

Since the purchasing price is \$4 and the sale price is \$6, profit is \$2. To find the profit ratio, we need to build a direct proportion

If   \$4 profits \$2
then   100 profits x

$x = \dfrac{2 \cdot \%100}{4} = 50\%.$

7) **The correct answer is (D)**

$$\frac{2x^2 - 98}{x^2 - 14x + 49} = \frac{2(x^2 - 49)}{(x-7)^2} = \frac{2(x-7)(x+7)}{(x-7)(x-7)} = \frac{2(x+7)}{x-7} = \frac{2x+14}{x-7}$$

8) **The correct answer is (C)**

$f(x) = x^2 + 4$ and $g(x) = 1 - x$, $f(g(x)) = (1-x)^2 + 4 = 1 - 2x + x^2 + 4 = x^2 - 2x + 5.$

9) **The correct answer is (A)**

If $f(x) = x^2 + 3x$, then $f(2x) = (2x)^2 + 3(2x) = 4x^2 + 6x.$

10) **The correct answer is (D)**

$6 - x = 8$, $-x = 2$ and $x = -2$. Replacing x with -2, $f(-2) = (-2)^2 + 2(-2) + 3 = 4 - 4 + 3 = 3.$

11) **The correct answer is (B)**

The total surface area is $6 \cdot a \cdot a = 6a^2 = 6 \cdot 5^2 = 6 \cdot 25 = 150$, and the volume is $5^3 = 125$, therefore the ratio is $\dfrac{150}{125} = \dfrac{6}{5}.$

12) **The correct answer is (C)**

Let there be x SAT books. Then the cost in the first situation is $C = 20x - 480$ and in the second $C = 16x + 180$. Since these two must be equal to each other, $20x - 480 = 16x + 180.$

13) **The correct answer is (B)**

$|BC| = \dfrac{|AC|}{2} = \dfrac{6}{2} = 3$ and $|AB| = \dfrac{|AC|}{2} \cdot \sqrt{3} = \dfrac{6}{2}\sqrt{3} = 3\sqrt{3}$.

Therefore the perimeter is $6 + 3 + 3\sqrt{3} = 9 + 3\sqrt{3}$,

and the area is $\dfrac{|BC| \cdot |AC|}{2} = \dfrac{3\sqrt{3} \cdot 3}{2} = \dfrac{9\sqrt{3}}{2}$,

and the ratio is $\dfrac{9 + 3\sqrt{3}}{9\sqrt{3}/2} = \dfrac{18 + 6\sqrt{3}}{9\sqrt{3}} = \dfrac{6 + 2\sqrt{3}}{3\sqrt{3}}$.

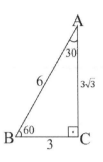

14) **The correct answer is (C)**

Since these two lines are perpendicular to each other, the multiplication of their slopes is equal to –1, therefore m·n=–1.

15) **The correct answer is (D)**

If these three points are on the same line, then their slopes must be equal to each other. ($m_{AB} = m_{AC}$). Therefore

$\dfrac{y_2 - y_1}{x_2 - x_1} = \dfrac{y_3 - y_2}{x_3 - x_2}$, and $\dfrac{7 - 4}{3 - 2} = \dfrac{y - 7}{6 - 3}$, $\dfrac{3}{1} = \dfrac{y - 7}{3}$, y–7=9, y=16.

16) **The correct answer is (A)**

A physics book costs $5 and 12 books cost 12·5=$60. Since a math book costs $4, x being the number of math books, 60=4x, and x=15.

17) **The correct answer is (E)**

$\dfrac{a + b}{b} = 11$ and a+b=11b, a=10b.

Replacing a in the second equation, $\dfrac{b}{a + b} = \dfrac{b}{10b + b} = \dfrac{b}{11b} = \dfrac{1}{11}$.

18) **The correct answer is (E)**

4(2m+3)-3m>-13, 8m+12-3m>-13, 8m-3m>-13-12, 5m>-25, m>-5

19) **The correct answer is (E)**

The equation of line d_1 is $\dfrac{x}{3} + \dfrac{y}{4} = 1$, therefore 4x+3y=12, and

4x+3y–12=0, resulting a=4, b=3, and c=–12. a+b+c=4+3–12=–5.

20) The correct answer is (E)

If f(2x–4)=x²+3x+4, and since f(6)=f(2x–4), 6=2x–4 and x=$\frac{10}{2}$ = 5.

Replacing 5 with x, f(6)=f(2·5–4)=5²+3·5+4=25+15+4=44.

21) The correct answer is (A)

Let the weight of box C be y and the weight of box D be x, then

A	B	C	D
y	x+44	y	x

A+B+C+D=424 and y+x+44+y+x=424, 2x+2y=380 and x+y=$\frac{380}{2}$=190kg.

22) The correct answer is (C)

Total surface area of a cube is calculated by 6a², where a is the edge length of the cube. Therefore 24x²=6a², a²=4x² and   a=2x. Therefore the volume of the cube is a³=(2x)³=8x³.

23) The correct answer is (D)

$\frac{x}{2} - \frac{x}{5} \geq 6$, $\frac{5x - 2x}{10} \geq 6$, and $\frac{3x}{10} \geq 6$, 3x ≥ 60, x ≥ 20.

24) The correct answer is (A)

If $\frac{x^2 + 6x + 9}{(x + 3)^2} = -3$ then x²+6x+9=–3(x+3)³=(x+3)²

therefore (x+3)²=–3(x+3)², simplifying by (x+3)², –1=3, therefore the solution set is empty.

25) The correct answer is (D)

f(x)=4x²–8x, g(x)=f$\left(\frac{x}{2}\right)$ = $4\left(\frac{x}{2}\right)^2 - 8\left(\frac{x}{2}\right)$. g(x) = $4\frac{x^2}{4} - \frac{8x}{2} = x^2 - 4x$.

g(4)=(4)²–4·4=16–16=0.

26) The correct answer is (A)

Student numbers in the most charity collecting classes are 12 and 16, and the ratio is $\frac{12}{16} = \frac{3}{4}$.

27) **The correct answer is (C)**

The total amount of charity collected is: 60+50+40+30+20=$200. The total number of students is 8+10+12+16+20=66. Therefore the average amount of charity is $\frac{200}{66} = \$3$.

28) **The correct answer is (A)**

Let the volume of the tank be 100x, then the full part is 90x. When 2/3 of this amount is used, the used amount would be $90x \cdot \frac{2}{3} = 60x$. Since another 10x of the tank was already empty, 70x of the tank is empty, which means 70%.

29) **The correct answer is (A)**

The sum of the area of the squares is $(3a)^2+(2a)^2+(a)^2=9a^2+4a^2+a^2=14a^2$.
The sum of the perimeters of the squares is $4\cdot3a+4\cdot2a+4\cdot a=12a+8a+4a=24a$.
Therefore the ratio is $\frac{14a^2}{24a} = \frac{14a}{24} = \frac{7a}{12}$.

30) **The correct answer is (C)**

$|AC|^2+|AB|^2=|BC|^2$, therefore $(4x)^2=x^2+|BC|^2$, and
$|BC|^2=15x^2$, $|BC|=\sqrt{15}x$, $\cos C=\frac{|BC|}{|AC|} = \frac{x\sqrt{15}}{4x} = \frac{\sqrt{15}}{4}$.

31) **The correct answer is (C)**

The teacher needs to be on duty for ten more times, which means 10·5=50days. Since there are 7 days in a week, dividing 50 by 7, the reside is 1, therefore we need to go on one day further than Thursday, which means Friday.

32) **The correct answer is (A)**

There are 12+14=26 candidates in the 79–100 interval who would be recruited. Therefore 40–26=14 more candidates need to be recruited. Since there are 16 candidates in the 68–78 interval, 14 of them would be recruited and 16–14=2 of them would not be recruited.

33) **The correct answer is (C)**

The farmer has sold 20% of the watermelons, which makes $\frac{20}{100} \times 3600 = 720$kg.

34) **The correct answer is (D)**

He has sold 40% of his watermelons in August, which is

$\frac{40}{100} \times 3600 = 1440\,kg$. Since the price of watermelons was \$4 then, he had

earned \$4·1440=\$5760.

35) **The correct answer is (A)**

Let us calculate his monthly sales one by one:

May: $\frac{10}{100} \times 3600 \times 7 = 2520$ June: $\frac{20}{100} \times 3600 \times 6 = 4320$

July: $\frac{20}{100} \times 3600 \times 5 = 3600$ August: $\frac{40}{100} \times 3600 \times 4 = 5760$

September: $\frac{10}{100} \times 3600 \times 3 = 1080$

Therefore he has performed the least sales in September.

36) **The correct answer is (A)**

Let the number of students who had donated \$10 be x, then the number of students who had donated \$5 would be (25–x) and 5(25–x)+10x=185.

37) **The correct answer is (D)**

Solve the recursive equation for r. $a_n = a_{n-1} \cdot r$, $r = \frac{a_n}{a_{n-1}}$, $r = \frac{18}{6} = 3$

$a_6 = a_2 r^4 = 18 \cdot 3^4 = 18 \cdot 81 = 1458$

38) **The correct answer is (B)**

$y = x^2 - 10x + 21 = (x-7)(x-3)$. Therefore, for x–7=0, x=7 and for x–3=0, x=3. |a–b|=|7–3|=4.

39) **The correct answer is (C)**

Since 100% would be shown in 360°, 1% must be shown by $\frac{360}{100} = 3.6^o$.

And since the rent covers 15%, its central angle needs to be 15x3.6=54°.

40) **The correct answer is (D)**

The rent makes up 15% while transportation makes up 5%. Therefore
If 15% costs 120,000
    5%   costs   x
$x = \frac{120,000 \cdot 5}{15} = 40,000$.

41) **The correct answer is (B)**

The unit price for 250 math books would be $4, therefore they would cost $4x250=$1000. Similarly 350 English books would cost $3 per book, which means $3x350=$1,050 must be paid and 602 science books would cost $2 per book, which means $2x602=$1,204 must be paid. Therefore the total price is 1000+1050+1204=3254.

42) **The correct answer is (C)**

Lets us calculate the perimeters one by one:
P(ABCD)=2(4a+3a)=14a
P(LEFK)=2(3a+2a)=10a
P(VMNO)=2(2a+a)=6a
Total Perimeter=14a+10a+6a=30a

43) **The correct answer is (D)**

Lets us calculate the area one by one:
$A(ABCD)=4a \cdot 3a=12a^2$ $A(LEFK)=3a \cdot 2a=6a^2$ $A(VMNO)=2a \cdot a=2a^2$
Total Area=$12a^2+6a^2+2a^2=20a^2$

44) **The correct answer is (D)**

If all three angles are equal, a triangle is an equilateral triangle, therefore all edges are equal to each other. Therefore $\dfrac{|BC|}{|FE|}=\dfrac{12}{18}=\dfrac{2}{3}$.

45) **The correct answer is (D)**

For complementary angles, sine of one is equal to the cosine of the other. Therefore, 90–32=58 and sin32=cos(90–32)=cos58, x=58°.

46) **The correct answer is (A)**

120 physics books have been bought in 2012, while 100 have been bought in 2013 which means (120–100=20) decrease.
If   120   decreases by 20
Then   100   decreases by x
$x=\dfrac{20 \cdot 100}{120} \approx 17$, which means 17% decrease.

47) **The correct answer is (B)**

The number of books bought in 2011 is: 140+100+90=330, while in 2012 it is 120+90+90=300. Since 6 parties of books have been bought, the average is $\dfrac{330+300}{6}=105$.

48) **The correct answer is (C)**

Let the number of tables for 8 be x, then the number of tables for 6 would be (18–x). Since there are 128 seats available, 8x+6(18–x)=128. 8x+108–6x=128, 2x=20 and x=10.
Then the number of tables for 6 would be 18–10=8.

49) **The correct answer is (E)**

$(-4x^3+6x^2+7x+4)+(4x^2-7x+8)= -4x^3+6x^2+4x^2+7x-7x+4+8=-4x^3+10x^2+12$

50) **The correct answer is (A)**

$\angle A=\angle C=x=66^o$, $x+y=180^o$, $y=180^o-66^o=114^o$, $y-x=114^o-66^o=48^o$.

51) **The correct answer is (E)**

Let the original length of the be x. Then the length of the long piece would be $\dfrac{x/2}{7}=\dfrac{x}{14}$ and the short piece would be $\dfrac{x/2}{11}=\dfrac{x}{22}$. Then $\dfrac{x}{14}-\dfrac{x}{22}=4$, $\dfrac{22x-14x}{22\cdot14}=4$, and 8x=14·22·4, x=154cm.

52) **The correct answer is (C)**

7x+3y+12=0, 3y=–7x–12,   y=-7/3x-4 and the slope is equal to $\dfrac{-7}{3}$.

53) **The correct answer is (E)**

Since ABCDEF is a regular hexagon, and exterior angles of a regular hexagon is 60° each, then $\alpha=180^o-60^o=120^o$, and AEF is an isosceles triangle, as |FE|=|AF|. Therefore $\angle FEA=\angle FAC=x$, and $\alpha+2x=180^o$. $120^o+2x=180^o$, and $2x=60^o$, $x=30^o$. $\alpha-x=120^o-30^o=90^o$.

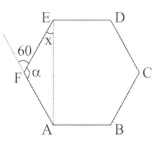

54) **The correct answer is (A)**

There are six numbers smaller than seven (1,2,3,4,5,6) and two prime numbers greater or equal to seven (7,11). Therefore the probability is $\dfrac{6+2}{12}=\dfrac{8}{12}=\dfrac{2}{3}$.

55) **The correct answer is (E)**

56) **The correct answer is (E)**

Let the purchasing price of this toy be 100. Adding the initial 30% profit on it, its sale price would be 130, and then adding the final 30% increase in the price, its final price would be 130x30%=169. Therefore the final profit would be 169–100=69, and the profit margin would be 69%.

57) **The correct answer is (E)**

The total number of aircrafts is 40+50+30+60=180, therefore 180 aircrafts would be presented in 360°. Since airline C has 30 aircrafts, we can built a proportion.

If   180 aircrafts are shown in 30°

Then   30 aircrafts are shown in   x

$x = \dfrac{360 \cdot 30}{180} = 60^o$.

58) **The correct answer is (D)**

There is an inverse proportion between the amount of fuel left, and the distance gone. Therefore,

If   (x+2) gallons left in   200 miles

Then   (x–1) gallons left in   400 miles

$200 \cdot (x+2) = 400 \cdot (x-1)$

x+2=2(x–1)=2x–2 and x=4 gallons.

59) **The correct answer is (E)**

$\angle A + \angle B = 180^o$,

$2x + 110^o = 180^o$, $2x = 70^o$, $x = 35^o$

60) **The correct answer is (A)**

d_1: 2x+3y=12,

d_2: y=3x+4.

$m_1 = -\dfrac{2}{3}, \quad m_2 = 3,$

$m_1 + m_2 = 3 - \dfrac{2}{3} = \dfrac{7}{3}$

TEST – 2.8
- Solutions -

1) **The correct answer is (B)**

According to the figure, $\dfrac{A}{100} = \dfrac{B}{140} = \dfrac{C}{120}$. Dividing each term by 20, $\dfrac{A}{5} = \dfrac{B}{7} = \dfrac{C}{6}$. Therefore A:B:C=5:7:6.

2) **The correct answer is (D)**

$7(x+7)+7=6(x+6)+6$, expanding the parenthesis, $7x+49+7=6x+36+6$, and $7x+56=6x+42$, $7x-6x=42-56$, $x=-14$.

3) **The correct answer is (B)**

The slope of the line $y=3x+4$ is $m_1=3$ and the slope of the line $y = \sqrt{2} + 6$ is $m_2 = \sqrt{2}$. Therefore $(m_2)^{m_1} = \left(\sqrt{2}\right)^3 = 2\sqrt{2}$

4) **The correct answer is (E)**

Find the vertex. The vertex is $\left(-\dfrac{b}{2a},\ f\left(-\dfrac{b}{2a} \right) \right)$.

In the equation a=-6, b=12. V(r, k)

$r = -\dfrac{b}{2a} = \dfrac{-12}{2\cdot(-6)} = \dfrac{-12}{-12} = +1$,

$k=f(r)=k=$ $-6x^2+12x+36=$ $-6\cdot1^2+12\cdot1+36=$ $-6+12+36=42$.
The vertex = (r; k)=(1, 42)

5) **The correct answer is (C)**

x being this number, half of its square is $\dfrac{x^2}{2}$, therefore $\dfrac{x^2}{2} + x = 6x$.

6) **The correct answer is (A)**

$\dfrac{A}{B} = \dfrac{2}{3}$ and $\dfrac{B}{C} = \dfrac{5}{7}$. Since B has different values in these equations, and they need to be equal, we need to take LCM (3, 5)=15, and expand both equations to equalize B. $\dfrac{A}{B} = \dfrac{2}{3} = \dfrac{2}{3}\cdot\dfrac{5}{5} = \dfrac{10}{15}$, $\dfrac{B}{C} = \dfrac{5}{7} = \dfrac{5}{7}\cdot\dfrac{3}{3} = \dfrac{15}{21}$, therefore A=10, B=15, C=21, A+B=25, B+C=36. The smallest number is A and the largest is C.

7)   **The correct answer is (A)**

8)   **The correct answer is (D)**

Shaded region=$\dfrac{6 \cdot 8}{2} = 24 \text{cm}^2$.

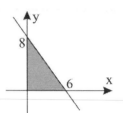

9)   **The correct answer is (B)**

Total surface area=$2(ab+ac+bc)=2(3x \cdot 2x+3x \cdot x+2x \cdot x)=$
$=2(6x^2+3x^2+2x^2)= =22x^2$ and the volume=$3x \cdot 2x \cdot x=6x^3$.

$\dfrac{\text{surface}}{\text{volume}} = \dfrac{22x^2}{6x^3} = \dfrac{11}{3x}$.

10)   **The correct answer is (D)**

Let the initial edge length of the square be a=10cm, which makes its area A(ABCD)=a^2=100cm². When the edge is increased by 20%, b=a+20%=10+20%=12, and the new area would be A(EFLK)=12^2=144, therefore there would be 44% of increase.

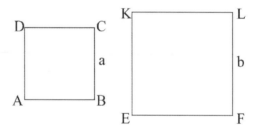

11)   **The correct answer is (A)**

If this parabola intercepts x axis at 4 and 3, then (x-4)(x-3)=0 and since it intercepts y axis at 12, c=12. Therefore y=ax^2+bx+c=x^2-(3+4)x+(3·4)= =x^2-7x+12, and a=1, b=-7, c=12. a+b+c=1-7+12=6.

12)   **The correct answer is (B)**

Let us call |AE|=|EC|=x, then |DE|·|EB|=x·x=x^2, 8·4=x^2, x^2=32, and x=$4\sqrt{2}$.

13) **The correct answer is (C)**

Female students   Male students
$$2x+10 \qquad\qquad y$$
$$40\% \qquad\qquad 60\%$$

If   40%   makes $2x+10$
Then   60%   makes y

$$y = \frac{(2x+10) \cdot 60}{40} = \frac{3(2x+10)}{2} = 3x+15.$$

Name	Score 1	Score 2	Increase	Percentage
Jack	500	620	120	$\frac{120}{500} = 24\%$
George	320	380	60	$\frac{60}{320} = 19\%$
Michael	120	160	40	$\frac{40}{120} = 33\%$
Jessica	820	1060	240	$\frac{240}{820} = 30\%$
John	100	124	24	$\frac{24}{100} = 24\%$

14) **The correct answer is (A)**

Therefore Michael has increased his points the most by 33%

15) **The correct answer is (B)**

George, by 19%.

16) **The correct answer is (C)**

$$3^{\frac{2}{3}} \cdot 3^{\frac{3}{2}} = 3^{\frac{3}{2}+\frac{2}{3}} = 3^{\frac{4+9}{6}} = 3^{\frac{13}{6}}.$$

17) **The correct answer is (C)**

$\tan C = \frac{1}{2}$, $\cot C = 2$, therefore $\tan C + \cot C = \frac{1}{2} + 2 = \frac{5}{2}$.

18) **The correct answer is (D)**

$(x+3)^2 = x^2+6x+9$, $(x-3)^2 = x^2-6x+9$,

$$\frac{x^2+6x+9+x^2-6x+9}{x^2+9} = \frac{2x^2+18}{x^2+9} = \frac{2(x^2+9)}{x^2+9} = 2$$

19) **The correct answer is (B)**

Summing both equations up,

$$\frac{1}{x} + \frac{1}{y} = \frac{1}{2}$$
$$+ \frac{1}{x} - \frac{1}{y} = \frac{1}{3}$$

$$\frac{1}{x} + \frac{1}{x} = \frac{1}{2} + \frac{1}{3}, \quad \frac{2}{x} = \frac{5}{6}, \quad 5x = 12$$

20) **The correct answer is (C)**

$y = ax^2 + 10x + 25a$ is tangent to x axis, therefore D=0.
$D = b^2 - 4a \cdot c = 10^2 - 4 \cdot a \cdot 25$, 100-100a=0, a=1, and 3a=3.

21) **The correct answer is (C)**

Let Jessica complete this task in x days.

Then, $\frac{1}{x} + \frac{1}{6} = \frac{1}{4}, \quad \frac{1}{x} = \frac{1}{4} - \frac{1}{6} = \frac{6-4}{24} = \frac{2}{24}, \quad x = 12.$

22) **The correct answer is (C)**

$\sqrt{2x+10} = 4$, taking square of both sides,

$\left(\sqrt{2x+10}\right)^2 = 4^2$, 2x+10=16, 2x=6, x=3.

The single root of the equation is 3.

23) **The correct answer is (A)**

$\frac{x}{-6} + \frac{y}{4} = 1$, and -2x+3y=16.

24) **The correct answer is (B)**

Let us call the classrooms as x and y. Then x+y=12 and 13x+12y=148.

25) **The correct answer is (D)**

3 hours 20 minutes is equal to 3x60+20=200 minutes.

| If | 200 minutes earns | $150 |
| Then | x minutes earns | $1240 |

$x = \frac{200 \cdot 1240}{150} = 1653$ min utes.

26) **The correct answer is (E)**

The number of female spectators at week 3 is 800, and at week 1 is 1000. Therefore

If   1000 decreases by   200
Then   100 decreases by   x

$$x = \frac{200 \cdot 100}{1000} = 20\%.$$

27) **The correct answer is (B)**

Let the number of students who donate $20 be x, then the number of students who donate $10 is (30-x), and 10(30-x)+20x=360.

28) **The correct answer is (D)**

Solving the above equation,
300-10x+20x=360, 10x=60 and x=6.

29) **The correct answer is (A)**

Since f(a)=$3x^3$-3 and f(a)=78, then $3x^3$-3=78, $3x^3$=81, x^3=27.   a=3

30) **The correct answer is (E)**

Since the two vehicles move towards each other, and the distance between two cities would be covered faster, we need to sum up the velocities.
Distance=(time) x (velocity), 90=t·(v+2V), 90=3V·t, and Vt=30.

31) **The correct answer is (A)**

f(x)=$3x^3$-x^3+$4x^2$+2,
f(i)=$3i^3$-i^3+$4i^2$+2=3$(i)^2$·i-$(i)^2$·i+4$(i)^2$+2=-3i+i-4+2=-2i-2

32) **The correct answer is (D)**

The marbles with prime numbers are {2,3,5,7,11}, therefore there are 5 marbles with prime numbers on them. Since there are 12 marbles, the probability is 5/12.Second draw is 4/11 so 5x4/12x11=5/33

33) **The correct answer is (D)**

Let us check out the costs of A and C:
=200+200=400 and sale price=400+400=800. Therefore profit is 800-400=400.

If $12 profits 12
Then   100 profits   x

$$x = \frac{400 \cdot 100}{400} = 100\%.$$

34) The correct answer is (A)

Average sale price (400+600+400)/3=1400/3
Average cost =(200+400+200)/3
The ratio=(1400/3):(800/3)=7/4

35) The correct answer is (D)

$\tan\alpha = \dfrac{7}{21} = \dfrac{28}{x}$, $\quad x = \dfrac{28 \cdot 21}{7} = 84$ kg.

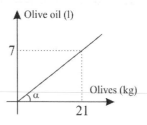

36) The correct answer is (C)

The general equation for a circle is $(x-a)^2+(y-b)^2=r^2$. Since 2r=10cm, r=5cm, and the center is located at A(3, 4). $(x-3)^2+(y-4)^2=5^2$.

37) The correct answer is (C)

Since 30% of the students are female,

If	30	out of 100 are female
Then	x	1200

$x = \dfrac{30 \cdot 1200}{100} = 360$. Therefore the number of male students is
1200-360=840, and the difference between the number of male and female students is 840-360=480.

38) The correct answer is (A)

Triangles $\triangle ABC$ and $\triangle ACD$ have equal heights, therefore the area of these two triangles are proportional with their bases.

$\dfrac{A(ABC)}{4} = \dfrac{A(ACD)}{16} = \dfrac{7}{4}$, $\quad A(ACD) = \dfrac{7 \cdot 16}{4} = 28$.

A(ABD)=A(ABC)+A(ACD)=28+7=35.

39) The correct answer is (D)

$\dfrac{\text{Okla hom a}}{2k} = \dfrac{\text{Kansas}}{4k} = \dfrac{\text{Arkansas}}{6k} = \dfrac{\text{Texas}}{8k}$,

2k+4k+6k+8k=360°, k=360°/20=18°. Oklahoma=2k=2·18=36°.

40) The correct answer is (D)

6 pencils + 3 erasers + 9 notebooks = 27, dividing both sides by 3,
2 pencils + an eraser + 3 notebooks = 9.

41) **The correct answer is (C)**

This student has read the maximum number of pages on Monday and Friday with 70 pages each.

42) **The correct answer is (A)**

Weekday average $= \dfrac{70 + 40 + 60 + 30 + 70}{5} = 54,$

Weekend average $= \dfrac{20 + 50}{2} = 35,$ The ratio $= \dfrac{54}{35}.$

43) **The correct answer is (D)**

Let us call the edge length of the cube as a.
Then $a^3 = 27x^3y^3$, and $a^3 = (3xy)^3$, $a = 3xy$.
Total surface area $= 6a^2 = 6(3xy)^2 = 54x^2y^2$.

44) **The correct answer is (A)**

$x = \dfrac{|AC|}{2} = \dfrac{10}{2} = 5 \, cm.$ $|DE| = |EF| = y$ and $|DE|^2 + |FE|^2 = |AF|^2,$

$y^2 + y^2 = 10^2$, $2y^2 = 100$ and $y = 5\sqrt{2}$, $\dfrac{y}{x} = \dfrac{5\sqrt{2}}{5} = \sqrt{2}.$

45) **The correct answer is (A)**

$A + B = \begin{bmatrix} 4+7 & 3+8 \\ 2+9 & 1+7 \end{bmatrix} = \begin{bmatrix} 11 & 11 \\ 11 & 8 \end{bmatrix}$

46) **The correct answer is (C)**

If 5 math=7 physics, then $\dfrac{math}{physics} = \dfrac{7}{5} = 1.4$

47) **The correct answer is (E)**

Let the number of cards with triangles be x, then the number of cards with rectangles would be 2x, and the number of edges would be 3x+4·2x=55, 11x=55, x=5. And the number of cards with rectangles=2x=10

48) **The correct answer is (D)**

Age groups of 24 and 26 use the Internet for 4 hours.

49) The correct answer is (A)

23 is between 22 and 24. $\left(23 = \dfrac{22+24}{2}\right)$

and their usage is $\dfrac{4+5}{2} = \dfrac{9}{2} = 4.5\,$ hours.

50) The correct answer is (A)

Daily average $= \dfrac{1+3+2+5+4+4}{6} = 3,16\,$ hours.

51) The correct answer is (B)

Since we are asked for (max), we need to take maximum value of x and minimum value of y, that are 6 and 2. Respectively $x^2 - y^2 = 6^2 - 2^2 = 36 - 4 = 32$.

52) The correct answer is (E)

The magazine has been sold at equal amounts at weeks 2-3, 4-5 and 6-7.

53) The correct answer is (A)

The 8 week average sale is

$\dfrac{200+400+400+800+800+1200+1200+1400}{8} = \dfrac{6400}{8} = 800$.

54) The correct answer is (E)

y=ax,   y=x,   a=1
y=bx,   y=-x,   b=-1
x=c,   x=3,   c=3
y=d,   y=4,   d=4
a+b+c+d=1-1+3+4=7.

55) The correct answer is (C)

$y=x^2 - bx + c$ intercepts x axis at 4 and 3, therefore
$x^2 - bx + c = 0$, 16-4b+c=0, and
$x^2 - bx + c = 0$, 9-3b+c=0, subtracting from each other,
    -(c-4b)=-(-16)
+   c-3b=-9
_____
-c+4b+c-3b=16-9,   b=7,
c-3b=-9, c-3·7=-9, c-21=-9, c=21-9=12,
c-b=12-7=5.

56) **The correct answer is (C)**

The volume of the prism is V=a·b·c=6·4·x=72, X=3

57) **The correct answer is (B)**

Total surface area is = 2(a·b+a·c+b·c)=2(6·4+6·3+4·3)=2(24+18+12)=108

58) **The correct answer is (D)**

$(\pi-3)^2+(3-\pi)^2=\pi^2-6\pi+9+9-6\pi+\pi^2=2\pi^2-12\pi+18=a\pi^2-b\pi+c$,
a=2, b=-12, c=18,   a+b+c=2-12+18=8

59) **The correct answer is (B)**

$\dfrac{6n+3}{4}=\dfrac{2n-5}{5}$ $\Rightarrow$ 5·(6n+3)=4·(2n-5),
30n+15=8n-20,   22n=-35

60) **The correct answer is (E)**

GCF (84,105)=21
84:21=4,   bottles of olive oil
105:21=5, bottles of flare oil.
We need (4+5)=9 bottles

TEST – 2.9
- Solutions -

1) **The correct answer is (B)**

4x+3y-12=0, 3y=-4x+12, therefore the slope is $\dfrac{-4}{3}$.

3x+4y-16=0, 4y=-3x+16, therefore the slope is $\dfrac{-3}{4}$. The sum of the slopes

is $\dfrac{-4}{3}+\left(\dfrac{-3}{4}\right)=\dfrac{-16-9}{12}=\dfrac{-25}{12}$.

2) **The correct answer is (B)**
The peripheral of the triangle is x+y+z=B

and the area is $\dfrac{x\cdot y}{2}=A$, 2A=x·y

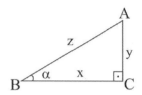

3) **The correct answer is (B)**

$x^2-2\sqrt{3}=-3$, $x^2-2\sqrt{3}x+3=0$, therefore $\left(x-\sqrt{3}\right)^2=0$, $x_{1,2}=\sqrt{3}$, and the equation has only one root.

4) **The correct answer is (E)**
3a=30cm, a=10cm,

b=a-10%·a=10-$\dfrac{10\cdot10}{100}=10-1=9$cm.

Therefore the new perimeter is
9x3=27cm.

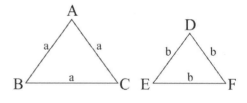

5) **The correct answer is (D)**

2x+3y=12, for x=0, 3y=12 and y=4,
 for y=0, 2x=12 and x=6

Since y=b=4 and x=a=6, 2a+3b=2·6+3·4=12+12=24.

6) **The correct answer is (D)**
Since α+α=90°, α=45°.

- Parabolas are symmetrical about the x axis.
- Peak points of the parabolas are (0, a) and (0, -a).

Therefore D is wrong.

7) **The correct answer is (E)**

(x+2)(x+3)+x+2=(x+a)(x+b).

Expanding the parenthesis, $x^2+3x+2x+6+x+2=x^2+6x+8=(x+a)(x+b)$

(x+2)(x+4)=(x+a)(x+b), therefore a=2, b=4. $(a+b)^{(a+b)}=(4+2)^{(4+2)}=6^6$.

8) **The correct answer is (C)**

Lets us solve the equation $x^2+3x=16$, $x^2+3x-16=0$.

$\Delta=b^2-4ac=3^2-4\cdot1\cdot(-16)=9+64=73$

$$x_{1,2}=\frac{-b\mp\sqrt{\Delta}}{2a},\ x_1=\frac{-3+\sqrt{73}}{2},\ x_2=\frac{-3-\sqrt{73}}{2}.$$

9) **The correct answer is (A)**

$$A(ABD)=\frac{|BD|\cdot h}{2}=\frac{14\cdot h}{2}=7h,\ A(ACD)=\frac{|CD|\cdot h}{2}=\frac{8\cdot h}{2}=4h,$$

$$\frac{A(ABD)}{A(ACD)}=\frac{7h}{4h}=\frac{7}{4}.$$

10) **The correct answer is (E)**

$$A-B=\begin{bmatrix}12-7 & 11-1 \\ 7-8 & 4-3\end{bmatrix}=\begin{bmatrix}5 & 10 \\ -1 & 1\end{bmatrix}$$

11) **The correct answer is (C)**

The diameter of a circle is twice the radius. (d=2r). Therefore the radius of this circle is, $4\pi=2r$, $r=2\pi$. The area of a circle is calculated by $A=\pi r^2$, replacing r with 2π, $A=\pi(2\pi)^2=4\pi^3$.

12) **The correct answer is (D)**

The probability of first egg being broken is $\frac{6}{12}$, while for second $\frac{5}{11}$, third $\frac{4}{10}$, and fourth $\frac{3}{9}$. Therefore it would be $P=6/12\cdot5/11\cdot4/10\cdot3/9=1/33$

13) **The correct answer is (B)**

$f(x)=x^2+10x+26=(x^2+10x+25)+1=(x+5)^2+1$,

Since $g(x)=(x+5)^2$, $f(x)=g(x)+1$.

14) **The correct answer is (A)**

$f(4)=-6$, $f(-2)=4$ and $f(3)=0$. $f(4)+f(-2)+f(3)=-6+4+0=-2$.

15) **The correct answer is (A)**

The volume of a cone is calculated by $V_{cone}=\dfrac{\pi r^2 h}{3}$, while the volume of a cylinder is calculated by $V_{cylinder}=\pi r^2 h$. Therefore $\dfrac{V_{cone}}{V_{cylinder}}=\dfrac{\dfrac{\pi r^2 h}{3}}{2\pi r^2}=\dfrac{1}{6}$.

16) **The correct answer is (B)**

$x+2x=90$, $3x=90$, $x=30$.

17) **The correct answer is (A)**

$4x-16\geq0$, $4x\geq16$, $x\geq4$, therefore the minimum integer value of x is 4.

18) **The correct answer is (E).**

$12=2x$, $x=6$; $24=3y$, $y=8$; $x+y=6+8=14$

19) **The correct answer is (B)**

Since $|AD|=|OB|=4$, and $\angle O=60^o$, then $\angle A=\angle B=60^o$. Therefore AOB is an equilateral triangle, and its perimeter is $4+4+4=12cm$.

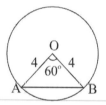

20) **The correct answer is (D)**

$A(ABCD)=|AB|^2=(3a)^2=9a^2$,

$A(LEFK)=|LF|^2=a^2$, therefore $\dfrac{A(ABCD)}{A(LEFK)}=\dfrac{9a^2}{a^2}=9$.

21) **The correct answer is (C)**

A math book and a physics book together cost $6.66+2.22=8.88$. Dividing 26.64 into 8.88, $2664/888=3$ therefore 3 math and 3 physics books have been bought.

22) **The correct answer is (A)**

Let this bookstore have sold x books in 2014 and y books in 2015. Then, $x+y=30$ and $12x+15y=420$, $12x+12y+3y=12(x+y)+3y=420$. Replacing $(x+y)$ with 30, $12\cdot30+3y=420$, $360+3y=420$, $3y=420-360=60$ and $y=20$. Replacing y with 20, $x+y=x+20=30$, $\underline{x=10}$.

23) **The correct answer is (D)**

The number of students who live
4 miles away : 50
5 miles away : 40
6 miles away : 30
Summing them up, 50+40+30=120.

24) **The correct answer is (E)**

Since we have a parallelogram, the sum of two adjacent angles are equal to 180°. Therefore $2x+2\alpha=180^o$, and $2(x+\alpha)=180^o$, $x+\alpha=90^o$.

25) **The correct answer is (C)**

According to the graph, (400-300)g of nuts cost (2.8-2.1)\$. Therefore 100g costs 0.7\$, and 900g costs 9x0.7=6.3\$.

26) **The correct answer is (A)**

The number of female students is 26, and the number of books they have read is 28, while the number of male students is 28, and the number of books they have read is 32. Therefore,

$$\frac{\text{The number of books read}}{\text{Total number of students}} = \frac{28+32}{28+26} = \frac{60}{54} = \frac{10}{9}.$$

27) **The correct answer is (A)**

Weekly average of the books read by female students is $\frac{28}{4}=7$. Total number of books read = 60. The ratio = $\frac{7}{60}$.

28) **The correct answer is (C)**

$\frac{x}{a}+\frac{y}{b}=1$, $\frac{x}{2}+\frac{y}{4}=1$, and 2x+y=4.

29) **The correct answer is (A)**

The average speed of the car is $\frac{160\,\text{miles}}{4\,\text{hours}} = 40\,\text{miles/hours}$.

Since x=υ·t=40·6=240 miles.

30) **The correct answer is (B)**

The prime numbers between 5 and 13 are 7 and 11. Therefore their geometrical mean is $\sqrt{77}$ and arithmetical mean is $\dfrac{7+11}{2}=9$, and the ratio is $\dfrac{\sqrt{77}}{9}$.

31) **The correct answer is (A)**

Let the number of female students be x, then the number of male students would be (3x+4). Then 3x+4+x=84, 4x+4=84, and 4x=84-4=80, x=20.

32) **The correct answer is (B)**

$\dfrac{|AB|}{|BC|}=\dfrac{1}{2}=\dfrac{x}{2x}$. By using Pythagoras theorem,

$|AC|^2=|AB|^2+|BC|^2=(2x)^2+x^2$ and

$|AC|=x\sqrt{5}$. $\sin\alpha=\dfrac{x}{x\sqrt{5}}$, $\cos\alpha=\dfrac{2x}{x\sqrt{5}}$.

$\sin\alpha+\cos\alpha=\dfrac{x}{x\sqrt{5}}+\dfrac{2x}{x\sqrt{5}}=\dfrac{3x}{x\sqrt{5}}=\dfrac{3}{\sqrt{5}}$.

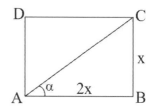

33) **The correct answer is (C)**

Since the cost of C is 600, the price would be 600+600·30%=780$, and this means $\dfrac{3900}{780}=5$ machines could be bought.

34) **The correct answer is (E)**

Profit margins would be 400·20%=80 for A, 500·25%=125 for B and, 600·30%=180 for C. Total profit would be 2(80+125+180)=$770.

35) **The correct answer is (D)**

The least profitable computer is D.
Sale price = 800+800·10%=880 and half of it =880/2=$440.

36) **The correct answer is (A)**

The volume of the rectangular prism is 3a·2a·a=6a³, while the volume of the cube is (2a)³=8a³, therefore the ratio is $\dfrac{6a^3}{8a^3}=\dfrac{6}{8}=\dfrac{3}{4}$.

37) **The correct answer is (D)**

The price of books would be

$A = \dfrac{1000}{20} = 50$, $B = \dfrac{1200}{30} = 40$, $C = \dfrac{1600}{40} = 40$ and $D = \dfrac{6250}{25} = 250$.

Therefore B and C are the cheapest.

38) **The correct answer is (E)**

The average fuel consumption would be $\dfrac{36 \times 100}{720} = 5$.

39) **The correct answer is (B)**

Each match takes two teams. Therefore we should calculate the

combination by: $C\begin{pmatrix} 8 \\ 2 \end{pmatrix} = \dfrac{8!}{(8-2)!2!} = \dfrac{8 \cdot 7 \cdot 6!}{6! \, 2!} = 28$.

40) **The correct answer is (C)**

Let us calculate how many hours 280 minutes is $\dfrac{280}{60} = \dfrac{14}{3}$ h. Therefore,

Jack needs to drive for $\dfrac{14}{3}$ hours. Since x=υt, (distance=time×velocity),

$x = \dfrac{14}{3} \cdot 60 = 280 \, \text{miles}$.

41) **The correct answer is (D)**

Let us call this number as x. x·30%=6, and $x \cdot \dfrac{30}{100} = 16$, and 3x=6·10,

x=20. 40% of 20 is $20 \cdot \dfrac{40}{100} = 8$.

42) **The correct answer is (A)**

$2A = 2\begin{bmatrix} 4 & 3 \\ 2 & 1 \end{bmatrix} = \begin{bmatrix} 8 & 6 \\ 4 & 2 \end{bmatrix}$, $3B = 3\begin{bmatrix} 1 & 2 \\ 3 & 4 \end{bmatrix} = \begin{bmatrix} 3 & 6 \\ 9 & 12 \end{bmatrix}$, $2A + 3B = \begin{bmatrix} 11 & 12 \\ 13 & 14 \end{bmatrix}$

43) **The correct answer is (B)**

If two lines are perpendicular to each other, multiplication of their slopes is equal to -1.

For 2x+3y=12, 3y=-2x+12, and $y = \dfrac{-2x}{3} + 4$, slope is $\dfrac{-2}{3}$.

For ax+7y=16, 7y=-ax+16, and $y = \dfrac{-ax}{7} + \dfrac{16}{y}$, slope is $\dfrac{-a}{7}$.

$\left(\dfrac{-2}{3}\right)\left(\dfrac{-9}{7}\right) = -1$, 2a=-21, a=$\dfrac{-21}{2}$.

44) **The correct answer is (A)**

Let there be 100x students in this classroom, then 70x students would be international. Since 30% of them are Asians, this makes $70x \cdot \dfrac{30}{100} = 21x$ and non Asian international students are 70x-21x=49x, and the ratio is $\dfrac{49x}{100x} = 49\%$.

45) **The correct answer is (B)**

The volume of sphere is calculated by $V = \dfrac{4}{3}\pi r^3$, therefore $160\pi = \dfrac{4}{3}\pi r^3$, r^3=120, and $r = 2\sqrt[3]{15}$.

46) **The correct answer is (A)**

From the first graph, $y=x^3$, and $m=2^3$, m=8. From the second graph, y=nx, y=x, and n=1. Therefore m+n=8+1=9.

47) **The correct answer is (A)**

Since 26l of water is divided into 0,8l bottles, we are asked to find the remainder of $\dfrac{26}{0,8}$. Therefore $\dfrac{26}{0,8} = \dfrac{260}{8} = \dfrac{130}{4} = \dfrac{65}{2} = \dfrac{64}{2} + \dfrac{1}{2}$, therefore the last bottle contains 1/2L of 0.8L, which is 0.4L

48) **The correct answer is (A)**

Total charity is (900+800+880+2400)=4980. Charity of school D is 2400. Therefore the ratio is $\dfrac{2400}{4980} = 48\%$.

49) **The correct answer is (D)**

Let us calculate average charities:

for A: $\dfrac{900}{30} = 30\$$, for B: $\dfrac{800}{40} = 20\$$, for C: $\dfrac{880}{44} = 20\$$,

and for D: $\dfrac{2400}{60} = 40\$$.

Therefore school D has the highest average charity.

50) **The correct answer is (B)**

The average charity per school $= \dfrac{4980}{4} = 1{,}245$.

51) **The correct answer is (D)**

Let the athlete run xm in the first day. Then second day=3x-100 and the third day is 3·(3x-100)-100=9x-400. Total distance he runs

7300=x+(3x-100)+(9x-400)=13x-500

13x=7300+500=7800, $x = \dfrac{7800}{13} = 600$m.

52) **The correct answer is (E)**

Let the number of algebra books be x, then the number of geometry books would be (8-x). Therefore 6x+4·(8-x)=44, 6x+32-4x=44, 2x=12 and x=6.

53) **The correct answer is (E)**

2x+3y=12, for x=0, 3y=12, y=4 and for y=0, 2x=12, and x=6.

$\tan\alpha = \dfrac{b}{a} = \dfrac{y}{x} = \dfrac{4}{6} = \dfrac{2}{3}$.

54) **The correct answer is (E)**

The prime numbers between 20 and 30 are 23 and 29. Summing them up, 23+29=52.

55) **The correct answer is (A)**

Let us find the angle for a single car first. The number of cars sold is

12+20+4+8=44. Therefore the angle for a car is $\dfrac{360}{44}$. Since the least selling

car is model C with only 4. Therefore multiplying with 4,

$\dfrac{360}{44} \times 4 = \dfrac{360}{11} \approx 33\%$.

56) **The correct answer is (E)**

The number of female students is 12+12+8+4=36,
The number of male students is 12+4+16+16=48.

$$\frac{\text{Female students}}{\text{Male students}} = \frac{36}{18} = \frac{3}{4} \approx 0{,}75.$$

57) **The correct answer is (E)**

Subtracting each other, $A \cdot 30\% - A \cdot 20\% = 10 = A \cdot 10\%$

$A \cdot \dfrac{10}{100} = 10$, $A = 100$, therefore half of A is 50.

58) **The correct answer is (C)**

Let the weight of the books be x and the weight of the empty box be y.

Then x+y=56, and $\dfrac{x}{y} = 13$ and x=13y. Replacing x with 13y, 13y+y=56,

14y=56, and y= $\dfrac{56}{14} = 4\,\text{kg}.$

59) **The correct answer is (A)**

$\dfrac{b}{a} = \dfrac{3}{7} = \dfrac{3k}{7k}$, Perimeter=2(a+b),

80=2(3k+7k), 40=10k, k=4
Shorter side = 3k=3·4=12

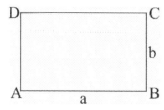

60) **The correct answer is (D)**

∠C=∠E=45°, CF=EF=x
∠E=∠A=45°, AK=EK=y
EF=KB=x, EK=FB=y
Perimeter(KBFE)=2x+2y=
=2(x+y)=2(AB)=2·16=32

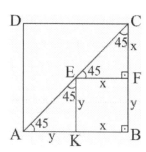

TEST – 2.10
- Solutions -

1) **The correct answer is (A)**

GCF (84,105)=21
84:21=4, bottles of olive oil
105:21=5, bottles of flare oil.
We need (4+5)=9 bottles

2) **The correct answer is (A)**

$\dfrac{b}{a}=\dfrac{3}{7}=\dfrac{3k}{7k}$, Perimeter=2(a+b),

80=2(3k+7k), 40=10k, k=4
Longer side = 7k=7·4=28

3) **The correct answer is (B)**

$\angle C=\angle E=45^{o}$, CF=EF=x
$\angle E=\angle A=45^{o}$, AK=EK=y
EF=KB=x, EK=FB=y
Perimeter(KBFE)=2x+2y=
=2(x+y)=2(AB)=2·24=48

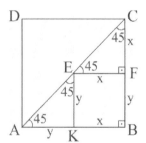

4) **The correct answer is (A)**

Two together = $\dfrac{1}{12}+\dfrac{1}{16}=\dfrac{1}{12_{(4)}}+\dfrac{1}{16_{(3)}}=\dfrac{7}{48}$

5) **The correct answer is (C)**

2a+b+c=14
a+2b+c=16
a+b+2c=18
+ ‾‾‾‾‾‾‾‾‾‾‾‾‾‾‾
4a+4b+4c=48, a+b+c=12

6) **The correct answer is (D)**

$\dfrac{1}{100}+\dfrac{1}{60}+\dfrac{1}{40}=\dfrac{1}{x}$, $\dfrac{1}{100_{(6)}}+\dfrac{1}{60_{(10)}}+\dfrac{1}{40_{(15)}}=\dfrac{1}{x}$, $x=\dfrac{600}{31}\cong 19\,days$

7) **The correct answer is (D)**

A) $\dfrac{\sqrt{3}}{\sqrt{2}} = \dfrac{\sqrt{3}\sqrt{2}}{\sqrt{2}\sqrt{2}} = \dfrac{\sqrt{6}}{2}$ B) $\sqrt{5}$ C) $\sqrt{7}$ E) $\sqrt{13}$ D) $\dfrac{\sqrt{100}}{\sqrt{289}} = \dfrac{10}{17}$

8) **The correct answer is (A)**

$\dfrac{4}{4+2} = \dfrac{6}{6+x} \Rightarrow \dfrac{4}{6} = \dfrac{6}{6+x}, \dfrac{2}{3} = \dfrac{6}{6+x}$

$3 \cdot 6 = 2 \cdot (6+x)$
$18 = 12 + 2x$
$6 = 2x, \ x = 3$

9) **The correct answer is (E)**

$2x + 3y - 8 = 0, \ 3y = -2x + 8, \ y = -\dfrac{2x}{3} + \dfrac{8}{3}$

10) **The correct answer is (D)**

$6a + 6b - 6c + 12d = 6(a + b - c + 2d)$

11) **The correct answer is (C)**

$7x - 6y = 15 \Rightarrow -6y = -7x + 15 \Rightarrow y = \dfrac{-7}{-6}x + \dfrac{15}{-6}$ Slope $= \dfrac{-7}{-6} = \dfrac{7}{6}$

12) **The correct answer is (D)**

Let's name the books the bookseller has: x
The first purchase price: 5x-120
The second purchase price: 4x+100
In this case :   5x-120=4x+100
                 5x-4x=100+120, x=220

13) **The correct answer is (B)**

Let's name the number of married couples: x
Now there are x number of men and x number of women joining the room.

$\left(\begin{matrix} \text{Number} \\ \text{of Men} \end{matrix} \right) = 3 \left(\begin{matrix} \text{Number} \\ \text{of Women} \end{matrix} \right)$

64+x=3(x+16),
64+x=3x+48,
64-48=3x-x, 16=2x, x=8

14) **The correct answer is (A)**

$$\frac{y^2 - 9}{y - 3} = \frac{(y-3)(y+3)}{y-3} = y + 3$$

y=-4, for (y+3)=(-4+3)=-1

15) **The correct answer is (C)**

$$\frac{\text{green marbles}}{\text{total marbles}} = \frac{5}{4 + 7 + 5 + 4} = \frac{5}{20} = \frac{1}{4}$$

About Author

Tayyip Oral

Tayyip Oral is a mathematician and test prep expert who has been teaching in learning centers and high school test since 1998. Mr. Oral is the founder of 555 math book series which includes variety of mathematics books. Tayyip Oral graduated from Qafqaz university with a Bachelor`s degree in Industrial Engineering. He later received his Master`s degree in Business Administration from the same university. He is an educator who has written several SAT Math, ACT Math, Geometry, Math counts and Math IQ books. He lives in Houston,TX.

555 Math Book Series

1. Tayyip Oral, Dr. Steve Warner. 555 Math IQ Questions for Middle School Students: Improve Your Critical Thinking with 555 Questions and Answer, 2015

2. Tayyip Oral, Dr. Steve Warner, Serife Oral, Algebra Handbook for Gifted Middle School Students, 2015

3. Tayyip Oral, Ersin Demirci, 555 SAT Math, 2016

4. Tayyip Oral, Geometry Formula Handbook, 2015

5. Tayyip Oral, 555 Geometry Formula Handbook, 2016

6. Tayyip Oral, IQ Intelligence Questions for Middle and High School Students, 2014

7. Tayyip Oral, Dr. Steve Warner, Serife Oral, 555 Geometry Problems for High School Students: 135 Questions with Solutions, 2015

8. Tayyip Oral, Sevket Oral, 555 Math IQ questions for Elementary School Student, 2015

9. Tayyip Oral, 555 ACT Math, 555 Questions with Solutions, 2015

10. Tayyip Oral, Sevket Oral, 555 ACT Math - II, 555 Questions with Answers, 2016

11. Tayyip Oral, 555 Geometry, 555 Questions with Solutions, 2016

12. Tayyip Oral, Dr. Steve Warner, 555 Advanced Math Problems, 2015

65388559R10203

Made in the USA
Lexington, KY
11 July 2017